Jane Moreland

Rock Paper Scissors

Gary's story

First published in the United Kingdom in 2021
by Jane Moreland

jane@janemoreland.com

ISBN 978-1-5272-8612-2

To Gary Shewan, whose story this is

Preface

I first met Gary in 2004. We were attending a conference on a cruise ship moored off Guernsey, where delegates would spend their days listening to talks and participating in workshops about human resources and training. In the evenings, supplier companies would host tables for dinner and one evening Gary turned up as a guest on mine.

The conversation flowed freely along with the wine. The women at the table were keen to gain Gary's attention and there was a lot of flirting mixed in with the laughter. Inevitably the subject turned to travel and I asked what was the most amazing natural sight he had ever seen. With a faraway look he replied, "I was once on a ship off Ascension Island, staring over the railings into the water, and I saw this hammerhead shark swimming underneath me."

Talk about attention grabbing. Why was Gary on Ascension Island? What was he doing there? Where was he going?

The details unfolded and as he related the tale, I grew more fascinated. Other guests were ignored, dinner was eaten and cleared away, and before the end of the meal I said, "It's such a great story, you really should write a book."

Gary agreed with some enthusiasm but acknowledged that he would never get around to it.

"Would you let me write it, then?"

Gary contacted me soon afterwards to find out if I was serious. After several emails and telephone conversations we met over coffee when I was next in London. He gave me a bag of letters, photographs and mementoes. Another time we met at the Royal Geographical Society to look at maps and research the geography and geology of the Falkland Islands. That summer he introduced me to his parents in Durham and walked me around the city. I contacted people who had worked at the NAAFI headquarters in London and the Kelper Store in Port Stanley, paid a visit to Falkland House in Westminster, even received a guided tour of HM Prison Weare in Portland Harbour, which had been one of the accommodation barges in the Falklands. Gradually, like a jigsaw, the story was pieced together. I spent hours at my computer, attended creative writing courses and welcomed all feedback.

Over a couple of years most of the writing was done but authorship of another person's memoir requires commitment. I had to earn a living and other priorities competed while Gary was busy with marriage, children and his career. The last two chapters would not write themselves.

Occasionally Gary would get in touch and there would be a short flurry of activity, but as the years went by the project disappeared further and further to the back of the cupboard.

Then in 2020 disruption came to all our lives - the coronavirus pandemic. After the first national lockdown was over, a text arrived out of the blue. Gary was visiting his parents in Durham and was planning to stop over in my area for one night on the way home. Could we meet up, socially distanced of course? For the first time in years he had had time to read the unfinished work and he was eager to see it through, if necessary involving another writer to get the job done. As we chatted, our joint enthusiasm for the story rekindled and just a few weeks later, with his input, the missing pieces emerged and fell into place. I could see my way to finishing the book.

Thus Gary's story sees the light of day.

I should add some important disclaimers and in particular must emphasise that this is my version of Gary's story. It is based on real places, real people and real events. As much as was feasible I have researched the facts, remained true to the chronology, the correspondence and what Gary has told me. However many details have been left out and where there were gaps in Gary's memory or where it suited the narrative, I have added my own elements and come away from the strict time line. I have never been to the Falkland Islands, despite a strong desire to visit. More importantly, I have had to give life to characters as I imagined them to be. The spoken words, actions and a few individuals are fictionalised. Some who appear in this book may feel that they have been unfairly represented. To them I apologise. To you, the reader, I hope you will enjoy the story.

Jane Moreland

February 2021

The Falkland Islands

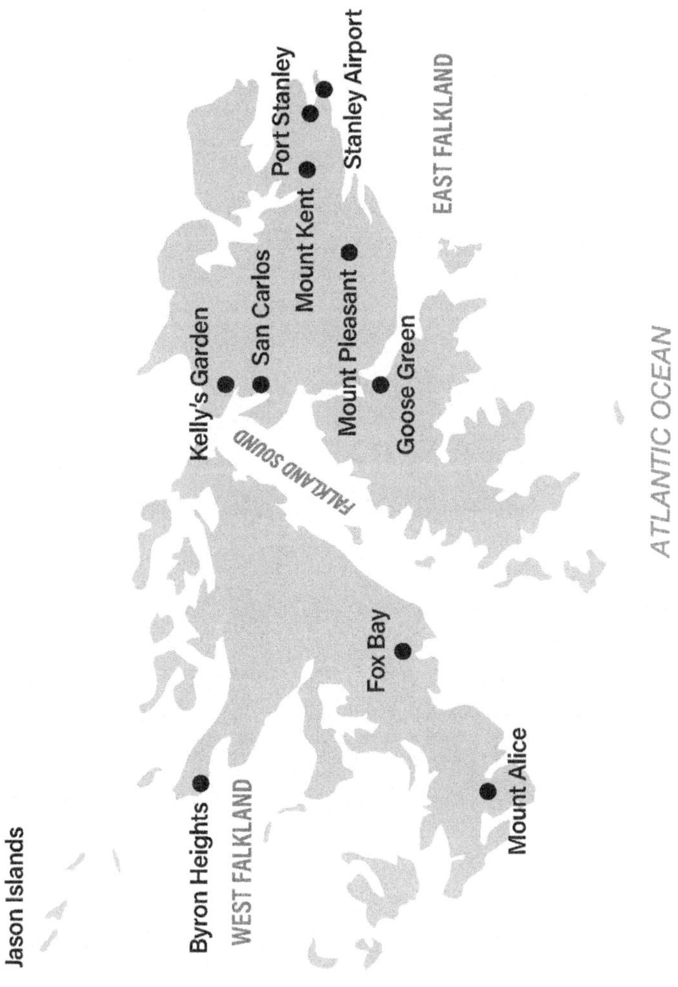

GLOSSARY

Beaver	Single-engined, high-wing, propeller-driven, short take-off and landing aircraft with amphibious floats
BFFI	British Forces Falklands Islands
Bristow	Helicopter operated by Bristow Helicopters Ltd; the company had a contract to supply three S-61s in support of the Falkland Islands garrison
BV	Tracked all-terrain vehicle
Camp	All areas other than Port Stanley; the countryside
Cessna	Small, piston-powered aircraft
Chinook	Twin-engined, tandem rotor, heavy-lift helicopter
CO	Commanding Officer
Coastel	Floating accommodation barge
Combat speed boat	Fast assault vessel
EFI	Expeditionary Force Institutes, provides NAAFI services in war zones

Eric	Nickname for helicopter operated by Bristow Helicopters Ltd
FIGAS	Falkland Islands Government Air Service
FILOG	Falkland Islands Logistic Battalion
FIPASS	Falklands Interim Port and Storage System
Forces Radio	Radio station operated by BFBS (British Forces Broadcasting Service)
Frigate	Medium-sized warship, a workhorse of the Royal Navy fleet
Gazelle	Five-seat helicopter, commonly used for light transport, scouting and light attack duties. The first helicopter to feature a fenestron tail rather than a tail rotor
Geordie	Native of Tyneside, especially Newcastle upon Tyne; can also refer to a supporter of Newcastle United Football Club
Gozome	Goes home

Hercules	Four-engine, turbo-prop military transport aircraft capable of using unprepared runways for take-off and landing
HMS	Ship prefix designating a Royal Navy ship: Her Majesty's Ship/Submarine
HMSO	Her Majesty's Stationery Office
HQ	Headquarters
Islander aircraft	Light passenger and utility aircraft
IRA	Irish Republican Army
Kelp	Large brown algae seaweed
Kelper	Native or inhabitant of the Falkland Islands
Mackam	Native of Sunderland; can also refer to a supporter of Sunderland Association Football Club. Also Mackem, Makem and Mak'em
MV	Ship prefix designating a merchant ship: motor vessel

NAAFI	Navy, Army and Air Force Institutes - official trading organisation of Her Majesty's Forces, providing retail and leisure services to the British Armed Forces
Phantom	Tandem, two-seat, twin-engine, all-weather, long-range supersonic jet interceptor and fighter-bomber
Portakabin®	UK brand of modular, prefabricated, portable buildings
R and R	Rest and relaxation
S-61	Civil variant of the Sikorsky Sea King helicopter, a versatile utility model which in the Falkland Islands seated six or seven passengers alongside cargo
Sea Harrier	Naval short/vertical take-off and landing jet fighter, also known as a jump jet
Sea King	UK-built version of the American twin-engine Sikorsky SH-3 Sea King, used in the Falklands War as a troop carrier and equipment mover, it also had an anti-submarine role
SS	Ship prefix designating a merchant ship: steam ship

TriStar	Converted, wide-body, trijet airliner, used for the air-to-air refuelling of Hercules as well as for the long-range transport of passengers and cargo
Vulcan	Jet-powered, tailless, delta wing, high-altitude strategic bomber

DURHAM

DECEMBER 1984

At the end of 1984, the average eighteen-year old living in the industrial north east of England had little reason to believe that their future held much promise.

Far away in the south Atlantic, Argentina had long asserted its claim to sovereignty of the Falkland Islands, a British dependency since 1841. When in April 1982 the Argentine military junta took possession of the islands by force, the British government reacted by sending a task force to oust the invaders. Prime Minister Margaret Thatcher had been in power since 1979 and the successful military action bolstered support for her government. The Conservative party won a landslide majority in the 1983 election and this victory legitimised and accelerated Thatcher's radical programme of transformation to revive the British economy and reverse what she called "the corrosive and corrupting effects of socialism".

In early 1984 the National Coal Board announced the closure of more of the remaining coal pits across the UK as another stage in Thatcher's free-market reform of nationalised industries. In a response intended to deprive the nation of its most important source of energy, the National Union of Mineworkers declared a national strike which dominated and overshadowed the rest of that year and would continue into the next. Violent clashes erupted and served only to underline the destitution, despair and division of close-knit communities who until that moment had always pulled together. The public, although largely on the side of the mineworkers, disapproved of the Union's methods. By Christmas 1984, Union funds were running out. Many strikers were on the last of their Union pay and, unentitled to social security benefits, would have to consider returning to work.

In Durham, factory closures had already hit the local economy hard. The closures of Bearpark, Herrington, Sacriston, and nearby Brenkley collieries were each a devastating blow.

Unemployment across the UK surged to a record high in 1984 at well over three and a quarter million people, of which youngsters under the age of 25 made up more than one third. School leavers were particularly badly hit. Teenage boys between 18 and 20 who were lucky enough to have a job would earn an average salary of £5,532.80. For men of all ages it was £9,807 while "an unemployed man with a wife and two children was expected to live on benefits of £61.80 per week plus a housing allowance, with little prospect of reemployment", according to Neil Kinnock, the Leader of the Opposition.

Privatisation was driving enormous social and economic change. While so many struggled with unemployment, yet others started to purchase shares for the first time as British Aerospace and then British Telecom were privatised. Home ownership was increasing across the country, partly fuelled by the Housing Act in 1980 which enabled council house tenants to purchase their freeholds; in the north the average price in 1984 was £23,540. Car ownership was also increasing and for those who could afford it the cost of a car in the north averaged £5,700.

These revolutions of the early eighties were matched by a transformation in popular culture. Punk then the New Romantics spawned flamboyant fashions, make-up and hairstyles while bands and singers such as Duran Duran, Spandau Ballet, Queen and Paul Young took British music to the USA and led a resurgence of interest which became known as "the second invasion". As news of an apocalyptic famine in Ethiopia hit TV screens late in 1984, the pop industry came together to form Band Aid and recorded a chart-topping Christmas song to raise money.

Meanwhile in the south Atlantic, Falkland Islanders were enduring a second invasion of their own. Nearly three years after the takeover by Argentinian troops in 1982 and subsequent relief by the sea-borne British task force, the eighteen hundred residents of the islands were still outnumbered several times to one. To deter and repel further armed attacks, thousands of UK service personnel were stationed both at sea and on land, maintaining vigilance in ships, observation posts and outstations across the islands, all supported by the NAAFI's recreational and retail services, while another army of engineers and construction workers built an international RAF station at Mount Pleasant, southwest of the capital Port Stanley.

Only once this airport was operational could the security of the islands be assured. The station would provide a new base for air-defence and transport operations while a new fleet of air-to-air refuelling aircraft would bolster the

RAF's long-range capability and ensure rapid back-up in case of attack. The target for opening was May 1985.

Rock

January 1985

Gary

The morning frowned so dark it collided with the sky and Gary wished he could do something different with his day. He stepped off the pavement at the usual place and turned up his collar, its leather smelling faintly of aftershave. Frost-chilled fingers fumbled to tug the zip as high as it would go.

Hands quickly back into pockets, his pace quickened and legs warmed to their familiar journey, past ice-encrusted cars and houses that blinked themselves awake. He looked up as he crossed the footbridge over the busy main road, the horizon dominated by the massive outline of the cathedral, an icon of Norman architecture but for him a symbol of all that was fixed and oppressive about life in Durham.

The glow of streetlights cast a yellow pallor on ancient houses while foggy air muted the sound of his shoes tapping against the paving stones. Impatient with the monotony of yet another day's walk to work, he ran the last hundred yards down the hill.

In one pocket he had been turning the shop key over and over in his hand, bitten fingers never still. He dug it into the key-hole shadow with an accuracy born of repetition. Once inside he shut the door quickly to trap any vestige of warmth, pausing to catch his breath and squeezing his eyes tightly to press out the ache of the cold. As he pulled the zip down on the leather jacket, he kicked away a polythene-wrapped Hairdressers Journal from the doormat and flipped the sign that swung from the door on a metal chain: Upstairs Downstairs - Open.

In the gloom he sought first the push button on the electric fan heater then switches for the lights, heading upstairs to fill the kettle while the neon strips flickered reluctantly into life. He measured out instant coffee and powdered milk into three glass mugs. The girls' work area with its tawdry plastic trolleys of rollers and pins always depressed him. The atmosphere was raw so he turned all the hairdryer hoods on; they chugged into action and exhaled metallic heat, greedy in their consumption of energy even though the business, and more particularly his parents, could ill afford it.

Going back downstairs to his barber's shop the coffee steamed, mixing with a cloud of his breath. He glanced through the front window, beyond the graphics that zigzagged up the glass, and across the road to the old Post Office where flickering strip lights meant that the counters were opening one by one. A few doors further along, his main competition, a chic hairdressing joint run by a team of sleek blondes, twinkled so brightly it was as if Christmas had come round again. He felt that all too familiar sense of inadequacy, jealous of their beauty and glamour.

Lynne burst in through the door in her usual way, lipstick-mouth in top gear, craning backwards to make sure that Pat behind her didn't miss a word, barely pausing for "Hi, Gary!" before heading up the stairs at full volume, trailing a long scarf and a whiff of body spray. Meanwhile Pat stopped for a moment to pull off her hat and gloves, running her hands through her blonde wedge to fluff it back into shape. “All right, pet?” she shivered, throwing Gary a bright smile and a wink.

“I made you both a coffee. It’s upstairs.”

Pat blew him a kiss and he grinned sheepishly, feeling the blood rush to his face. Even though she was a friend of his mother's he could never help but get embarrassed at any female attention. He pressed play on his tape recorder to drown out the banal sounds of Radio Two which Lynne had turned on upstairs as always.

Outside, darkness grudgingly gave way to a murky grey. January-wrapped women trundled in and hauled themselves up the stairwell for their hairdos. He knew many of the customers from childhood. Some were old friends of his Mam’s. Others used to come to him for cheap haircuts when he was training at Durham College; at the salon they grumbled about paying real prices, but nothing could deter their loyalty.

On the ground floor, the men would line up for Gary, awaiting their turn on the row of wooden chairs under yellowing spotlights, at least on busy days. Old boys would shuffle in on a Monday after collecting their pensions, asking for a trim or wanting a tidy-up of their ears and noses. Most of the demands were routine and predictable, but occasionally a lad would come in asking for a New Romantic look like a pop star and Gary would enjoy imitating a particular style, the more ambitious the better, crafting hair into a work of art.

There was one customer he dreaded, a man who returned every six weeks for a footballer perm. Gary was convinced he was the host of one of the Saturday evening shows on TV and that was quite exciting but at the same time the man seemed to like him a bit too much and his suggestive winks would give Gary a queasy feeling. It made him uncomfortable as he stood beside the man's face to trap the long hair in perm papers and wind in the rollers, unsure where the probing eyes were lingering. The girls upstairs always took the piss.

Despite the excitement of opening the salon the previous spring, now ten months in to running his own business all novelty had worn off and the days were dragging.

He swilled down his coffee and changed the tape. The combs, clippers and scissors were perfectly lined up, but he adjusted them a little and brushed the shelves down although they were already hair and dust free. He glanced sideways into the big mirror, trying to catch himself by surprise. He felt twitchy and fretful, bored with the slow start to the day and wondering what it would bring. Black and white pictures covered the walls in tidy rows, photographs of handsome men looking down on him with their perfect teeth and glossy hair.

He ripped the plastic wrapper from the Hairdressers Journal and threw himself into one of the chairs.

His thumb flicked the pages, but he had bitten the nail just a little too hard and now it was sore and weeping. He put it into his mouth and sucked to numb the pain.

At the back of the magazine were two pages of situations vacant. One of the advertisements caught his eye, unmissable with its bold frame and block capitals.

WANTED: HAIRDRESSER IN THE
FALKLAND ISLANDS.

He read it through and read it again.

He looked up blankly at the maroon flock wallpaper and faded artificial plants. In the corner, brown striped gowns hung from the coat-stand like empty skins. In the stairwell the noise of hairdryers and the radio accompanied the hum of women's chatter while a sickening smell of ammonia rolled down like a sea fog.

He had heard of the Falkland Islands from the war coverage just a few years before: all those soldiers who left by ship, the excitement and the promise that it would be over quickly. Patriotic enthusiasm might have seized the country but the news on television each night was shocking: grim horrors and battle darkness, Exocet missiles, explosions, heroes dead, the Sheffield, the Sir Galahad and so many men brutally burned and mutilated. The Prime Minister always spoke in that frog-spawn voice amid a violent flashing of photographers' bulbs. And then our gallant lads yomped to victory and returned in ships festooned with Union Jacks and bunting. We really did think that Margaret Thatcher was our saviour. The sailors stood along the decks raising their button-mushroom hats while on the quaysides the nation cheered and wept.

Gary was not sure exactly where the Falklands were except that they were a long way from Durham, away from everything he knew, from school and college and the shop, far from the depressing hopelessness of downtrodden miners and famished businesses; a place that meant escape.

He headed upstairs to the telephone and looked around furtively. Bitten fingers shook in the dial, wheeling the numbers back to make them go faster while his other hand cupped the receiver so that the girls wouldn't hear him.

"I've seen your advertisement in Hairdressers Journal."

"Ah, good. Let me ask a few questions first then we can talk about it. Name?"

"Gary Shewan."

"Age?"

"Nineteen. In a few weeks."

"Any hair-cutting qualifications?"

"Diploma and advanced diploma."

"Experience?"

"Quite a lot. I've been running my own salon nearly a year."

"Right. I'll tell you a bit about the job. Then there'll be an application form in the post."

Gary had never filled in an application form before, at least not for employment. As a kid, if you wanted a paper round or a milk round you only ever had to go and see the local newsagent or get Mam to ask for you. It was no different when he decided to become a hairdresser at sixteen. Mam got him his first job, she just went in and asked at Vince Barbaro's down by the County Hotel. Vince, who always smelt of garlic, had said OK and gave him Saturday work, washing hair and cleaning up. It was good experience, even if Gary didn't always get paid. And then after he completed his training at college and was ready to launch himself into the profession of hairdresser, his parents had helped him by buying Upstairs Downstairs so that he could run his own business and pay them a bit of rent to cover the overheads.

The gloom barely lifted all day and it had gone properly dark long before he closed up. Usually Gary waited across the road for the 63 bus but this evening he was filled with a fizzing energy which rushed in his ears. He headed up the hill on foot and took the short route home, through the council estate, watching out for the bully boys although they held no fear for him these days. When he was little he had been too scared to face them alone so would depend on the protection of his big brother Glenn.

Today his heart was beating fast not from fear but from the anticipation of telling the family his news.

He raced past the school, down the back alley which marked the end of the council houses and past his Mam's salon, already shut for the evening. One hundred yards further on he turned into their street and home.

When he opened the door the steam of mince and potatoes was wafting thickly in the air inside.

"Is that you, Gary? Half an hour till tea, it's your favourite," Mam called from the kitchen. "Dad and Paula have taken the dog out for a quick walk."

"OK." He bounded upstairs and shut himself in his room. He removed the heavy jacket, buttoned it onto a hanger and hung it neatly in the wardrobe, smoothing the leather and straightening the arms. A new set of darts sat atop the chest of drawers, their barrels heavier than his old set, and to calm his nerves he threw them one by one at the pock-marked and fading dart board on the wall, competing against himself in Round the World.

When he went down for dinner he was rumbling inside not so much with hunger as with the butterflies.

"What's up with you, son?" asked his Dad, prodding him on the arm. "You're all quiet. It's not like you not to be talking shite or jabbering away about something or other."

Gary's teeth forced themselves under the edge of the nail on his sore thumb, feeling their eyes on him – Dad, Mam, his sister Paula.

"I've got something to tell you."

They all paused what they were doing, Mam's ladle in mid-air, a steaming glob of mince gravy wobbling from its underside, Paula with her waiting plate in both hands, Dad with a glass of beer raised partway to his lips.

Gary took a deep breath. "I saw an ad for a job and I rang up to find out about it."

He looked at them one by one. They remained motionless, apart from his Dad's thick eyebrows, which creased together until they joined and become a single, black line across his forehead.

"A job?"

"You won't believe where it is."

His mother's eyes were wide, but her mouth went small and round.

"It's in the Falklands. Working for the military, cutting hair. The man told me it's based in the main town of Stanley but a lot of the men live in these lookout places around the islands, so it means travelling all over." He drew breath and glanced at each of them in turn.

Gravy plopped into the dish. Paula's mouth dropped open. Dad sat back in his chair.

“Well, son, good joke.”

“It’s not a joke.”

Mam sat down heavily, clutching the serving spoon.

“I don’t understand, Gary. You mean you’re leaving the shop? But I thought it was everything you wanted."

"It was, Mam. But think about it. It is an amazing chance."

"And the Falkland Islands, of all the places. What about the war?”

“There isn't a war anymore.”

“It could start up again at any time. They keep saying so on the news.”

“Don’t be daft. The man I spoke to said they’ve got thousands of military there, even more than during the fighting. That's why they need a hairdresser. Come on, don’t you think it’s exciting? I can see the world and get paid for it!”

He looked to his Dad, grinning, wanting support, heart still thumping.

“It’s a bit sudden, son. We thought you were settled what with your own business and everything. You’ve never said anything about seeing the world before.”

“Well, I never thought about it before. I won’t be leaving for good. It’s only for six months, and then I’ll be back.

And Paula will still be here to keep you company, eh Paula?"

"You can't go, Gary, it's bad enough since Glenn moved out," she pouted like she always did when things weren't going her way. "I'll get the blame for everything."

"What about Lesley? What's she going to say?" interjected his mother.

Gary felt a jolt in his stomach. It was going to be hard telling his girlfriend, no question. She would be mad at him, but then she always was, whatever he did. It was a wonder she was going out with him at all, the times she got angry. But they always made up and after nearly three years it just seemed to be the way that things worked.

The family resumed their meal. He wanted them to share his excitement or at the very least to show interest, but they remained strangely quiet, intent upon their food as if something unspeakable had happened.

"Aren't you going to say anything, then? What do you think?"

Mam looked up and smiled weakly. He hadn't noticed before but she looked tired and there was a wrinkle at the corner of her mouth which stayed there even when her lips were not turned down.

"Well, son, it's not for us to tell you what to do. Just so long as you're happy."

*

After tea, Gary borrowed his Mam's car to drive over to Lesley's place in Bowburn, about ten minutes out of Durham. It was a detached house, a lot bigger than his family's, with ostentatious bay windows and tiling underneath as if to emphasise the point. He rang the front-door bell, fingernails between his teeth out of habit and twitching his foot against the step. She came to the door in a low-cut red top that suited her colouring, her eyes glinting and a curling smile on her lips that made her look even sexier than usual.

"Mum and Dad are out."

She grabbed his arm and pulled him in, laughing. He followed her up the stairs watching the tight-jeans swing of her hips. She gave him a devilish look and dragged him into her room, turning the music up. He sensed her mood and they danced, swaying to the rhythm, holding their bodies close, feeling the heat. Every contour of her body was pressed against his, her warmth radiating through layers of clothes to his skin. Their lips met. Her mouth was hot and moist and giving and his whole body shivered. He ground his hips into hers and she backed towards the bed, where they tumbled in a tangle of fingers and tongues.

"Won't your grandparents hear us?" he gasped.

"They've got their TV on."

Afterwards, he lay with her snuggled up against him, curving his body around hers. He spoke into the smooth hair.

“Lesley? I’ve got to tell you about this job advert. I'm going to apply. It’s abroad.”

She turned around, stared into his face with eyes like pin pricks. He started to explain but before a full sentence was out, she exploded.

“What the hell are you saying?”

“It’s only for six months.”

She kicked him off the bed, grabbed some clothes from the floor and threw them at him. The belt of his trousers slapped his face, catching his lip.

“Hey, watch it!”

“I hate you!”

“Hang on; don't give me a hard time."

"Why not?! How could you come in here and act like normal when you knew you were going to tell me this!"

"Look, I’m sorry. It’s the routine and the shop, it’s driving me mad,” his voice started to rise.

“But all you ever wanted was that shop, what do you mean it’s driving you mad?”

His lip started to swell, a lump like jelly. “I know I should be grateful. But I feel trapped in that place and it will always be the same. Surely there’s got to be more. I can’t explain it, I just feel like taking a bit of a risk, seeing what happens.”

Lesley picked up her hairbrush and aimed it at him.

“A risk? Well thanks a lot! What about me? I suppose I’m just a part of your bloody routine too!" The angry colour of her cheeks was spreading down her neck.

“Oh, Lesley, come on. You know we’re great together and this job, it’s only for a few months, you’ll hardly notice. I’ll be back before you know it. Try to see it could be a great opportunity for me.” The words sounded pathetic even to himself. Lesley threw herself onto the bed and shrieked into the pillow.

He stood there helpless to deal with her temper, knowing that it could last for hours, maybe days, but that he was not going to change his mind.

“Listen, it should be good pay and I don’t suppose there will be much to spend it on. I’ll save it all up and come back with more money than you can imagine. We can go away for a really good holiday, I promise.”

Her cheeks were blotched and mascara had smeared across the pillowcase.

“Listen, I’ve got to do a written application.” He moved towards her, doing his best to put on a winning smile.

"You know me, Lesley, I'm rubbish at that kind of stuff. Chances are I won't get the job anyway."

Her fury started to subside, and she quietened down. He pulled her to him, enfolded her in his arms and wondered just where the Falklands were, exactly.

They sat for a long time in silence.

Next morning early the letterbox rattled and from his room Gary heard the plop of an envelope on the front door mat. "I'll get it!" he yelled, hurtling down the stairs while buttoning his shirt. The dog bounded into the hall, barking excitedly, wanting to join in the game. He stumbled over her and she yelped.

"Schweppes! Out of the way, you daft mutt!"

The dog backed off, tail wagging. He gave her ears a tickle and cuffed her gently. He knew before his hand was on it that the envelope was addressed to him.

"Hey, Paula," he made his way to the breakfast table, "It's here."

He read the short letter and the long application form while he poured cornflakes and milk one-handed. He quickly sprinkled several spoonfuls of sugar over the top before Mam would notice.

"You'd better write out a practice one first and let us check it. You know what your spelling's like," jibed Paula.

He paid little attention to his breakfast, concentrating on the paperwork rather than his cereal. On his way out he gave his Mam a big kiss on the cheek.

“Hey! What’s that for?” she flapped him away.

“Cos you’re beautiful. See yas later.”

He took his time over the form, completing it carefully with the best pen he could find during a quiet spell in the morning. He checked it again at lunchtime and made a few corrections. In the afternoon he gave it a last read-through and folded it into the reply-paid envelope. “I’m just popping across the road!” he shouted up the stairs.

The post-box was countersunk into the wall of the Post Office, mouth agape. He fed it the envelope, holding on until just the corner was pinched between thumb and forefinger. It hung there for a moment until he dropped it. He crossed the road back towards the salon with a mix of elation and fear.

The response came within days: he was invited for an interview.

Travelling alone for the first time, he arrived at King’s Cross station where he made his way across the concourse to the tube. He stopped beside the underground map to work out his route, checking and re-checking, counting stops. Down the rattling escalators he went, the tunnel smelled hot and acrid, the blackness roared with an angry wind. The carriages screeched to a halt, doors opened furiously and slammed again and the train lurched off into the dark.

At Vauxhall there were so many exits it took him a while to work out which one he needed. He stepped out into dull air where the remnants of last year's leaves swirled in the gutter, mixing with the pages of abandoned newspapers and a flattened burger box. Trains scurried across a bridge overhead. Even in the middle of the day taxis and buses had their sidelights on, distrustful of the gloom. He looked up and down the busy street, orientated himself then swung the overnight bag onto his shoulder, right into the face of a sullen youth who pushed by, muttering threats in a strange patois.

Half a mile down Kennington Lane the Navy, Army and Air Force Institutes headquarters occupied a wedding cake of a building complete with pillars and carved icing. To Gary it was a replica of Buckingham Palace and just as awe inspiring. With a deep breath he handed his letter to a security guard at the gate, crossed a tarmac approach and climbed the steps to the front door. Inside, grandeur gave way to very ordinary functionality. A receptionist showed him to a dreary corridor where three worn chairs stood in a line, peeling varnish. "Wait here please. You will be called in."

His palms felt clammy and he cleared his throat, wishing that he had had a drink. He tried to gather his thoughts and to concentrate on all the things everyone had said he should do and say.

After some minutes a man appeared at the door and called him in.

"Journey all right?"

Gary swallowed and re-activated the saliva in his mouth. The man's desk was neat and tidy, with papers stacked in a pile on one side and a large green blotter in the middle covered in ink marks and writing.

When the interview began in earnest the man was reassuring. Gary remembered his Dad's advice not to talk too much and focused on thinking before he replied to the questions. The man nodded and listened and made notes on a form using a pen with HMSO stamped on it.

"Why do you want this job?"

Gary swallowed hard. "Business isn't good in Durham; there are lots of people out of work and trade is getting slower and slower. This looks like a good opportunity."

The man scribbled and responded. "We see a lot of men from the north east."

"The strike has been making things worse for everyone, not just the miners." Gary pulled himself up short, wanting to avoid politics and no use at them anyway.

The interviewer told him all about the contract and the living arrangements and the weather in the Falklands. He peppered his talk with questions and listened carefully to the answers. He said it was a tough assignment, hard work.

“That's OK, I like being busy.”

The man gave him a smile. “Well, Gary, you seem self-reliant and it sounds as though you should be able to handle the responsibility. I can tell you straight away you’re our best candidate. The job holds the rank of Corporal. The contract says nine to five, five days a week but that's not actually how it is in real life. A lot of flexibility is required – you’ll work when and where needed, and that means all around the islands, sometimes at unsocial hours. You're to manage the cash as well as cut hair.”

“I’m used to that.”

“You’ll be employed by EFI; it stands for Expeditionary Force Institutes. It’s part of the NAAFI, but you'll be in full military uniform. EFI personnel are on a kind of secondment from the NAAFI to the Army - it's because the Falklands are still considered a war zone, not actively at war, obviously, but because of the security risk. Don’t worry, you won’t actually be in the Army but if conflict should start up again, you do need to understand that you will be required to provide support to the troops.”

Gary’s brain was whirling, trying to make sense of the new information. “When you say secondment, what is that? And what do you mean, support to the troops?”

"You'll be employed by EFI under NAAFI terms and conditions. Support to the troops would depend on the situation but mostly it means doing your normal job in different circumstances. Keeping the supply chain going, making sure the troops are looked after. Although things have been quiet, the Falklands are still on full invasion alert. Anyway, as I say, don't worry about all that. You'll get a week's EFI training before you go."

Gary nodded silently, bewildered by alien phrases such as supply chain and invasion alert but digesting the fact that he was the best candidate. The job certainly sounded different from anything he could have imagined.

"Can you tell me what the pay is, please?"

The man's hands went to a manila file and withdrew a sheet covered in figures. He traced down a line with his finger. "The basic's £18.61 a day, that's £6,793 a year. There's an additional £1 a day during your first six months and a bonus of £700 if you choose to extend your tour beyond that six months. How does that sound?"

"It sounds great."

Gary's head had grasped the financials quickly. The package wasn't just great; it was amazing, better than anything he could ever hope for from the shop or any job up north. He was going to be rich.

"Got your overnight bag? Good. Your medical is scheduled for tomorrow. I'll tell you how to get there. A bed has been booked for you. Assuming that goes all right, we'll send the papers through in the next couple of days."

Gary's medical was to take place at the EFI headquarters and NAAFI residential training centre, Wingham, which was half an hour's journey out of town, down the railway line to Claygate in Surrey. Gary was getting used to catching a train on his own. Once at the station he hopped into a taxi, which wound its way through a maze of leafy lanes and smart commuter-belt houses. He stared wide-eyed as the car pulled up the drive. Wingham's architecture was quite different from the palatial design of the London office, although to his eyes no less imposing: a brick-built country house, with enormous bay windows overlooking sweeping lawns and mature trees. The taxi driver twisted round in his seat.

"Are you going to get out or not?"

After Gary had checked in at the reception office and been shown to a room, there was time to phone home. "Hey, Mam, you're going to have to address me as Corporal from now on."

"Does that mean you've got the job, Gary? Well done, son." She sounded proud, even though he knew she didn't want him to go. "But what do you mean, Corporal? Are you an officer?"

"Yeah. But don't worry; I'll be in the EFI not the Army. I wouldn't join up to be a soldier!"

“Well that’s one thing to be grateful for. We’d never get you back if you did that.”

He told her all about his day and everything he could remember about the interview and the job.

“I’ll make a fortune, Mam.”

“Good luck with the medical, love.”

“Let’s just hope the doctor doesn’t notice my bow legs, eh?”

“You don’t have bow legs, pet.”

“I know.”

At the end of the medical the next morning the doctor patted Gary on the back. “That’s you done, all fine. Go and see your GP at home straight away and get him to sort out this list of inoculations as soon as possible. We’ll see you back here in a few weeks when your training starts.”

It had happened so quickly that Gary gave no thought to the decision. In fact he wasn’t entirely sure afterwards that he had made a decision. On the train going home his mind wandered haphazardly while his eyes stared into the flickering landscape without seeing it. He found it difficult to imagine where he was headed. He had no points of reference other than those news stories and none of them showed the Falklands in a very good light. Yet if the islands were worth going to war over, they must be something special. He couldn't wait to find out. Were they somewhere near Scotland?

Over the next fortnight the phone never stopped ringing and for the first time in his life Gary felt like something of a local celebrity. Lesley wanted to spend as much time with him as she could, not just evenings out but visiting all the family to say goodbye: his brother Glenn and his girlfriend Julie in their new flat in Durham, Uncle Alan and Aunty Nancy with cousins Paul and Joanne in Washington, Gran and Grandad Shewan up the road in Washington Old Town, and, dearest of all, Gran and Grandad Davison over in Whitburn.

Lesley seemed to be enjoying the attention more than he was, she talked about the job interview as if she had been there and as though it was all her idea in the first place. The family insisted that she must come round and visit them while he was away, which Gary thought was generous since he knew none of them really liked her all that much. Everywhere they went she made sure that people saw the article in the local paper, with an embarrassing photo which had caught him looking smug.

On St Valentine's Day, his nineteenth birthday, she presented him with a teddy bear wearing a T-shirt printed "I love you", only there was a heart instead of the word love.

"Thanks, he'll keep me company," he said, brushing the toy along her nose, not quite able to say "I love you" back even though he was almost breathless with emotion and could sense it was what she wanted.

On the last day Mam lent him her car to drive across to Lesley's. It was awkward, having to make polite conversation with her parents and grandparents over tea, thinking about the last-minute things he must remember to put in his rucksacks, the clock ticking cruelly towards the time when they would say goodbye.

When the moment came, the parents each shook his hand then Lesley followed him out. He squeezed her close, felt her warmth, smelt her soft hair. He kissed her quickly then got into the car. Her fingers were on the door handle, gripping tight.

"Hey, Lesley, don't do what you did the time we had that big argument and you hung onto the car door so I couldn't drive away. Mam will kill me if you scratch her paintwork."

A smile played at the corner of her lips despite the tears dissolving her mascara.

"I'll phone tomorrow when I get to Wingham. Write lots, promise? Wish me luck." He blew her a kiss, started the car and pulled out of the drive, checking in the mirror through the mist of his own tears to make sure she was still there.

Early next morning his parents and sister piled him and the two rucksacks and the holdall into his Dad's car and they drove to the station.

"Have you got everything, son?"

"Think so."

"Take care, Gary love. We'll miss you. Let us know as soon as you have an address in the Falklands and we'll write."

"OK. Write often."

"Gaz, can I have your blue sweatshirt?"

"Paula. Honestly."

The train pulled in and suddenly their arms were around him, hugging and laughing and pushing him in with his big bags so that the door could slam shut. He struggled to get the window down but it wouldn't go so he was mouthing goodbyes and waving and the three figures were mouthing things back that he couldn't understand and the train was moving and Durham was gone.

Elizabeth

It was hard enough when Glenn decided to move out but at least the house had remained full of Gary's background music or foreground carry-on. Now she would feel a second loss and although Paula was still home it was bound to be quieter. However there was no time to get sentimental, she had more than enough to think about with her own salon to run and there would be Upstairs Downstairs to manage, too.

One night soon after the interview but before he actually left, Gary and Paula had both gone out, giving Elizabeth and her husband a rare moment on their own.

"What's up, pet? Why are you fretting?" He always knew what her mood was, especially when she tried to hide it. And this evening she was feeling anxious.

"It's the shop, Mattie, we're going to have to put it up for sale. The business is barely making enough profit to cover the bills as it is. We'll never replace Gary so the men's trade is finished. And the women's side might stagger along on its own for a while but it is only going to get more difficult."

Mattie raised his eyebrows and wrinkled his forehead in a query. He was her good-looking man and those eyebrows gave his face character and strength.

“We know the Post Office across the road is closing next month and as if that isn’t bad enough, I just heard that the Council has confirmed the new road scheme. I reckon that will kill trade stone dead,” she continued.

Mattie was reluctant to give up on Upstairs Downstairs. “I see what you mean, pet, but it seems a pity after everything we put in. The money and all that effort.”

“What’s the alternative? I can’t imagine Gary will want to come back to it.” She knew in her bones that the shop would only be a liability, whatever Gary decided to do.

He sighed. “Of course, you’re right, though it does seem hard. Well then, I suppose if we are going to sell up, we need to get on with it, try to get rid of the place quickly rather than waiting. We could put an ad in the paper this week.”

“I’ll have to tell Pat and Lynne first. It’s a shame, they’re good workers.”

Elizabeth managed not to cry when Gary’s train pulled out of the station. The next day, Monday, was her day off and she used it to catch up with housework. From the kitchen she could hear the muted sound of the oxygenator in the fish tank, bubbling into her consciousness. She was sorting out some laundry when the telephone rang and made her jump. Hoping it might be a someone interested in the shop, she threw down the bundle of towels and ran to grab the receiver. But the voice was her mother's, calling breathlessly from a payphone.

"Elizabeth? Your Dad's had a stroke. I'm at Sunderland General, can you get over?"

It was all Elizabeth could do not to drop the phone. "Oh, God. Mam, is he going to be OK?"

Her mother's voice sounded tiny down the line. "They don't know, love."

"I'll be right there."

She hated ringing Mattie at his work but there was nothing else for it. He must have known it was an emergency as soon as she spoke.

"You'd best get straight over there, pet. I'll tell Paula when she gets home. Stay as long as you need to, just ring and let us know."

She grabbed her coat and keys and drove to the hospital as fast as she could, finding it difficult to concentrate properly on the road because her heart was pounding so fast she could hear it thumping in her ears.

Elizabeth's Dad, Tom, was a strong man, a miner just like his father had been, still as hard as the coal he used to extract although he'd been disabled by a stroke six years previously. Gary said his Grandad reminded him of John Wayne. She could see why because the actor's characters always kept fighting even when wounded, but she knew another stroke would flatten her Dad one day.

She found the others in the waiting area, Mam and her brothers Alan and Roy, who had also dropped what they were doing and raced to be there. They sat together in anxious silence, jumping every time a door opened or a nurse raced through, willing their Dad to be well. Eventually the doctors told them to go home, their hanging around wasn't going to make any difference.

It was an exhausting few days. She made the same trip and stayed much of the day on Tuesday, on Wednesday she panicked because her mother rang to say come quickly, then on Thursday they all felt more optimistic because he was doing better.

During the week Gary rang several times from his training at Wingham and she had to reassure him that Grandad was all right. Gary had such a special relationship with his grandfather that he was all for throwing in the promise of adventure in order to come home.

"Listen, Mam, I can forget about going to the Falklands, it doesn't matter."

"No, son. He's proud of you and what you're doing, he'd want you to go."

GARY

Wingham was less imposing the second time around and the training was nothing like he had expected. Each morning the raw EFI recruits assembled outside and were put through exercises. Gary soon learned to march and turn, to swing his arms, to stop smartly on cue with everyone else. He concentrated hard to avoid a shouting and that stopped him thinking about Grandad for a few hours, which was a good thing. One day they were told to queue up by the door and each of them was issued with a gun. When it was his turn, the drill sergeant thrust a semi-automatic into his arms.

“I can’t believe this!" Gary muttered to the next lad in the line. "The only time I ever touched a gun I swore I'd never go near one again."

He felt the weight in his hands, the brutish handle pressing into the crook of his arm, remembering the two policemen who came to their house to give him the telling-off of his life, even though setting off his mate’s air pistol had been an accident and he hadn’t actually hurt anyone. He had been messing about in Belmont Park with a load of other teenagers and it was just unfortunate that one of the girls was much closer than he had realised to the line of fire. He couldn't look his Mam in the eye for a week and the girl never spoke to him again.

"Get out on the parade ground and stop mincing about!" barked the drill sergeant behind him.

Gary jumped out into the thin Surrey sunshine with the killing machine in his hands, the stiff leather of standard-issue boots chafing at his ankles. He stood in his appointed place in the line, other recruits to the left and right of him in identical clothes – camouflage jackets and trousers cinched in with webbing belts, berets each tipped over the right ear with a shiny badge pinned to the front. He was proud of his corporal's stripes and cap badge which had three cannons and three balls and a motto in Latin that meant absolutely nothing to him.

He couldn't see the point of marching up and down the square of tarmac in columns nor of presenting arms and standing at ease, least of all carrying a gun which he would never need to fire, but the drill sergeant bellowed so they paid attention to their formation. He obeyed orders and despite all the doubts he could feel his back straighten and out of the corner of his eye could see that their line was neat and starting to look professional.

Afternoons were easy. Sometimes they had training lectures or gentle sessions of PT which he enjoyed, being light on his feet. It was all surprisingly relaxed and in between times Gary was detailed to undertake practical jobs around the grounds. One day he was told to mow the grass and he thought at first that the sergeant was joking because the lawn was the size of a football pitch and probably hadn't last been trimmed since the autumn, and there was just an ordinary garden mower that would cut a strip twenty inches wide.

He pulled at the starting handle and the machine roared into life with a cough of smoke, spluttering and choking before it settled into a regular low-toned roar. He set off down the middle of the grass, defining a line as straight as a parting. He turned at the end and followed his template back and forth to comb a neat pattern of stripes. The day was bright and though it was fresh it felt good to be outside with the smell of the grass and promise of spring coming soon. When he had finished one side he returned to the middle and worked his way meticulously on the other side. To finish he trimmed tidily around the borders with a pair of edging shears. It took hours and looked great.

By the end of each day he was reasonably tired but sleep didn't come easily and most nights he would lie awake for hours in the dark, listening to the snoring and thinking about Lesley and the family back home and especially his Grandad.

On the night before they were due to fly, Gary queued for the telephone in the booth under the stairs, jangling a pocketful of change. After he had spoken to Mam and been reassured that Grandad was improving, he dialled Lesley's number. He ignored the lads who grumbled outside as he pushed coin after coin into the slot.

"Did you get my letter?"

“Yeah, thanks, it was nice. Your Mam asked if I’d heard from you and I went all red because I couldn’t tell her what you'd said.”

“I miss you loads.”

“Don’t give me that, Gary. I didn’t want you to go.”

“Listen, I’ll write as soon as I can. Please be the first person I see when I get back.”

“Of course. I’ll come down and meet you in London.”

The pips went and while she was wishing him a good flight the line went dead. Gary’s finishing words disappeared into a vacuum. He replaced the receiver in its cradle and turned around to let the next lad take his place.

Bet

When Tom had lost consciousness in his bed in the kitchen on Monday morning Bet was so terrified it was all she could do to dial 999. She cushioned his heavy head in her lap until blue lights heralded the arrival of the ambulance men. They marched in like stormtroopers, bundling her out of the way so that they could check her husband's vital signs, manhandling him firmly onto a stretcher and into the waiting vehicle. Travelling next to him in the ambulance she felt a similar helplessness as the first time around, only now she knew that Tom's chances could only be worse.

Once at the hospital she found a payphone and called Elizabeth, Roy and Alan in turn. She didn't know how to spare them the shock, so she just told them as it was. One after the other they dropped what they were doing and drove over. They hovered about for hours, waiting for news, fetching cups of tea. Her boys forgot their usual differences and sat quietly together in mutual anxiety.

Bet hoped fervently that this crisis would not stop Gary flying out of the country in a week's time. She was so excited by his plans; the last thing she wanted was to create a diversion. Bet and Tom adored all their grandchildren but Gary was the closest. It wasn't favouritism; as a little boy he had formed an intense relationship with them both. She sat in the plastic hospital chair thinking about when Elizabeth and Mattie used to bring the three children over to Whitburn and leave them for the weekend. The best times were Sunday mornings when they would pile wriggling and squealing into bed with her, while Tom went downstairs to make breakfast for them all. After they had filled the bed with crumbs and left milky ring marks all over the bedside table, they would pull on their clothes and she and Tom would wrap them up in their raincoats and balaclavas to take them winkle-picking along the beach under the lighthouse or to play crazy golf or walk over to the allotment to look at the chickens and the rabbits. Gary worshipped Tom, with his strong arms and skin engrained with decades of coal and his unique brand of unsentimental kindness.

She and Tom lived in Whitburn because of the colliery and after it had closed down in 1968, Tom commuted four miles to the pit at Monkwearmouth for eleven years until he had his first stroke. That explosion in his head was like a bomb blast through their lives. It changed everything, he no longer even looked the same. The stroke left him twisted and speechless, paralysed down one side, unable to walk. Bet insisted that she would be able to manage, both with the change in their finances and with the job of looking after him. They moved a bed into the kitchen and the hospital supplied a hoist. Friends came over and built a concrete ramp over the steps and down into the garden.

Tom was brought home in a wheelchair and never again managed to move unaided, other than from chair to chair and into bed. She would shave and dress him every morning then wheel him outside to look at his precious garden or to sit out the front and wave at the schoolchildren as they passed. He tried to speak to them, but the words wouldn't form and he would grow more and more frustrated until he became wild and angry and would end up barking indecipherable animal sounds. His speechlessness exhausted them both but they persevered and little by little she began to interpret his grunts and expressions. It was not what she had anticipated for their retirement but it was better than losing him.

She couldn't have all the children to stay anymore but on a Saturday Gary would get on his bicycle and pedal the twenty-two miles from Durham up to Whitburn on its cliff top, where beautiful green land served as an Army rifle range. He would arrive flushed and bright-eyed and ready for something to eat and drink and would sit and play dominoes with his Grandad and help her in the house and sometimes go to tend the allotment and generally make himself useful until he left the next day.

Gary grew before their eyes, taller each year, full of chatter. After he had passed his driving test he would borrow Elizabeth's car and come over with Lesley, and Tom would tilt his head from side to side and make faces and she knew he thought Lesley was very pretty. She and Gary made a good-looking couple but they did argue a lot and that was not a good sign in her books.

The day Gary came to tell them he was going to work in the Falklands, she thought Tom was going to burst he was so thrilled.

"You never did think much of me being a hairdresser, did you, Grandad?" Gary said and Tom gave a long, slow wink. "But who would have thought this would happen? What do you think about me going abroad, eh?"

Tom nodded and grimaced and stuck his thumb up.

"Did you say you are going to have a uniform, Gary? You'll look smashing," Bet said. "Don't forget to come and say goodbye to us before you go."

When that moment came, of course she had to hug Gary for both of them. Lesley stood awkwardly in the background, putting on a brave face, she thought. Bet wished her grandson luck, torn between wanting to hang on to him and wanting to push him away.

"I'll write often, Gran, and tell you all about the penguins." She could see tears in his eyes.

"Don't worry about us, Gary love. I expect you'll be too busy for that but I'll write every week and we'll be thinking about you all the time, won't we Tom? That's a promise."

Tom sat pathetically in his wheelchair, waving with his one good hand and grinning lopsidedly, but she knew he was as proud as he had ever been.

Within days Tom's second stroke threw them both full tilt into a whirlwind of a crisis from which her husband might not return. When none of the family was available to ferry her, she was able to get a lift of an evening to and from the hospital with some local friends or could catch the bus. In the daytime she tried to keep things as normal as possible in the house, but when Glenn told her he had decided to tidy up the garden at his and Julie's new flat her automatic response was to offer him the spade and the hoe. She had neither the time nor the inclination to maintain the allotment and anyway there was a neighbour who she knew would be grateful for it.

Everyone was kind and the family and neighbours buzzed around but when she was there on her own the house seemed deathly quiet. Bet found the television poor company and it sat faceless and blank in the corner of the front room, a sullen reminder of how the life had gone out of their home.

On the sixth evening after the stroke, Saturday, she got in from the hospital, put the kettle on and sat herself down to write to Gary for the first time. He was still training at Wingham but would soon be on his way to the Falklands. She had bought a pad of light blue writing paper and matching envelopes and some airmail stickers.

Hello Gary, just got back from seeing Grandad, he is fine, she wrote. Mam and Paula were there. Grandad looks well and was asking after you. It took me a while to get who he meant but then Mam gave him all your news, pleased to hear you are enjoying it. Don't forget I would like a photo in your uniform when you can manage to get one taken to show off to my sisters. Haha! My handsome grandson!

No-one else had a grandson like Gary. It was small comfort, but the tea and writing the letter soothed her. When she had finished she licked the envelope down to post in the morning, then locked the back door and gazed for a minute or two at the empty bed. She patted it tenderly, switched off the lights and headed upstairs.

GARY

In the narrow confinement of the plane, he found it difficult to get comfortable. His knees were pressed hard against the seat in front and next to him a snoring colossus with shoulders as broad as a house overflowed the armrest into his space. Outside the window and a long way beneath them, clouds formed an infinite duvet of white. He found himself reliving that last telephone conversation with Lesley, over and over.

Even after three years he still couldn't believe that such a gorgeous looker really was his girlfriend. And although her parents were never less than kind and polite he knew that they must be disappointed with her choice, that they would prefer their daughter to be with some educated and ambitious man who had prospects and was more of everything that he was not.

Yet against all the odds he was the one who had won Lesley's heart on that school skiing holiday when they were both sixteen. It had been such a stroke of luck. One day she had fallen over and ended up with her leg in plaster, while the teachers had banned Gary from the slopes for a day as a punishment for missing classes and skiing off with another lad. So there was nothing better to do than hang around with the best-looking girl on the trip and keep her company.

She seemed to like his jokes and the attention he lavished on her and once they got home she still had her leg in plaster for a few weeks so he carried on. They enjoyed spending time together, sometimes doing stuff and sometimes not, and joining in with their families, and when one day she actually conceded in public that he was her boyfriend he was so proud that he found it a small compromise to put up with her self-centredness.

After GCSEs, they went to the same college in Durham, he for hairdressing, and she for secretarial studies. For two years, he was the only lad in a learning cohort of thirty women. He worked hard and it was the one time in his life he was top of the class. That was a good feeling, even if there did seem to be endless opportunities for Lesley to get jealous.

One day he was in the student bar showing one of his female classmates how to line up a shot on the snooker table. He was leaning over to help her to form a bridge with her hand, his face bent low next to hers so that he could feel the warmth of her breath and if he had wanted to, he could have kissed her. It was all perfectly innocent but at that moment Lesley had to walk in. She went berserk and ran out again screaming hysterically. He trailed her all the way through the buildings to the car park and she shrieked and swore then drove off in her car far too fast. He followed in his Mam's car to her house where her mother came to the door and told him with tight lips that he had better leave it for a few days.

“We are commencing our descent to Ascension Island. Please fasten your safety belts.”

He shook himself back to the moment and looked out of the window to a great ocean of blue and in it a tiny brown blot of an island. All around men were waking and stretching, with a hum of excited conversation. The plane descended fast and before he realised how close they were they landed with a heavy bump and the engines screamed into reverse. All the lads were craning their necks to look out of the portholes at the new sights.

When the door opened Gary grabbed his holdall and joined the line to get out of the confined space where they had been cooped up for over ten hours. As he approached the exit the light grew brighter, then he was outside and blinking on the top step of the gantry. The sunshine was the brightest he had ever known and vibrant heat rushed up from the tarmac to greet him.

He squinted at the barren landscape, where the only hint of green was on the upper slopes of a volcano which dominated the view. Beyond oil cans at the edge of the strip the ocean glinted in a wide bay, and on the far side of that stood a settlement, just a sprinkling of low buildings. He had never seen a place that looked anything like this and the rush of adrenaline at knowing he was just south of the Equator added to the sweltering heat. He was still wearing the warm jumper and army jacket that had been needed before take-off in England and would doubtless be right for what lay ahead, but right now he felt that he was cooking.

He and a few of the EFI lads took photographs of one another then stood around in a loose huddle complaining about the temperature. Some men headed straight indoors to the prefabricated buildings. Gary peeled off his layers, folded them neatly in a heap, preferring to sit down in the glaring sunshine. Luggage and cargo were being unloaded from the plane's hold and a waiting helicopter started to relay supplies to the ship.

When his name was eventually called, Gary joined others walking over to the helipad and clambered into the helicopter. There was an enormous pile of luggage in the middle, secured down with netting. He had to sidle his way around it to wedge himself in with his back to a porthole and his knees pressed into the luggage, shoulder to shoulder with other recruits. The engine noise was so loud that speaking was pointless. When the machine took off it was exhilarating and he craned around to look out at the view but he was too tightly squeezed between the other bodies to be able to see.

Their destination was a converted cross-Channel car ferry, the MV Keren. For more than thirty-two hours they waited while the ship was filled with stores and people. In the cramped four-berth cabins there was barely room to turn around and anyway it was so dark and dingy below decks that Gary found it more comfortable to while away time up top, leaning over the railings. He peered into the water and spotted the extraordinary shape of a hammerhead shark swimming just below the surface. He recognised it from one of those wildlife programmes on television and wished he hadn't left his camera in the cabin. Every now and then flying fish would break the surface in a whirring dazzle of silver.

Conversations between the passengers ebbed and flowed like the lazy tides lapping the anchor ropes. He introduced himself to two friendly types who chain-smoked at the rails; they reciprocated with ready smiles and handshakes and their names: Rob and Steve.

"Why are you going to the Falklands, then?" Gary asked.

"I've worked in the main NAAFI warehouse in Amesbury since I left school," replied Rob, the older of the two, probably in his mid-twenties. His hair was black with a straight fringe, and he had a thick moustache. "Me and the wife had a second baby seven months ago and we're finding it really expensive having two kids. Going abroad for five months seems like the easiest way to get some extra pay."

"Five months? I've got to do six. I thought everyone did."

"We marrieds get a shorter tour of duty. A few of my workmates have done it before and said it's not too bad; you just have to grit your teeth, do your job, watch the money roll in and hope the wife misses you."

Gary turned to the other lad, Steve, who pulled in his chin and raised his eyebrows.

"Me? I'm a forklift truck driver. Been working in a big warehouse at home in Nottingham but like everything else it closed down, then my girlfriend ditched me. So there didn't seem much point being home and there are sod-all jobs available; the Job Centre suggested this and a tour in the Falklands sounded a lot better than going on the dole. It's good money and after six months maybe the employment situation might be better. Who knows, it might improve my chances of finding a new girlfriend. How about you then, Gary?"

"I'm a hairdresser."

Steve backed away, scrutinising him sideways. "You're not a poof, are you?"

"No."

"Then here's a piece of advice, mate. Call yourself a barber not a hairdresser, right? And mind your back. There are plenty of rough types on this ship."

When the Keren finally set sail a schedule of lectures, first aid and PT helped them forget the tedium of the long journey and filled the time between meals.

"I can't understand why this is meant to be the high point of the day," Gary complained to his two new friends a couple of days later over a plateful of tasteless brown gristle. "This food's puke. It sums up the whole ship."

"Mine's a lump of old whale," said Steve.

Rob was pushing his fork around. "Is either of you lads going in for the darts tournament?"

"Yeah, I'd like to," said Gary, "Only I'll need to borrow your darts if that's okay, I didn't bring mine. And as long as it's not tomorrow night; I'm on guard commander duty."

The others chewed and grimaced.

"Not exactly sure what I'm guarding against," muttered Gary. "I reckon it's just another way to keep us busy."

"I've heard some of the squaddies can get a bit frisky," said Rob. "I remember one time the NAAFI sent over some fruit machines for the clubs. Apparently a gang of idiots got down into the hold and found them, I guess they were looking for money but of course the machines were empty, so instead they heaved one all the way up to the deck and tipped it over the side."

Gary fervently hoped he wouldn't have to deal with any squaddies larking around.

"This is disgusting," Steve spat his mouthful out. "I'll give a fiver to the first one that catches me a penguin."

"You wouldn't be able to unwrap it!" quipped Rob.

"P-p-pick up a penguin!" chanted Gary.

"Fuck off," said Steve.

The ship ploughed southwards day after day for thousands of miles. The monotony lulled them into a strange timelessness and the cramped physical conditions in the cabin below were intolerable. One evening Gary found himself sitting up on deck with a crowd of men as a glowing sunset gave way to a velvet canopy shimmering with a billion stars. Dolphins arced out of the water and were gone as quickly as they had appeared.

“Hey, lads, look, a whale!”

A great grey hump moved along in the viscous swell beside the ship, moonlit foam glistening as it cascaded off the animal’s sides. They watched it snort spray from its blowhole then shift direction and disappear into the dark horizon.

One of the men played a saxophone and a lazy melody drifted out on the warm breeze.

For a blissful moment Gary forgot the trials of the journey, filled with wonder at the huge ocean through which they were making their southerly way and excitement about what lay ahead.

ELIZABETH

The trips to the hospital ate up so much time that if there had been a buyer for Upstairs Downstairs, Elizabeth wouldn't have been able to deal with them. At her own salon she was fortunate to have two very competent girls who kept things going – Julie and Sadie – and between them they managed to cover all the appointments that Elizabeth had to miss. Julie had come a long way since Elizabeth took her on through the youth opportunities scheme. She was a real star, totally reliable and she had turned into a great stylist, too; she always used to give Gary a run for his money in the competitions. Glenn had fallen for Julie immediately and asked her out within weeks of her joining and now they had set up home together.

Meanwhile Paula was proving to be less of a treasure. It wasn't her daughter's fault; the poor girl missed Gary terribly and could not stop moping, no matter how nice her young boyfriend was to her. Now she had taken to her bed with a temperature and needed checking every hour or two. Elizabeth sat back in the sofa and looked at the dark window, too weary to get up and close the curtains. Fine sleet was falling, white silence in a black night.

The latest edition of the newspaper sat open on the armchair with their ad circled, begging for attention. They had had no interest, even after two weeks. The only person who phoned to say she had seen it was Pat, who enquired how Gary was getting on but soon worked her way round to the real reason for the call and handed in her notice. It was another blow which meant that Elizabeth would have to find someone else short term until they were rid of the business.

"Right, pet," Mattie appeared at the sitting-room door in his coat and jangled the car keys. "I'm off down the Coal Hole for a pint and a game of dominoes. Coming?" Mattie was President of the Lions and took his role seriously; he had something going on just about every night, a fund-raising event or a meeting or just the social down at the pub.

"No thanks, love. You go. I'll stay in and write to Gary. I'm dead beat anyway and I don't want to leave Paula on her own upstairs. Schweppes can keep me company. Pour me a sherry before you go, will you?" She picked up the lined pad.

Mattie headed for the sideboard. "Ask him if he's all right for money. Tell him we'll keep an eye on his account."

"I think he's more concerned that we keep an eye on Lesley."

"He'll be pleased to hear she rang and is coming round to see us, then. Here you are, I'll put it on the side. Won't be late."

She glanced over to the mantelpiece and the three Mother's Day cards, speckled with pollen from a vase of desiccating daffodils, and settled to her task.

Hi, Son, she wrote. She sipped at the sherry and felt its oaken sweetness relax her as it went down. She told him not to worry about Grandad or the shop, mentioned all the people who had asked after him and by the time the headlights of Mattie's car swung back into the drive she had fallen into an exhausted sleep.

Gary

The temperature had dropped and the churning sea turned flat and the colour of steel. Gary looked out of the cabin porthole at a drab morning and saw a darkening patch on the horizon which gradually formed into low shapes and an outline of land. He felt a surge of anticipation and rushed up on deck. They passed grassy islands then, in the lee of moss-coloured hills, turned into the narrows which formed an entrance to a harbour. Chilly drizzle misted around them as the ship inched forward between two low spits. Straight ahead, multi-coloured two-storey buildings dotted the port and gently rising ground behind.

The Keren approached a massive floating dock where they tied up next to a naval supply ship, whose battle grey blended with the clouds and wet concrete and wind-chopped water.

The loudspeakers crackled.

"All personnel are to proceed immediately to the dining room for disembarkation procedures. We will be welcomed to Stanley by the Commander of British Forces, Falkland Islands."

Gary dashed downstairs to squash in with the rest, his damp jacket steaming gently, tight-lipped, wondering what lay in store. A hush fell upon the gathered crowd, all eyes turned to the swing doors. The ship's captain led the Commander in, a good-looking man with grey hair showing underneath his beret, a stern yet kindly face, his body lean and fit in regulation camouflage.

“I’ve seen him in the paper,” whispered Steve. “I think he used to be in charge of the SAS.”

“Shh!” Gary hissed, not wanting to miss a word.

“Good morning,” the Commander started, his voice resonating effortlessly across the room. “My name is Major General Peter de la Billière. Welcome to the Falkland Islands."

He paused and the men shuffled, coughed and murmured like kids at a school assembly.

“Three years ago, the British armed forces won a decisive victory here in the Falklands against the invading forces of Argentina and reminded the world that British sovereignty is not easily usurped. Lives were lost and sacrifices made. The scars of those dark months will never leave the Falkland Islanders or the British people.

“You all have an important job to do, whatever your particular role. Your posting takes place during the most exciting phase of development in the Falkland Islands’ history, the building of an international airport at Mount Pleasant. This facility will transform the way the military operates here and will enable British forces to respond rapidly to any enemy attack in the future.”

The Commander allowed another pause for shuffling. Gary looked at Steve and raised his eyebrows.

"They'd better not attack before it's finished or we're toast," whispered his friend.

"Shush!" replied Gary.

"Here on the Falklands, members of the armed forces and EFI outnumber the islanders almost two to one. This is an important fact. We all have a duty to be as unobtrusive as possible, to allow islanders to go about their business and not to cause disturbance to the people or to the natural environment any more than is absolutely necessary. Please ensure you uphold the reputation of the British military by behaving at all times with discretion and responsibility. Whatever your role, be it in the armed forces or in EFI, be assured that you have a contribution to make to the long-term security of these islands and their people. Good luck to you all."

Although cutting hair hardly seemed significant compared to repelling an invasion or building an airport, the words were stirring. Gary was eager to get off the ship and go to work.

Another army officer stepped forward to address the assembled passengers. "Before you leave the ship, some very important safety information." Gary had twisted around to leave but turned back and groaned at Steve, who rolled his eyes heavenwards. It took a minute for everyone to settle down again.

"This is a standard briefing for everyone arriving on the islands. Listen carefully. Your lives may depend on it."

Gary felt a nudge from Steve and elbowed him back.

"Despite the Geneva convention, the Argentinians did not feel it necessary to mark their minefields. In fact they scattered mines indiscriminately and left no signs or records. The Royal Engineers have been doing a great job to identify where these mines are and have either cleared them or fenced off the areas where mines have been found. You are not, I repeat not, to venture inside those fences. You could lose a limb or your life. Be under no illusion, if you enter one of those areas and come out alive, we won't congratulate you. The opposite. You will be liable to court martial or summary dismissal."

Steve was making silly faces which Gary tried to ignore. He wondered how far inside a minefield you would get before you trod on something. Ten feet? Twenty feet? Or just one step? What if someone you knew went in and got injured, were you supposed to stand there outside the fence and do nothing?

The officer fished into a large wooden box and pulled out two objects. They all leaned forward. The first was large and flat like a pan lid with a fluted top.

"This is an anti-tank mine. It is designed to disable a tank by blowing the tracks off it. If you step where this is buried, the chances are it won't go off. However, in a Land Rover it would do significant damage, possibly kill you."

The boys looked at one another, more serious now. The officer held up the other mine, more compact, like a canister of camping gas.

"This is an anti-personnel mine. Step on this and you are guaranteed a major injury, possibly death. It only needs a pressure of between twenty-two to thirty-one pounds to set it off. That's a lot less than the pressure of your foot when you step. Both types are usually buried beneath the ground. You will not see them. On the other hand if you do see one, it could be a booby trap – what you see might be attached to a larger bomb nearby. So, I repeat, no going inside the fences. And if you see anything at all suspicious outside the marked areas, do not approach but report it immediately."

Gary felt slightly queasy.

"Remember, movement on the islands must remain strictly within the road network and checked areas."

This was all feeling a bit real. Gary shifted uncomfortably, wondering what it would be like to step on a mine. What would happen first, the flash or the bang? How much would you know about it? What if it blew your leg off, how much would that hurt? He imagined arriving home with one leg, on a stretcher with a bandaged and bloody stump, dependent on help for the rest of his life. How would Mam react? How would he get over to see Gran and Grandad? Would Lesley still fancy him?

"Gary!" Steve was pushing him. "Come on, we're going!"

He looked around to see that the canteen was emptying. Through the window and across the harbour to the east Steve pointed out three buildings.

"Look, those must be the coastels."

Gary peered out for his first sight of where they would live. Three monoliths, the same uniform colour as the sea and the sky, loomed above the water of the inner harbour. From here they looked like industrial units or warehouses.

A coach took them in batches along the shore. The EFI personnel were despatched to the largest coastel, number two. It was moored fast to the beach by long chains and cables, not built into bedrock at all but floating, a massive barge about fifty feet wide and over two hundred feet long. The accommodation was a mass of containers welded together on five floors, painted a uniform grey and punctuated by rows of windows. At the rear, machinery pumped out steam and water which trickled down in lines of rust.

Access to the coastel was via a long bailey bridge built on pontoons from the beach, with a flexible section at the far end to allow for the rise and fall of the tide. Gary pulled his two rucksacks and his holdall onto his shoulders and set off into wind-driven rain to join the new arrivals queuing at the entrance for room numbers.

He was directed to the first floor. After the conditions on board the Keren the room was a pleasant surprise. Reasonably spacious even if strictly functional, it had four bunks each with a reading light and a curtain for privacy and some headphones which plugged into the wall for Forces Radio. There were two lockers each and a table and chairs against one wall. A row of coat-hooks provided somewhere to hang stuff.

He threw his kit down and said a brief hello to his new roommates then went to find Rob and Steve, who had been sent to the second floor.

"What do you think, Gaz?"

"Not bad," he responded optimistically, singing out a favourite track about wherever he lay his hat, that was his home.

"My poor ears!" joked Rob, screwing his face up. "Come one, let's have a proper look around."

The whole of the front section of the coastel was taken up by sleeping accommodation, thirteen bedrooms on the outside and twelve on the inner side of two parallel corridors, with a well between them that gave the inner bedrooms a little natural light. Arranged over five storeys, he worked out that this made two hundred and fifty bedrooms, so there must be beds for one thousand men. On each floor there were communal showers and toilets as well as a lounge area. In one of the lounges there were a few billiard tables and on his floor there was a video room. The whole place smelt faintly of cigarettes, old socks and trainers.

A wide stairwell marked the division between the accommodation and the amenities in the rear half. Underfoot, shiny lino absorbed the noise of their boots. The atmosphere was dry and although the coastel rode the tide, there were no waves in this corner of the harbour and the floor was steady. Nonetheless, after the long sea journey he still felt like he was going up and down and he clutched the rail for security.

At the top of the double staircases they found the gymnasium, built like an aircraft hangar with air-conditioning pipes running the length of its high roof.

The gym was laid out with benches and barbells, while football, badminton and other courts were marked out on the floor in different colours.

"These weights and stuff look all right." Gary picked up a barbell and did a few bicep curls. "Flipping heck," he puffed.

"Stick to hairdryers," said Steve.

On the next floor down was the canteen and below it the kitchens, where staff in checked trousers and white jackets stirred huge, steaming aluminium pots and music blared.

"Smells all right," said Rob, sniffing the air for a hint of their first meal.

On sea deck were the laundry and offices and some secure areas they couldn't visit, and down below the water line, with no natural light, were two squash courts and a swimming pool.

“These facilities are OK,” Steve said, scratching his head, something Gary had noticed he did quite a lot, just out of habit.

“Either of you two play squash?” asked Rob.

“I could give you a game,” said Gary, making a mental note to ask his parents to send his racquet along with his darts.

“I’ll thrash you.”

“You good then? Bet I can run the legs off you.”

“Oh really?”

“Yeah, really. I may not be great at sport but I’m quick on my feet.”

“Where’s the bar?” Steve asked.

They went back to the reception area to ask the guard, who sniggered.

“No bar in this hotel, boys. You’ll have to go to Coastel One for that. Good luck.”

The next day was a Sunday and the new arrivals were given most of the day to recover from the journey and get their bearings. Gary stood on the beach looking out over the lagoon in which the coastels were moored. The sun broke through and gilded distant hills the colour of mustard. Weed was stranded by the retreating tide and twitched with tiny flies. The tangy smell brought back happy childhood memories of his Grandad, along the coast at Whitburn, wading in rock pools for starfish and crabs. Meanwhile far out on the water, a single bird with a long, thin neck paddled smoothly along the surface. It would dive down for minutes at a time, only to reappear somewhere completely different.

He surveyed the full sweep of Stanley Harbour, enclosed protectively by two great arms of land. Northwards, across the water, a long, low ridge interrupted the view of background heights. The crook of its wrist provided shelter for a naval station and two great cylindrical tanks like the ones on the quay in Tyneside.

Following the arm leftwards, to the west, the land rose up to a shoulder of bare hills, while the diminutive capital, Port Stanley, snuggled into the land's grassy breast, breathing wisps of domesticity from its chimneys. Along the beach at irregular intervals lay the abandoned remains of antique ships, their hulls torn apart by the Atlantic or having abandoned their journeys in storms near Cape Horn, condemned as scrap and left to rot at the water's edge. The jetty where the Keren had tied up floated out on the deep water just this side of Stanley with the loathsome ferry still moored alongside.

Now his eyes returned to the coastels and along the beach where he stood, to the collection of Portakabins that made up a temporary hospital and other support services. Then his gaze followed the shoreline as it extended to the right all along the other arm that enclosed the harbour. The elbow of the land formed a wide, knobbly peninsula that shielded the port from the Atlantic. Behind his back, invisible across the narrow but uneven isthmus, he could make out the rumble of the great ocean. He was glad of the regulation issue windproof jacket over his jeans and sweater.

“Hurry up, dreamer.” Rob’s voice broke his reverie.

Steve and others had gathered and were already striding away, drawn by the roar of surf, so Gary followed, his boots sinking a little into spongy ground dotted with tussocks of tough grass. It wasn't far to cross the thin neck of land that separated them from the Atlantic. Beyond the rise, there was nothing to see or hear but the ocean which crashed against the tilted rocks and pale sand of a bay. Huge wave tops were whipped into a froth of white foam by the wind. The sun glinted.

“Hey!” he shouted above the thunder of the rollers, while oystercatchers danced a skimming flight over the waves. “Who’s going in?”

It was only a joke but Steve gave a whoop and started to pull off his shoes and socks.

Not to be left out, Gary kicked off his footwear, rolling up his jeans above his knees while the others removed their boots, exposing pallid skin to the air.

“Last man in buys a round in Coastel One!” yelled Steve and hurtled towards the water with a loud yodel.

Gary pushed off like an athlete down the sand, the others hard on his heels. The wind rushed into his eyes and made them stream while spray dampened his face. He opened his mouth as he ran and tasted its saltiness.

“Shiiiitt!” screamed Steve, first in, though only just. “That’s fucking freezing!”

Gary felt the water grab his feet and ankles, the icy cold taking his breath away and squeezing a gasp from his lungs. One by one behind him yells and expletives marked the moment that the other lads hit the sea. To resist the suck of the waves Gary ran backwards for a few paces then turned to escape up the sand panting with shock and laughter but still too late to catch Steve, who was already ahead and had grabbed his shoes.

“Catch!” he shouted, throwing them in opposite directions. Gary quickly grabbed another pair. Soon footwear was all over the beach.

Eventually he sat down victorious with his own shoes in each hand and squeezed his chilled feet in. He rolled down his wet trouser-legs and Steve pushed him over. The other lads were wrestling for a boot. A red and white helicopter flew low overhead whirring like an insect.

Rob cupped his hands to make a megaphone. “Come on, you lot, there’s more to look at.”

Gary picked himself up and shook the hem of his windcheater to drain the sand out. They headed away from the beach, northwards to the gravel road and over a gentle rise which led them towards the airstrip which was RAF Stanley. It was good to feel the sun on his face, though odd to think that was north. It was a welcome contrast after the dismal grey of their arrival.

Over the hump in the road he looked down on an irregular collection of buildings and a sturdy control tower, beyond them an apron with air-force jets and a Hercules and, on a circular pad, the helicopter they had just seen flying over, its rotors still turning and men climbing out.

He wondered if any guards would come to stop them as they walked around the side of the hangars but the figures they passed seemed unconcerned about their presence. For all it was a military station, Stanley Airport had the air of a suburban backwater.

At the runway he instinctively looked right-left-right before stepping out although it wasn’t really like a street. The surface was laid in prefabricated strips crosswise, rather than being metalled with tarmac.

"Strange," he murmured.

"Yeah," muttered Rob, behind him. "Not like any airstrip I've ever seen."

"As if you'd know," yelled Steve, who started to run about with his arms horizontal, banking and turning and making sounds like automatic gunfire.

"Hey, come and see these!" Rob's shout drew Gary's attention to wreckage that lay beyond the airstrip. Gary jogged across for a closer look.

Sections of aircraft were spread in disarray over the grass, their pieces scattered as if by bombs or maybe they had crashed or been gunned down. One complete cockpit lay intact, grounded with its undercarriage flat on the turf, its tail nowhere to be seen. He approached it tentatively at first, unsure of the protocol, nervous of trespassing. The others joined in and stood around it bashfully with their hands in their pockets.

"D'you think these were ours or theirs?" he asked.

"Theirs," answered Rob. "You don't think we'd leave bits of our own planes littered about, do you?"

Gary's hand was on the plane now, at the junction of the curved front windscreen and the body. "It must be great to be a pilot."

"I dare you," said one of the others.

He hesitated for a moment. "OK. Come on Steve, you get in the back."

He heaved himself up into the front seat and handed his camera out.

"Here, Rob, take a good one."

Steve clambered into the rear section.

Gary looked out sideways for the photo, hands holding imaginary controls. Behind him, he could hear Steve fiddling about. "Concentrate, would you?" he directed over his shoulder.

"Roger, Roger," replied Steve through his hands.

"Turn your head and watch the birdie, you clown. How do we look?" he cried, while Rob fumbled with the camera.

"Ready. Say cheese."

"Argie pilots wouldn't say cheese," yelled Steve, "They'd be going OOOH SHIIIIIIIIIIIITTTTT!"

The lads all burst out laughing.

"Who else wants a go?" Gary got up to clamber out and three pairs of hands seized him, dragging him from the cockpit. "Leave off, will you?"

"Quick! Casualty!"

"Kiss of life for the hairdresser!"

"Very funny. Let me get myself out."

Further along he spotted another cockpit, nose stubbed, one wing cocked above the grass, the other broken off beyond its engine housing where it had hit the ground. It was like the skeleton of an ancient bird, bones stripped bare and bleached by wind and sun. He couldn't help wondering about the airmen who had flown the planes. How old were they? What did they look like? Had they died here?

*

That evening he met his predecessor, who would be going home in ten days' time. They sat over hot drinks from the machine in the canteen. The barber's face was pale and drawn and he spoke with the weariness of an old stager, although he couldn't have been more than a few years older than Gary.

"It's a bloody relief you're here."

"Yeah, I'm really looking forward to starting tomorrow." Gary sipped the insipid coffee.

"Hopefully you'll manage. At least you're young and you look fit. There's over two thousand military and EFI people here and you'll get to cut all their hair, plus the sailors on the ships that come into harbour."

"It sounds great. I like to fill my time." Gary had grasped the figures that would make up his pay but had paid little attention to the numbers of people who would need haircuts every month. It started to dawn on him that the job was going to be very demanding.

"You have no idea."

"Any tips?"

"Yeah. Take every hour and every day off that you can and never volunteer for anything extra." The barber rubbed his forehead and gave a deep yawn, exposing the wet cavern of his mouth, the fillings and his slimy tongue.

"Actually, I meant the money sort."

The barber rubbed his eyes. "Oh yeah, you'll go home loaded. I'll explain how the percentages and things work when we're at the store tomorrow."

"That's all right then."

"Listen, I know you're keen, but the most important thing you have to do is learn how to survive here."

"Gary, wait for us!"

He paused for his friends; Rob sprinted towards him down the causeway while Steve limped behind in squeaking boots. The end of March was coming around soon and after a week in their jobs they had adapted to their new routines.

"How come you're always so keen to get in to work early?" Rob pulled alongside, just a little out of breath.

"Not keen, I just can't stand being late. I like to be sure I'm ready before I have to start."

The morning breeze had a freshness like clean laundry and it felt good to be outside.

Steve trundled up behind, puffing and wheezing. "I can't work out how you do that, Rob, the amount you smoke, you bastard."

"You should play more squash, I keep telling you," said Rob.

Gary paused to salute a seal that lounged by the rocks in its usual place, unperturbed by the busy foot traffic. "Morning, Sammy." It lifted its mournful velvet head in response, eyes and whiskers moist, while the lads made a parade line in mock deference. "You know, I think he's starting to recognise us."

"I think he's a she," quipped Rob.

"Hey, lads, is it OK if we take the road instead of the footpath today?" said Gary

"Why?" asked Steve.

"You'll see."

The soles of their boots drove the surface chippings into the gravel, crunching a brisk rhythm. Steve hummed while Rob whistled through his teeth. A few minutes later, Gary stopped and crossed a ditch to where the desiccated remains of a cow were caught in eternal grimace, limbs and bones scattered by the blast of a land mine, wind-tanned hide framing its shocked face in a gruesome halo.

"What are you doing?"

"Just taking a photo to go with those ones of the wrecked Argie planes we took at the airstrip."

"You're sick."

"No-one at home's ever seen a blown-up cow before." He clicked the button then stuffed the camera back into the pocket of his jacket. "No wonder they never managed to clear all the mines; they must've run out of cows."

The wind performed its endless dance, whirling in off the sea, into his right ear and down his neck. He pulled his cap down harder and rubbed his hands together. Sea birds wheeled above, wings curved to embrace the breeze.

The friends descended into the small town, following the rough road down to the seafront near the floating harbour. Rob and Steve left for their dockside warehouse while Gary carried on a quarter of a mile to John Street. The barber's shop occupied a cramped room in a house adjoining the Kelper Store, a double-fronted shop requisitioned for the NAAFI. It sold a bit of everything and was where the garrison came to spend their pocket money.

Light filtered through the window onto paintwork that was discoloured and peeling. The only fittings were a stackable chair, a battered worktop, a dustpan, broom and bin. Gary was already numbed by the work although he was happy enough about his percentage of the takings which meant that he walked back to the coastel each night with heavy pockets. A daily bag of sweets and a carton of orange juice hardly made a dent in the cash that was accumulating in the box in his locker.

The other barber had gone to complete a final circuit of the outstations before leaving for home. Gary knew that his own day in the store would be busy, not from any sixth sense, but because a stream of customers was as inevitable and relentless as the wind and the tide. He might recognise a few faces from the coastel but generally it was a sea of anonymous heads that ebbed and flowed. For most customers a shear with number two clippers was enough, although some of the men, mostly officers, still wanted a proper cut, which at least demanded some of his skill and dexterity with the scissors even if it did take a bit more time.

In just three days the other barber would be gone and Gary would take on the whole workload alone. He was looking forward to the added responsibility and to travelling around the islands, but it was already obvious that the demand for haircuts would exceed his capacity to deliver them.

This working day unfolded just as predictably as he might have expected until at the end of it a couple of nurses from the military hospital appeared, making a welcome contrast to the usual masculine flow. They stood at the doorway in their white lace-up shoes, coats over their uniforms, a look of hopeful enquiry on their faces.

"I know there's a sign advertising Unisex Hairdressing on the window of the store," one of them made a gesture to indicate the lack of facilities in the miserable little barber's shop. "But could we persuade you to come and do us a cut and blow dry at our house?"

He could feel his cheeks redden under their direct gaze.

"The last barber wouldn't cut women's hair at all," the other one said.

He went to pick up the broom and swept up a few stray clippings to cover his discomfort, cross with himself for looking embarrassed, as if he'd never met any women before.

"So we're a bit desperate."

"You'd best not let any of the men hear you say that or you'll have them all knocking at your door," he joked, unable to stop himself before it was said, sneaking a look at them to see if they minded.

They laughed and he calmed down; they were just ordinary women, after all.

"How about if we cook you dinner? Shall we say Friday?"

It would mean missing the monthly entertainment, a singer, but home cooking sounded tempting.

"We've already ordered a goose."

He wasn't sure what to make of that. "Why, is it a special occasion?"

"It will be if you cut our hair," the first one laughed and winked at him. "Actually, we eat goose quite often. There's so many of them about that the farmers shoot them to keep the numbers under control."

"I've never tried goose before."

"It'll be a new experience for you, then. You'll be helping us out."

That Friday after he had finished at the store he set off to find their house, which was easy enough in the simple grid pattern of Stanley's streets. The white weatherboarded bungalow had a rusting green corrugated roof and a pillar-box red front door. He pushed the gate open and walked up the path through a neat garden with bobbing roses.

"I'm Denise, by the way," said the taller one, greeting him at the door with a towel around her shoulders to catch the drips from her just-washed hair, ushering him in to a large kitchen. "And this is Lorraine."

An appetising smell of roast dinner wafted from the oven and the spitting and bubbling of hot fat accompanied background music from a tape player. Lorraine said she would prepare the vegetables while he started on Denise's hair. It made a welcome change from short cuts with clippers or scissors to think creatively about what would suit her. She had a natural wave and if they had been in England he would have suggested a fashionable flick, but it was obvious that she needed something practical that would keep its shape; he cut it close to the nape of her neck with soft layers to lift it. It only took minutes to dry. The women swapped places, Denise now attending to pans boiling on top of the stove, while he concentrated on Lorraine's longer bob, which needed a good inch and a half off it to give it some shape and to get rid of all the split ends but had to be long enough to tie back at work. They talked mostly to each other, letting him concentrate, and occasionally they would all sing along with the music. He wondered if they had boyfriends and was sure they must be popular with the doctors and the officers.

"You'll have to give us a wave when you walk past our Portakabins now," Lorraine said, shaking her head so that the shiny bob swung from side to side. "Did you hear about last year's fire at the old hospital? It was dreadful. Really dreadful. There was nothing left. But at least we'll get a nice new building out of it in a few months' time."

When he had finished tidying his tools away Gary sat down at the kitchen table while the nurses rushed about to drain the vegetables and transfer food to plates.

"Da-daa!" Denise fanfared triumphantly as she set the goose down heavily on the table. He couldn't believe its size; it was bigger than any Christmas turkey he had ever seen, more like an ostrich. The skin was salty and crisp on the outside, oozing with fat, and the roast potatoes were the best he had ever tasted, better even than his Mam's, although he would never tell her that. He enjoyed the fresh greens from the garden. After he had finished his first plateful, he readily accepted another.

"You must think they starve us on the coastel."

He ate until his stomach hurt, revelling in the feast and the homely surroundings and the women's company. They enquired about his family and life in Durham and did he have a girlfriend? "Of course you do, silly question, a handsome boy like you. I bet she's pretty."

"Yeah, she's good-looking all right," he said, putting his knife and fork down at last, feeling his face warming.

"Doesn't she mind you being away?" they asked.

He exhaled through his nose, lips pressed tightly together, and his forehead tightened as he remembered how angry she had been when he told her about the job.

"OK, you don't need to answer that!" The nurses broke into peals of laughter. "Keep her keen, eh? Absence makes the heart grow fonder!"

"I hope so," he replied. "To be honest, it all happened so quick, I didn't really think about things from Lesley's point of view. She took it all in her stride, though, once she got over the shock. She's going to be the first person I see when I get home."

When dinner was finished he offered to help wash up but they shoo-ed him away, telling him to hurry up so that he could catch the end of the show. Instead, he stopped on the way back and sat on a rock looking at the sea and the blackout-darkened coastel in the moonlight, aching with indigestion and wishing that Lesley would somehow appear out of the night.

Soon after the evening when he had cut the nurses' hair, Government House called to say that if he could please fit in a haircut for the Governor's wife, she would be most grateful. When he heard that a car would come to collect him, Gary was thrilled at the prospect of a ride in a shiny limousine.

On the appointed day he worked right through without any break for lunch and was ready to leave the Kelper Store at five on the dot. A vehicle pulled up outside and he peered anxiously through the window but instead of a uniformed chauffeur in peaked cap and braid, there was a snowy-haired man in a dark blue Ford Fiesta. It must just be a local calling in on some business. He gave the worktop an extra wipe and wished the official car would get here soon; he was looking forward to his commission and hated having to wait.

"Corporal Shewan?" a soft voice said. "I'm Don Bonner from Government House."

Gary started. The white-haired man stood at the doorway, neat but informal, in dark trousers and a black V-necked sweater over an immaculate white shirt and dark tie. His shoes were worn but they shone as if polished every day.

Gary grabbed his bag and followed the man towards the Fiesta. "Should I sit in the front or the back?" he couldn't resist asking.

"Whichever you like," replied Don, pulling open the door and holding it ceremoniously, with what would have passed for a straight face had his eyes not twinkled so much. Gary folded himself into the back seat and grinned.

They drove through the town, past low houses with corrugated iron roofs painted in pastel colours, past the new hospital building site and up a gorse-lined drive where the prickly bushes were dotted with yellow flowers, despite the lateness of the season.

“Do you take the Governor around in this?” Gary asked.

“No,” twinkled Don some more, gliding smoothly through the gears. “This is Lady Hunt’s private car; she calls it Fifi. For official business we use a red London taxi – the Governor’s very proud of it. And there’s a Land Rover for crossing the camp.”

“Which camp is that?”

Don turned to look at him and paused for a moment, as if checking that Gary wasn’t joking.

“That’s what we Kelpers call the countryside,” he said.

Gary had worked out who the Kelpers were.

The car pulled up at the front entrance, by a neat lawn with a pole and a fluttering Union Jack. He tucked his bag under his elbow and walked to the glossy front door. On each side of the step there was a miniature cannon pointing out, two brave mice, something that echoed from his childhood somewhere, maybe a visit to some stately home. He looked back at Don, who nodded and waved a finger towards the bell, which he rang. It jangled from a long way within.

A woman in her mid-fifties came to the door, simply dressed in a pair of working trousers, a checked shirt and flat shoes.

“I’m the hairdresser,” he said, and then, just in case the woman didn’t know, “For Lady Hunt.”

“That’s me, come on in,” she said with a beaming smile.

For a moment, Gary thought she was joking.

“We’ll go through to the back. I’ll ask Nanny to organise us all a cup of tea while Don parks Fifi.”

He followed her through the house to an enormous kitchen with a pine table in the middle of its red-tiled floor. Her hair was thick and wavy and reached to her shoulders. She moved effortlessly, without a sound. Behind them, another woman tapped in on peep-toed sandals. Her lilac overall was buttoned up tightly and she carried a flowerpot with an overflowing geranium. This was probably the housekeeper, though he was learning that it was dangerous to make any assumptions.

“This is Nanny,” said Lady Hunt, which didn’t shed a great deal of light on the matter.

“Tea, I imagine?” Nanny nodded her head and smiled at him. “Or coffee?”

She stood the plant on the draining board and then she made drinks in four very ordinary mugs and Gary blew and sipped his coffee while Lady Hunt held her tea and explained how much she needed a style that would look less of a mess in the incessant wind.

The Governor's wife reminded him of Gran Shewan, not Gran Davison but the other side of the family, his father's mother. There must be something about being married to an important man that gave such women their confidence; in the case of his Gran Shewan, she was married to the mine manager, which may not be as grand as being married to a Governor but was nonetheless quite significant in Sunderland. It was funny how Lady Hunt drank her tea like his Gran, sipping at it daintily with a little beak like a bird's.

They went through to a bathroom so that he could wash her hair then returned to the warmth of the kitchen to start cutting. The conversation flowed easily, although he was careful to listen rather than to prattle on about himself. Her dark brown hair was flecked with silver strands - a shorter style would suit her, make her look younger. Locks fell on the floor all around the chair.

"I'm so glad you said yes," she said. "I thought I was going to have to get Nanny to cut it."

Nanny looked up from her ministrations on the geranium and gave a light-hearted shrug, secateurs in hand. "Pruning, that's about all I'm good for. Lady Hunt usually waits for trips to London rather than trust me with the scissors."

He was dying to know what it was like for them when the Argies invaded, only he was too shy to ask. He had noticed the shell holes that scarred the wall outside.

"If you've got a hairdryer I'll dry it for you," he said.

"That would be a real treat," said Lady Hunt.

He took his time smoothing the thick waves to a neat finish then unplugged the drier and stood back. She looked at herself from all sides in a hand-held mirror. She gave him a broad smile, touching her hand to the back of her head.

"I hope you like it," he said. "It's an easy style for you to manage and it should last quite a long time before it needs re-cutting. You'll be able to blow-dry it yourself."

"It's simply lovely, thank you." She found her purse and paid him and then said, "Wait a minute," and pressed another couple of coins into his hand. "Don will give you a lift."

He found Don outside the back door by the galvanised metal garage where he was polishing the red London taxi, parked next to Fifi, with his crisp white shirtsleeves rolled up above his elbows. Behind him the sun sank low in a fireball of dark orange.

"Sure you don't want to sit in the back again?" Don asked straight-faced as Gary went for the front seat of the Fiesta. "I'll drive you all the way to the coastel if you like."

Gary enjoyed being driven in the small car, its whirring motor, Don's careful steering around the numerous potholes and his distinctive burr describing the history of the places they passed and the mounds of peat, which the islanders burned to keep the houses warm and their cookers stoked. Sweet-smelling smoke rose from the chimneys in the town and flew away across the sea. They passed a few straggling EFI boys walking back up the road, hopeful of cadging lifts from passing vehicles, then he spotted Rob in the dusky evening light.

"Actually, Don, you can drop me here. That's a friend of mine. I'll walk the rest of the way with him."

Don pulled up and Gary unfolded his legs, reaching into the back for his bag. "Thanks very much."

There was a look of surprised amusement on Rob's face.

"How did you get on with Lady Hunt? Hope you didn't muck up her hair," he said as soon as Gary was out.

"Course not. She was really nice. "

They stood on one side while Don manoeuvred the car in a three-point turn then sped off with a cheery wave and a flick of gravel. The friends fell into step, hands in pockets. Gary related his experiences while his stomach rumbled and he stifled a yawn.

"D'you know, I've done over two hundred and fifty haircuts in my first ten days and I'm shattered. There's a few nice people like the nurses and Lady Hunt but mostly the job is no different from shearing sheep. I can't imagine why they think one person on their own is going to be able to do it all."

"I think you're right," said Rob.

"I've got to get out of hairdressing. It's a killer job."

"But you've only just got here."

"I mean when I get back. The trouble is I don't know how to do anything else."

They headed straight in for tea. Gary wolfed down soup and a double helping of toad in the hole and added extra custard to his pudding.

Afterwards he dug out his writing pad and pen. He plugged in the earphones to Forces Radio and lay down to write home about the Governor's wife. He thanked Mam and Dad for parcels that had just arrived - his darts and the squash racquets from the back of his bedroom cupboard and he told them how well he was getting on and about all the new things he had seen and how great the food was and how much money he was making. He asked after the family and made jokes and asked them to send his no.3 and no.4 clippers, because not everyone wanted to look like a skinhead.

Then he wrote to Lesley and he told her how meeting the nurses and Lady Hunt were fun but made him feel homesick, how dreary it was at the Kelper Store, how relentless and hard the work was, how much he was missing her despite the big adventure. He got out his diary and counted up the days until he would see her again and there were a lot. The little bear with its heart T-shirt was wedged between the pillow and the wall and he reached up and held it and pressed his face into it. His body ached for her.

A few days later there was a big sort-out of rooms at the coastel to group similar personnel together. The EFI boys were all to move to the fourth floor rather than be mixed up among various troops. They spent the best part of Saturday morning packing and establishing their new arrangements. Gary got on well with his boss, Dita, who was in charge of security at the big EFI warehouse, and had asked to share a room with Rob and Steve. When he looked at the list he saw that Dita had fixed it for them. Their fourth roommate was Shaun, who worked with the others at the warehouse.

"Which bunk do you want, Gary?"

It already looked as though a bomb had gone off in the room and exploded eight bags in all directions. Gary had to lift his feet over piles of uniforms and boots and cassette tapes to get to the far end.

Steve upended his rucksack onto his bunk and added to the confusion with stray underwear, socks, and a pack of playing cards that slipped off the bed one by one to form a slick on the floor.

"Bloody hell, guys, how can you create such a mess?"

"What's your problem?" said Steve. "It's called unpacking."

"It's chaos."

"Make yourself useful, Gaz," said Rob. "We might as well decorate the place." He threw a pile of dirty magazines at Gary, who had taken refuge on the bottom bunk, waiting for calm before sorting his own stuff out.

"Hey, Rob, I bet your wife doesn't know what you read when you're away from home." Gary started to leaf through the magazines. "Right then, lads, which hair colour do you prefer?"

"Gary, don't tear all the pictures out, for God's sake!" interrupted Steve. "Leave some over."

"What's your problem?"

"Just like to keep a few for a bit of quiet reading, know what I mean?" His hand moved as he winked.

Within an hour order was restored, clothes were folded and stacked in lockers, coat hooks claimed, territories established and the place was their own. Naked women adorned every inch of the communal walls. They stared out provocatively, breasts jutting, legs splayed, mouths open.

Gary had bought two maps of the islands illustrated around the edges with different types of helicopter. He fixed them to the wall next to his bunk, tearing the sticky tape between his teeth, placing them close to his pillow so that he could see them when he was lying down.

He stuck prints of Lesley and Paula and Schweppes next to the maps. He balanced his battery alarm clock on the little strip-light on the wall and sellotaped a few of the letters from home above and below.

"Hey, who's that smasher, then?" Steve was pointing at the photos. "And I don't mean the dog."

"You mean Paula?" He looked round to check. Steve had seen his photo of Lesley before. "That's my sister. It's not a brilliant shot."

"She's a looker!" Steve whistled. "Has she got a boyfriend?"

"Yeah, she's going out with a local lad but I don't think it's serious. Why?"

"Do you think she'd mind if I wrote to her?"

"I'll ask her."

"This your girlfriend, then, Gary?" Shaun asked, pointing at the other photo.

"Yeah."

"You lucky bastard."

Gary grinned and blushed.

"Quite a trophy, eh, Gary?" said Steve.

Rob gave him a playful punch. "I think our Gary is beginning to wonder why on earth he left her behind, eh, Gaz? Wondering what she's up to while his back is turned!"

He felt the redness deepen. "Stop it, lads. Don't joke about her."

"You're mad to leave a girl like that," said Steve. "All the blokes in Durham will be round her like flies."

"She's waiting for me. She can look after herself."

"Yeah, I bet she can."

He squirmed under their mocking eyes.

"You're just jealous."

He busied himself with the pile of letters from the bottom of his rucksack, more than a dozen already, full of news and gossip. The envelopes from Lesley were covered in acronyms, M.L.F.Y.W.N.D. and A.M.L.F.N.A.E.M., and he worked them out and read what she said and knew that he had nothing to worry about. But the conversation had unsettled him; he couldn't stop an uneasy sensation rolling in over his spirits like cold mist on off the sea.

That afternoon he scribbled a note to Paula.

I have plenty of mates and we are all missing our girlfriends. I've told them how good looking you are, so send a photo and I'll sell it to them. They think I'm stupid for leaving Lesley having seen her picture.

He felt better for confiding in his sister.

Tell Schweppes I am missing her. You can tell her it is RUFF out here.

ELIZABETH

Elizabeth pushed the vacuum cleaner around the sitting room for the second time that day. "Honestly, Schweppes, I've never known you moult like this before." The dog followed around forlornly, tail at half mast, attempting a wag but achieving little more than a droopy wave. "I think you're missing him, too." She turned the machine off and straightened her back. "I've never seen you look so miserable."

She put the machine away and found her coat amongst all the others on the hooks by the back door. Schweppes looked up at her with head cocked to one side, whiskery eyebrows moving up and down inquisitively, mouth opening and starting to pant in expectation.

"Right then, where's your lead? Where are my keys? Let's think about how much time we've got for a walk. I must get over to the hospital and you'll need a good brushing before you come back into the house."

The clocks had gone forward at the weekend to summer time. It was extraordinary how much better it was having an extra hour of light in the evening and the weather had turned mild.

The path leading down to the river was slippery, winding between fallen branches and the tattered brown stalks of last year's weeds. The dog ran on ahead, happy to be off the lead, pausing to sniff and leave her scent at every plant and tree.

Elizabeth tucked her hair behind her ears and breathed in the fresh air. Below, the river flowed fast and silent, in spate after the rain and snow of the previous weeks. She passed the steep bank where generations of children had worn a muddy slide. Memories of her three little ones running up and down through the trees, distant echoes of their laughter, rebounded all around her and off the tree trunks.

She wished those days could have stayed forever in freeze frame, capturing that innocent joy of youthful parenthood when the future looked as bright as the summer sunshine that danced in the children's hair and kissed their pale skin. How cruel time was. Look what it was doing to her father, holding grimly on to what was left of his life, not yet an old man but a broken one, his bear strength gone for ever. Look what it was doing to her Mam, already weighed down with the relentless effort of caring for him and now with the worry of what the next stage might be, undermining the optimism which was her mother's hallmark. Now time had taken both Glenn and Gary out from under her wing and before too long it would take Paula, too. What would her life be then?

In the brown swirl of the river, sticks and leaves floated past to who knew where, joining the dizzy rush of the water, twirling and circling in a frantic dance, borne along on the irresistible flow. The greedy water bit at the bank by her feet, taking small mouthfuls of earth away from between the tree roots.

She called to Schweppes, who appeared from the undergrowth with a panting grin that could only mean she was having a lovely time. They headed back up the hill and the dog repeated her usual sniffing and peeing ritual, revisiting all the same bushes and shrubs and pausing to mark each again.

When they arrived at the back door, Paula was already home from school.

“Don’t let the dog in, Paula, her paws are filthy and she needs a brushing. Her coat’s falling out in lumps.”

“I’ll do it if you like, so you can get on with dinner and I can put off my homework.” Paula grabbed the towel and the blue brush that were lying on the back step and took Schweppes by the collar. “Come here, mutt.”

Hair started to fly past the kitchen window, floating off in the breeze.

“Hey, Mam, do you think if I put all this in a bag it would be possible to spin dog hair into knitting wool?” Paula’s voice called from outside the back door. “We could sell it.”

Elizabeth smiled to herself as she prepared vegetables for their tea. Paula was bound to do well in her life, she was so entrepreneurial. She was always making things and thinking of business opportunities. Even though she was a bit listless without Gary, she hadn't lost her flair for new ideas.

"Well, I don't know about that. Mind you, we need to come up with something ingenious. I hoped we would have got rid of the shop by now and the bills just keep mounting up."

"Haven't you had any interest, what about those people you showed round?"

"No, love. Let's just keeping hoping."

"Mam, can I come with you to see Grandad?" Paula was puffing with exertion.

"What about that homework?"

"I'll do it after we get back."

Paula let go of Schweppes at the back door and the dog shook herself from nose to tail, working her skin back into the right position. She slunk into the house and took refuge in her basket.

"Right, then, we'd better get going."

Elizabeth left the supper cooking in the oven and the two of them jumped into the car for the drive to Sunderland. Grandad had been moved out of the general hospital to a private room in the small Havelock Hospital on Hylton Road. They said he was out of danger although he needed nursing care and would have to make significant progress if he was ever going to go home again. It was not great news but at least the immediate crisis was over. And Mattie had an interview tomorrow at a large furniture store over in Billingham, which needed a new manager. That might help the cashflow. Perhaps spring really was just around the corner.

GARY

The nightfall announcement resounded through the coastel every evening.

"Blackout precautions now in force. Blackout precautions now in force!"

They pulled down the blinds in their room. It was a grim daily reminder that the Falkland Islands were still on invasion alert and it always made the back of Gary's neck prickle. Today was Wednesday, it was April and they were into the second day of a three-day invasion exercise. The enemy hadn't landed yet. After a hard day's work Gary did not relish what was coming, wishing instead he could relax as usual playing cards and darts and hating the idea of playing soldiers.

The EFI corporals had been allocated into pairs for lookout duties and would be called to the gym in turn to be given their instructions. The Paras and Gurkhas were acting as the enemy invaders. They had a fearsome reputation.

"Did you hear about the ruckus yesterday in the bar on Coastel One?" Gary was always the first to hear the latest news and gossip at the Kelper Store and liked to pass it on to his roommates before they heard from other sources. "One of the Paras bit off the ear of this guy he was fighting."

“I have heard that if they catch you on exercise you get one hell of a beating,” said Rob.

There was no reason to disbelieve it.

“Shewan! Pownall!”

“Shit,” said Steve, “No sleep for you and me then, Gary.”

“Good luck, guys,” said Rob and Shaun simultaneously.

Gary and Steve reported to the gym where they lined up with a dozen or so EFI lads for a small piece of blacking which they had to rub all over their faces and the backs of their hands. It would have been funny except that Gary felt too tired and apprehensive to mess about. On the next table was a pile of radios, then a mountain of helmets. At the end of the line a sergeant thrust a sub-machine gun into his hands.

“Hope I don’t need to use this thing. I can only do present arms.”

He turned to his friend.

“Hey, point that gun in the opposite direction!” cried Steve, eyes staring out nervously from his blackened face. “Blanks or no.”

An instructor checked that they were familiar with the two-way radio and gave them some code words. “You’re to keep your eyes and ears peeled and radio in if you see or hear anything. Any movement. Any sound. Remember, the enemy could arrive from anywhere at any time. Make sure you know where you are on the map. You will be relieved in the morning. Got that?"

"Yes, sir," they chorused.

Across the causeway in the dark a line of vehicles was waiting.

"You two. Get in that Land Rover over there. Move!"

Gary climbed into the back, behind the driver and an officer, and helped Steve who seemed to have got tangled up with the radio. The Land Rover headed out into the dark night, bumping slowly over the camp for miles, its headlights hooded so that it gave only enough light for the driver to see the ground a few feet ahead. Eventually the vehicle pulled up in the middle of nowhere.

"Right, this is your position. You are lookout 36." The officer shone a torch on the map and pointed with his finger. "This is where you are. Got it?"

Gary and Steve both peered at the map.

"Yes, sir," Gary said, even though the markings on the map were as meaningless as Chinese to him. He hoped that Steve understood what he was looking at.

"Right. Good luck."

They clambered out and exchanged greetings with the two Corporals they were to replace. By the light of their dull lamps, they found their positions in the dugout and hunkered down, cursing the darkness and the cold. The

Land Rover was gone, swallowed up by the wind and the night and the lumpy ground.

Gary listened and watched. He strained his ears and eyes into the black nothingness, in which after a time he could make out clouds and the shapes of the land. When he grew tired of staring he sat down with his back to the wall of the dugout and shrank into himself to keep warm. They spoke little, conscious of the need to keep quiet, their ears alert to the noises of the night. Time passed slowly. From time to time he or Steve would shuffle about, get up and look over the top, to see if there was anything.

The silence was so profound that he felt he could identify the microscopic sound of the breeze in each individual blade of grass for miles around. It was as if he was alert to every tiny nuance, each miniscule flutter of a leaf or stalk.

Time dragged. Rain came and went. He was tense. Every now and then Steve's breath would go completely quiet then he would suddenly inhale with a great rasp.

"For God's sake, I know you're listening hard but just breathe normally, will you?" Gary muttered, his nerves on edge. They had already been waiting for at least two hours and the next five stretched ahead of them as if into infinity.

And then, just perceptibly, the tiny sounds changed, a feeling before it was a hearing. His ears seemed to be reaching out, trying to trap every wavelet of noise. He strained to work out if there really was anything and the harder he listened, the more he was sure that it was not just the sound of the wind in the blades of grass but the wind in the rotor blades of a helicopter.

He jumped to his feet, eyes straining into the darkness as the unmistakeable *wok-wok-wok* grew louder.

"Shit!"

His eyes had grown accustomed to the darkness and through the gloom he could make out a Chinook coming towards them.

"Steve! Get the radio!"

Steve fumbled for the machine while Gary grabbed the sub-machine gun. His heart was crashing against his ribs.

"Lookout 36 to base. Do you read me? Over," Steve hissed into the machine.

There was a crackle of static.

"Shit." Steve was twiddling the knobs. He tried again. "Lookout 36 to base. Do you read me? Over."

"Base One. What's your password? Over."

"Speedwell."

"Go ahead, lookout 36."

"There's a Chinook and it's coming towards us."

Gary kept his eyes on the helicopter, which stopped less than a quarter of a mile away and was hovering steadily.

"Tell them to hurry up!" With horror, he saw a line of ropes thrown out from the machine, black figures sliding down, like drops of tar, more and more of them, until he lost count.

The radio voice crackled. "Can you give us the grid reference? Over."

"Gary! What the hell is the grid reference?" Steve sounded panic-stricken, waving the map about hopelessly.

"I don't know. I can't do grid references." Gary passed the gun to Steve and grabbed the radio. "Lookout 36 here. They're about a quarter of a mile away from us. They're coming out of the helicopter now."

"Which direction are they coming from?"

He looked at Steve, at a loss to know which direction they were facing.

"Straight ahead. They're straight ahead!"

"Can't you do better than that?"

His mate turned the map round and round, the sub-machine gun resting in the crook of his elbow. "This is hopeless."

"We don't know. Come and get us, please!"

"Aren't there any features that would help us identify the direction?"

"Just get the hell over here and get us out!"

"Ssshhhh!" Steve was tugging his sleeve. "The helicopter's going. That means they're all on the ground. Shit, I really don't want a beating."

Gary looked out, terrified, adrenaline thumping through his veins, trying to make out figures from the shadows. Any minute now he expected to be jumped. He could see nothing; hear nothing now but the sound of the wind in the grass and the crashing of his heart. Suddenly there was another noise, behind them, a vehicle heading across the camp. It appeared out of nowhere and in half a minute was upon them, a Land Rover. It screeched to a halt.

"Right you two useless idiots, get in!" The driver revved the engine and Gary threw himself in head first, landing in a heap and scrambling to sit up while Steve sprawled across him as they sped across country in the dark.

"Shit, that was a close call." Steve's eyes were staring out madly from under his helmet.

"Bloody hell," Gary replied. "We were rubbish but that was so unfair. None of the training prepared us for that. We're going to get a roasting."

Sure enough, the debriefing proved to be an excruciating embarrassment. The older EFI hands showed great delight in seeing two new boys take the wooden spoon as most useless lookouts and teased them mercilessly. When the exercise was finally over and everyone was dismissed, the hapless pair went for showers and had their towels stolen by a gang of laughing men who chased them naked down the corridor.

They banged through the door of their room and barricaded it with the table, glad of sanctuary.

"Well, that's settled one thing," Gary said as he dressed.

"What's that?" Steve asked.

Gary pulled on his warm sweater. "There's one career worse than hairdressing and that's being a soldier. I will never, ever sign up for the Army."

Steve grinned. "Nor me."

After work the next evening Gary went to his locker and pulled out the cash box, filling his pockets with high denomination coins before sneaking to the telephone booth, hoping that none of their tormentors would see him.

He was surprised at how nervous he felt. It was four weeks since he had called Lesley from the phone box at Wingham. Although he had written many times and received numerous letters in return, he wondered what it would be like to speak from eight thousand miles. He ran through imaginary conversations in his head.

Now the phone was ringing at the other end. He pictured the house, its slightly showy furniture and precisely positioned ornaments. The line clicked as someone picked up the receiver.

“Hello?” said her voice.

The sound was almost more than he could bear. He faltered.

“Hello?” she repeated.

He forced his mouth to speak. “Lesley?”

“Gary?” She sounded unsure. “Gary?”

“Yeah.”

“Gary!”

“Hi.” He felt breathless. “How are you?”

“I’m all right. How about you?”

“I’m shattered. Haven’t slept for two nights.”

Once he got started he talked and talked. He turned the drama of the previous night into a joke and enjoyed telling her how ridiculous he had been.

“I’m missing you something terrible, Lesley. I think about you all the time. How are you getting on?”

"Oh, you know," she said, "I had a cup of coffee with your Mam yesterday. We talked about you. I told her I lie in wait for the postman every morning; he must think I fancy him. She says she does the same. She's great, your Mam. She looks tired, though. She's been awfully worried about your Grandad."

"He's all right, isn't he? Gran wrote that there is a chance he could live at home again."

"Your Mam says he is starting to look better. Gary?"

"Yeah?"

"You are a very long way away."

"I know." Gary paused. "Listen, I'm making so much money you wouldn't believe it. I've already sent a couple of hundred quid home and I haven't even had my pay yet. And I'm learning a lot, it's really good experience."

"I wish you hadn't gone."

"Oh no, my coins have run out. What are you wearing? What have you got on underneath?"

"Honestly, Gary, is that all you think about?"

"No," he lied. "I just want to picture you… there go the pips. I'll phone again when I can. Keep writing. Take care."

"You take care, too."

He stared at the telephone for a while, chewing his nails, until someone pulled the door open.

"You finished or what?"

There was a great buzz around the canteen at dinner. He was so tired that he was impervious to the jibes and taunts about the exercise.

"Well done, mate," Rob said, coming over from the counter. "Ignore them and they'll soon shut up." Rob was usually right about things. He put his tray on the table next to Gary's and sat down. "Have you heard? The pay slips are in. We should get them tonight. At last, confirmation that we are all getting rich."

"That's good. I've earned my money. Five hundred haircuts in two and a half weeks." Gary was almost too tired to eat.

"You're not still counting?"

"Yeah, I'm keeping a book. I thought it would be good to have a record of what I did. My first Friday I did 49, that was the busiest so far, but when I start travelling next week it will probably get worse. It's a kind of diary, something to remember it all by."

"I don't think I'll need a diary to help me remember my Falklands experience," smirked Rob. "Every day is the same. Walk to the warehouse. Work in the warehouse. Walk back from the warehouse. I'm not complaining, mind, but I reckon you've got the best job on the islands. You meet different people and you make extra money and you'll get to travel. And that's to say nothing of slap-up dinners with the only available women on the island. And you went to the Governor's house for heaven's sake."

"Hey, Gary," Steve wandered over to join them, "Could you maybe introduce me to those two nurses? Do you think either of them would go out with me?"

"No."

"Worth a try, though, eh?"

"No."

They slurped their soup and tucked into mutton pie. Shaun appeared through the door. He was waving a handful of brown envelopes.

"Hey, guys, payslips. I picked yours up for you."

Gary looked up, wiping his hands in anticipation. Shaun ambled over slowly, flourishing his opened slip at them with a silly grin on his face. "Happy Easter, everybody. We're rich!"

Gary, Rob and Steve grabbed at the fan of envelopes in Shaun's other hand, eager to read the good news. Wages were paid directly into their bank accounts but they were impatient to see the figures. All around the canteen others were going through a similar performance and there was a hum of excitement.

The envelopes were small and had a little window of transparent paper where you could read the person's name, "Corporal G. Shewan, 24664113". The payslip inside was a paper strip with pre-printed blue boxes and small typewritten figures in the spaces.

Gary's eye travelled from top to bottom, scrutinising the figures. At the top, his gross pay was as expected. Then there was national insurance and tax, a lot of tax. And at the bottom, his net pay, the amount that would go into his bank account.

"What the hell?"

"What?" asked one of the others.

"How much did you guys get? Mine must be wrong."

"Let's have a look." Steve grabbed the slip out of Gary's hand and squinted at the paper. "Crikey, you must have done something to offend somebody." Steve proffered it back. "There must be a mistake," said Gary. He took the slip and tried to make sense of the figures, scratching his head, hoping that he had mis-read them and that if he looked at the numbers again, they would magically transform into reasonable compensation for his efforts.

"I can't believe this; I just can't believe it." Emotion suddenly swept over him. "You mean to say I left my job, my home and my girlfriend and got a pathetic week's training which didn't prepare me in any way for what I've actually got to do then I travelled thousands of miles and I work harder than anyone else then I get put in a terrifying hole in the ground for the night without any sleep and am expected to be a soldier and am made a laughing stock and all I get is a few insulting quid?"

He stood up, hot in the face, the hard work and exhaustion and indignity of the last few days compounding unbearably with a deep sense of injustice.

He abandoned the rest of his dinner, left his tray on the table for someone else to clear and hurried back to the room. He threw himself on his bunk and plugged the radio earphones in to shut himself off from the world. His eyes were smarting and he could feel hot blood pounding in his cheeks and neck. He turned the volume up loud, heavy metal guitars shrieking and wailing.

"Shit, even the music's crap."

He lay in boiling silence for a while then found his writing pad. "Dear Mam and Dad, I am going through one of those phases when I wish I was home, though they only last a few hours. Can you give me some advice about my pay?" The stress eased a little as he unloaded the dramas of the last few days and he chewed at the stubs of his nails and the end of the pen in between sentences. His Dad would be able to help, could go to the tax office or speak to the NAAFI or ask someone who knew.

After filling several pages and signing off, he pulled the curtains on his bunk so that he wouldn't have to speak to the others and fell fast asleep in his uniform.

PAPER

APRIL 1985

BET

The single room in the Havelock Hospital had a television so Tom could choose whichever station he liked to watch, which meant he would be able to follow the football team's fortunes.

Bet felt some sort of duty to be grateful that Tom was here, with the individual room and the television and the specialist nurses, and that he had made it out of the emergency ward. But there was a terrible sense of finality about his move to the Havelock. It meant he was likely to depend on nursing care for the rest of his life, however long or short that might be, which made the possibility of his coming home such a faint one. Most of the time he just lay there listless as if defeated. She could see him giving up and slipping away.

She travelled in religiously every day to cheer him and it was a relief when anyone else from the family could come too. That Saturday her son, Alan, himself struggling with poor health, came along with his wife Nancy and children, Paul and Joanne. Eight-year old Joanne was prancing around, showing off an over-sized ring on her little-girl finger. Bet thought she was behaving like the Queen of Sheba the way she was flashing it about.

"Hey, Grandad!" Joanne said, waggling her finger in front of his face. "Look what me boyfriend gave us."

Tom jerked his head and opened and shut his mouth.

"Does this mean we need to buy you an engagement present, Joanne?" Bet enquired.

"Of course," replied Joanne. "But don't worry, Gran, you won't have to buy us a wedding present as well." The girl sat herself down at the end of Tom's bed.

"How come, love?" Bet asked.

"Oh, he's much too small for me to marry," Joanne stated with a defiant flick of the head.

"Joanne, that's enough silliness!" Nancy remonstrated.

"And get off Grandad's bed!" Alan chimed in.

Bet couldn't hold in her laughter while Tom stuck his tongue out and dribbled.

At the end of the visit they offered to drive Bet home so she went with them and left Tom watching the wrestling on television. He loved it. On Saturday afternoons at about tea-time the entertainment always revolved around Mick McManus and Big Daddy and Giant Haystacks and Kendo Nagasaki. It was the best thing on the telly, that and the football. At other times he left the television on but seemed to withdraw increasingly into himself.

The nurses responded to this depression by wheeling Tom into the day room most mornings, where at least there were a few people about.

When Gary's letter arrived, saying he had arrived and describing the voyage, Bet couldn't wait to read it to Tom.

She fished it out of her handbag and walked through the door into the day room brandishing it as if she had won the pools. Tom wagged his head at the descriptions of flying fish and stuck his tongue out when she read that Gary had done well in the darts competition and not so well in the tug of war.

She had brought the newspaper to the hospital as well so that she could read him the article about Sunderland's match the previous afternoon.

"I think I'll cut this out and send it to Gary, he's bound to want to know how they are getting on," she said. "Maybe I should send him a Sunday paper every week. What do you think, Tom, do you reckon the team are good enough to win the Milk Cup this year? The Mackam fans would go mad and forget about their troubles for a while, wouldn't it be great?"

Tom rocked and twisted his head about and sounded like he was trying to articulate something only it came out all strangled and shapeless.

She nodded and patted his arm. "That's it, love. Yes, let's hope they are in with a good chance."

Bet had thought to bring the box of dominoes, which had split along its tattered, red, cardboard sides years ago and was held together with an elastic band. Tom could just about push the tiles around one-handed.

In the tall chair in the far corner there was an old lady propped up on pillows. She was so shrunken that her transparent skin had settled in thin folds over her tiny bones, and they poked out as if through gauze. A little girl came in with her mother to visit but soon grew bored of sitting and listening to them talk. She sidled over towards Bet and stood by, watching. While Tom slowly pushed his next piece into place with a shaking back of the hand, Bet explained how the game worked. The little girl remained wide eyed, saying nothing.

When they had finished their round, Tom motioned for the girl to have a go. Bet showed her how to shuffle the tiles by sliding them around the table with the flats of her hands. The chink of the pieces against one another and their shiny scrape against the Formica table reminded her of happy days with her grandchildren. The little girl soon picked up the idea and after two games she beat Tom.

"Hey, it's time to go now," her mother called from the other side of the room. "Come over and say goodbye to Granny."

The little girl tore herself away from the table and went to kiss the old lady, who responded with a silent stroke of her hair.

"Mam, will you buy me some dominoes?" Bet could hear the wheedling voice fading down the corridor as they left.

She took Tom's hand and gave it a conspiratorial squeeze. "See," she said, "Another convert, just like our Gary. I wonder how he's getting on this week. I hope he isn't walking around with his nose in the air after doing

Lady Hunt's hair. He'll be too grand for us now!" Tom nodded but although he was smiling a tear rolled down his cheek.

GARY

The inlet where the coastels were moored was called the Canache, and Stanley Airport lay just a mile up the road to the north east, on the wild and windy peninsula that Gary and the lads had explored soon after their arrival. After the war, during which British Vulcan bombers and Sea Harriers had attempted to disable the runway and caused damage to both it and the Argentine aircraft on the ground, the RAF had immediately set about reinstating and lengthening the hastily repaired airstrip. Not long enough to take wide-bodied jets, nonetheless it was busy with military and civilian traffic. Twice a week, Hercules aircraft that had to be re-fuelled several times en route from the UK would bring in the post and supplies and a few passengers.

An international facility called Mount Pleasant was being built at a new site an hour southwest of the main town but for the time being, Stanley Airport still formed the focus of operations for much of the activity on the islands. Apart from the RAF, it was the base for the FIGAS air service, which maintained two tiny Islander aircraft for use by Falkland Islands Government staff and civilians. They would fly to every farm and settlement scattered across the islands, taking supplies and visitors and the vet, relying on farmers to clear birds and obstacles from grass airstrips for a safe landing. A third FIGAS aircraft, a Beaver floatplane, lived separately in a hangar on the shore beyond Government House. Bristow Helicopters, which had a contract with the military to provide transport to and from all the outstations, also had their offices and base at Stanley Airport. In addition, private hangars housed numerous Cessnas and other individually owned aeroplanes.

On Easter Sunday Gary should have enjoyed his first day off after four oppressive weeks working at the Kelper Store, but the sky remained heavy with clouds like sodden wool while driving rain forced him to stay inside. He had a work-out in the gym. He did his washing and ironing, paying meticulous attention to the creases in the sleeves, getting everything just right. He polished his boots until he could see his reflection. He played cards for hours then beat Steve at darts as usual. It was a disappointing break, nonetheless he was looking forward to the new phase of his job that was to start the next day.

In the morning it made a welcome change to turn left instead of right at the end of the causeway. Gary took a deep breath of fresh air full of sea spray and strode out towards Stanley airport. He headed away from the control tower towards a low line of buildings occupied by the RAF. The air filled with the scream of jet engines and the flinty smell of kerosene. A pilot revved his Phantom jet down at the far end of the runway. A number of Portakabins and prefabricated concrete hangars with rounded metal roofs dotted the grass alongside the airstrip, all dark green to blend in with the peaty grassland. Gary made for the RAF office buildings and a serviceman in a blue jumpsuit came out to greet him.

“Aha! You must be Corporal Shewan!”

“Yes, that’s me.”

“We’re glad to see you. Come along to the mess. We’ve got a place sorted out for you to work and an appointment system. It should all work pretty smoothly.”

The arrangements were simple: a chair and table in a corner; they would work well enough. Gary got out his brushes and combs and scissors and clippers and gown and spray gun and set to work straight away, with a long queue of servicemen lining up for their haircuts. Mid-morning a cup of coffee appeared and at midday he had a short break for lunch. The food wasn’t as good as at the coastel but it was hot and filling and he appreciated sitting down for half an hour. All day the air exploded with the noise of Phantoms taking off and landing, screaming to a halt hooked on the steel cables that were stretched across the short airfield, so loud that all other sound was drowned out. When the last cut was done it was only mid-afternoon. He swept up for the final time and said goodbye to the officer in charge.

“Good job, corporal, very efficient. We’ll look forward to seeing you again.”

Gary walked all the way to the Kelper Store to account for his takings and returned to the coastel with his percentage heavy in his pockets. For once he was in before the rest of the lads. He went straight to his locker, stashed the money in his cash box and pulled out his fountain pen and a green cardboard-backed diary. It was a spare HMSO duplicate book that someone had given him in the store, with a note printed on the inside front and back covers, "The duplicate copies (unperforated) must be used on both sides. Write all originals on right-hand side only, then reverse book and continue on right-hand side." The carbon paper was missing, maybe that's why the book was free. He had rubber-stamped four king penguins on the front for decoration and in the back he was already keeping a daily count of haircuts.

Gary unscrewed the lid from his fountain pen and wedged it onto the end of the barrel. He bit the tip between his teeth while he geared himself up for writing. On the front page he had already written his plan.

Dear Readers,

This book will give a write up of every outstation I have visited during my tour of the Falkland Islands, March 85-Sept 85.

There will be a mark out of 10 for the station, for each of the following:

Food (quality)

Relations (with officers and servicemen)

General (place itself).

This book will also give an up-to-date number of haircuts I have done, also a list of all the transport I have travelled on.

He had signed the inscription.

Now it was time to complete his first report. In the top left hand corner he wrote RAF Stanley and underlined it, using his ruler carefully so that it didn't drag the ink, adding the date in the top right-hand corner. He took a deep breath.

My first station I visited, in the fourth week. It is quite a large place where all flying takes place. I was made welcome immediately by officers and servicemen.

He recounted his day and when he had finished, he considered what score RAF Stanley merited.

Food 5/10

Relations 7/10

Generally 7/10

19/30

He signed the page and stamped a penguin in the square of space that was left.

Elizabeth

With scrupulous impartiality, Elizabeth had bought Easter eggs for each of their three children and the respective boy- and girlfriends but the two for Gary and Lesley were waiting out of the dog's way, next to the fish tanks on the partition wall that divided the sitting room from the dining room. Elizabeth had rung Lesley a few times and each one her mother said the girl was just getting out of the bath. She had hoped that Lesley would pop in sometime over Easter to collect her egg but the holiday had passed and it was Wednesday already. When the front doorbell rang, Schweppes growled and rushed to the hall, hackles up.

"Good girl, shush now." She pushed the bristling animal back into the kitchen and went to the door. Lesley stood smiling, eyeliner thick around her eyes; it was rather too much make up for Elizabeth's taste but she had to concede the girl was stunning.

"Hi, Elizabeth. Sorry I'm a bit late to say happy Easter."

Elizabeth ushered her in. "That's all right, love. It's nice to see you."

They went through to the kitchen and Lesley leaned against the door jamb while Elizabeth busied herself with the kettle and mugs and retrieved the milk from the fridge. She opened a new packet of biscuits, Gary's favourites, and made conversation.

"Did you hear about that group of local lads who won all that money on the pools?"

Lesley nodded. "Yeah, shame I don't know any of them, it was nearly a million pounds. Thanks," Lesley accepted the mug of coffee and they went to sit down in the lounge. "Where's Paula?"

"Upstairs." Elizabeth wished her daughter would come down. "She's in a bit of a sulk. She's been miserable since Gary left. She says I do nothing but tell her off."

Lesley smiled. "I'm sure you don't."

Elizabeth laughed. "Oh, I don't know. Maybe I am a bit hard on her. It's been a difficult few weeks with Grandad in hospital and Easter and everything. She needs to knuckle down and revise for her exams but she doesn't seem too bothered."

"How is Grandad Tom? Gran sent me some Easter money; it was really nice of her."

Elizabeth sighed; her father really wasn't making the sort of progress they had all hoped for. Initially there was the odd panic call from her mother, to come quickly. Each time Elizabeth's pulse would race and she would drive across to the hospital fearing the worst, but her father's underlying strength had pulled him through those crises and now he was off the critical list. But that was where the improvement had stopped. "I took him a couple of beers last night to cheer him up but he's on a new course of tablets so he can't drink them." She changed the subject. "I had two letters from Gary this morning."

She went and fetched the two envelopes from the hall but before looking at them Lesley told her all about his telephone call and she realised Lesley already had his news. They laughed about his experiences in the foxhole.

"He's really fed up with cutting hair, you know," said Lesley. "He says he's dreading having to come back to it. Is there any news about Upstairs Downstairs?"

"Mattie and I were down there on Monday evening showing a couple around and taking them through the books. They say they want it but a few people have said that and then they just disappear into thin air, so we'll wait and see. The man promised to phone so I'm keeping my fingers crossed."

They drank to the end of their coffee.

Lesley looked at her watch and proffered her mug. "I'd better go."

Elizabeth stood up. "I'm organising a fund-raising evening for the Lions in a couple of weeks. Would you come? It's a coffee evening with a fashion show. You could bring your Mam and Gran."

"I'll ask them, thanks," said Lesley, heading towards the hall.

Elizabeth put the mugs down and went to retrieve the Easter egg from the partition. She pushed it into Lesley's hands and received a dazzling smile in return. She couldn't help but feel sorry for the girl, left to wait while Gary swanned off on his adventures.

She watched until the car had pulled out of the drive and pushed the front door to. The telephone rang. It was a man's voice.

"Mrs Shewan? I was wondering if I could have another look at the salon."

Bet

Bet became a regular on the bus between Whitburn and Sunderland and she liked to sit in a seat two rows back, so that she could watch out of the window. The past few days it had been pouring so hard that all she could see was the water streaming against the glass, in slashes and trails of beads which were dragged backwards by the speed of the vehicle.

Today her friend Dot was travelling to Sunderland with her, in a voluminous raincoat and a headscarf that was leaving puddles on her shoulders. She was bemoaning the dreadful weather and the fact that her shoes let the water in. Their conversation inevitably turned to football, the match against Liverpool at the weekend resulting in a 3-0 defeat for Sunderland. The woman sitting in front of them, who had a big, canvas shopping bag on her lap, swivelled around to join in. The discussion absorbed them completely, Bet was analysing how the goals had been set up and Dot was arguing that the free kick should never have been given, when without warning the driver pulled the bus sharply to a stop with a screech of tyres on wet tarmac, jolting them all in their seats.

The woman in front was caught off balance, her bag dropped onto the floor with an almighty clatter and tipped over, then a dozen glass jars started to roll all over the bus. The driver opened the gate by his seat and came to apologise and check that the woman wasn't hurt.

"It's all right, it's only my jam-jars that fell over, not me."

The driver and the other passengers immediately set about retrieving the jars which had disappeared under the seats and into the corners. When they were all safely collected up and counted back into her bag, the woman piped up, "I wouldn't care, but I started off with thirteen jars and took one out in case it brought bad luck." Bet caught Dot's eye and burst out laughing, then everyone on the bus joined in, including the driver, and the woman herself roared the loudest.

Bet spent a good ten minutes telling this story to Tom as they looked out at the clouds sailing across the sky and it cheered them both up.

"You know, it was a good job the jars were all empty although they must have been made of tough glass because not one of them broke."

They had a game of dominoes which he won 6-2 without cheating, although he was very slow. She was happy that his brain was functioning even if his body was so useless and she gave him a big kiss when she left. His eyes looked up at her with a mixture of love and regret and she prayed to whatever God there might be that he would find the determination from somewhere and enough strength to come home eventually.

The next morning it was still pouring with rain and she was glad she had given up the allotment, or else she would have to go down there and work in the mud in her wellingtons. Her feet were killing her but despite the pain she had to laugh at the way she was walking, just like an old woman. She supposed her grandchildren must think of her as ancient but at sixty-eight she really wasn't. She decided to give her feet a good soak later and have a go at cutting the calluses off.

The telephone rang.

"Hi Mrs Davison... Gran... I just wanted to thank you for my Easter egg money."

Lesley always had good manners.

"Hello, love. You're welcome. Have you spent it yet?"

"Well, I was thinking, if you don't mind, I'll save it rather than buy a treat. I want to go down to London to meet Gary when he comes home."

"That's a nice idea. You must be missing him."

After her hospital visit that evening, Bet had time for a warming bath then sat in front of the fire with a cup of tea on the side table, her writing pad on her lap and her feet in a bowl of hot water.

Hello Gary,

I think you have sent your terrible weather over here. Grandad is OK and sends his love.

She told him all about the dominoes and the jam-jars. She wondered if he had read the article about the football team and he hadn't answered her previous questions yet but would he like her to send a Sunday paper each week? She remembered he had said she could write to him free of charge by forces' mail but she had forgotten to ask about it at the Post Office and anyway she didn't care about spending 17p on a stamp, he was easily worth that. It was amazing that he had telephoned Lesley from eight thousand miles away. What about the lads out there and the food and what language did the people on the island speak? And she mentioned that Lesley had rung to say thank you for the Easter money.

She misses you, Gary. It must be love.

It was only a tease but she couldn't resist.

GARY

On clear mornings looking westwards from the coastel Gary would enjoy the view of royal blue water whipped up into peaks of white, the sweeping shoreline and low, grassy slopes scattered with the jewel-coloured houses of Stanley. Beyond the town were the hills which rose in successive waves and he was learning their names: Sapper Hill directly behind Government House, the rocky outcrop of Tumbledown neatly framed by the two peaks of the Twin Sisters, Mount Longdon over to the right and behind them all, standing sentinel over the capital and the harbour, Mount Kent.

The radar station on the top of this high point was just twelve miles away but with no road, the only way to get there was by helicopter.

His first flight took off from Stanley Airport on a wild and stormy Friday, with high clouds scudding across an angry sky the colour of slate. The wind blew in from the north, howling across thousands of miles of ocean in ferocious gusts.

The Bristows S-61s always flew fully laden, making the most of every cubic inch of space to make sure the outstation servicemen had treats from home as well as military supplies and fresh food, all secured in place along the right-hand side of the fuselage with a web of red netting. Down the left-hand side, a line of seats provided a porthole each for the passengers. Gary had quickly adopted the servicemen's affectionate nickname for the helicopters, Erics, after Eric Bristow, the much-loved world no.1 darts player.

They lifted from the pad and the machine was sucked violently sideways. During the short flight to Mount Kent he gripped tightly all the way, glad of a safety belt and surprised at the nonchalant calm of the other passengers despite the bucking of the aircraft. Out of the window, between the clouds, clean air gave a view for miles in every direction – the Canache and the coastels, Port Stanley in its neat grid pattern, land and water, rivers, grasslands and strange, long runs of stones like dried-up riverbeds. The helicopter rose over the familiar line of hills, their contours flattened by the angle except where bare, rocky peaks punctuated the baize covering. Within minutes the two green, golf-ball domes on Mount Kent were in sight, surrounded by a scattering of shipping containers, duckboards and tracked vehicles that made up the station at the top of the mountain. The helicopter turned in to land, buffeted by the wind, battling to gain balance.

As soon as they were on the ground the passengers all piled out, crouching low to avoid the rotor-blades, eager to get into any shelter. The wind pulled fiercely at their clothes and whipped their faces.

He followed the others towards the main office, holding on to his beret with one hand and his bag with the other as the duckboards of the walkway squelched into the mud beneath their boots. The door of the container banged outwards and he was blown inside.

An RAF serviceman appeared, proffering his hand in greeting. “Aha! You must be the barber. Welcome to Mount Kent. Call me Nick. We’re pleased to see you.” He led Gary out into the blasting gale and across more duckboards to another, identical container.

It was already one o’clock and Gary followed in to find three men waiting. They raised an appreciative cheer at his appearance. He was glad to feel welcome, to enjoy the high-spirited banter as he worked, which continued jovially as each neatly trimmed man left, to be replaced by a scruffier colleague.

“How come you’re all in such high spirits, then?” he asked.

“Going home, mate. It’s the end of our tour this week. Thank fucking Christ. We’re all going to get laid.”

Gary took extra care over their haircuts, made sure that they would look good for the reunion with their families. He carried on for a full seven hours without a break until the last man went away with a handshake and a salute.

Nick showed him to a dormitory with a spare bunk where he could lay out his sleeping bag.

“Thanks,” said Gary. “Can I still get an evening meal? It’s so late and I’m ravenous.”

“There’s a gozome party tonight.”

"What's that?"

"You know - goes home. The lads have been saving into a kitty for months."

"Oh right. But I just need something to eat, I don't want to gate-crash their party."

"No problem. You're invited."

They made their way across the site, sloshing in the mud, holding their jackets tightly around them and leaning against the ferocious wind. The station was too small to have a NAAFI team but RAF support staff provided a cramped bar in a cabin that, from the outside at least, was indistinguishable from the others, except that it had Puffin Club painted on the door in big white letters. Inside there was a steamy gathering of men all holding pints and smoking, talking loudly over music, a table groaning with food in one corner and free drinks available at the bar in the other. Gary tucked in hungrily to a plateful of sandwiches. After a couple of pints and a good laugh, he found himself singing along at the top of his voice in the smoky, beery atmosphere. He knew the words to the songs better than everyone else. They were all in great spirits. They called him Geordie and he put them right because he was a Mackam and they slapped him on the back a lot. He recognised many faces from earlier in the day and plenty of them came over to offer him a drink and have a chat. He finally staggered back to bed well after midnight.

The next morning he was working again before nine, his throat sore and voice gruff. During the day he drank mug after mug of coffee to soothe it back to its usual pitch and to ease his tired head. The queue for haircuts was steady until five when he cleared up and swept the last trimmings away, yawning. He couldn't stop a creeping, insidious jealousy as he thought of all the men going home to their girlfriends and wives in a few days' time.

One of the officers offered to show him around the radar facilities, even though the wind was blowing even more fiercely, so much so that it was hard to stay on their feet. The wire of the high perimeter fence screamed and the armed sentry nodded them both through from his hut, as they leaned into the gale. Gary instinctively ducked his head as they went into the monitoring room, small and dark, filled with a confusion of technology and screens, their blips and green lights incomprehensible. Four operators wearing headsets sat at the consoles looking at the screens and occasionally pushing buttons or flipping switches. There were radio microphones on the desk. Gary's host told him they were fighter control officers and aero systems operators whose job was to track approaching aircraft over Berkeley Sound, Ports William, Harriet and Fitzroy, and beyond. Gary asked a few questions but the only machine he could really understand was the one that showed the wind speed - 70 mph gusting to 100 mph.

He slept badly that night, woken periodically by the wind's slamming into the metal box that constituted the dormitory. Everyone else breathed regularly, oblivious to the commotion outside, the benefit of four months' acclimatisation. Someone in the far bunk was snoring. Gary tossed and turned, winding his sleeping bag tighter and tighter around his body. He tried holding his hands over his ears but could not keep up the pressure for long enough. Every time he dozed off another thudding gust would crash into the site, pulling at the containers which strained at the steel cables securing them.

Sunday morning dawned no better. He did a favour to the last few men who found him at breakfast and begged him to trim their hair before he left. The Eric was due mid-morning and he looked forward to getting back to the coastel. Nick came to find him just as the last customer was paying.

"Sorry, Gary, the helicopter can't fly up here this morning, the winds are too strong."

Gary had not considered this possibility. "How do I get down, then?"

"Not sure at the moment. It looks like you might have to stay on for a bit."

"But today's my day off." It was a rare occasion and he had planned to go for a walk with some of the lads to Gypsy Cove, where there was a breeding colony of penguins.

"I'll see what I can do, but you might as well settle down for a wait."

Gary hung around disconsolately, muttering under his breath and frustrated at losing his free time on the top of a hurricane-blasted mountain with nothing better to do than watch clouds tear across the ragged sky from left to right. He kicked his heels and waited for a miracle.

Eventually, after an early lunch, Nick came and found him.

“Right, we’ll take you down by BV.”

“What’s that?”

“You’ll see. Get your things, it’s waiting.”

Gary grabbed his bag and braced himself again for the wind, holding his beret to his head with its badge pressing into the palm of his hand. A boxy all-terrain vehicle stood at the perimeter gate, like a cuboid Land Rover only with caterpillar tracks in place of wheels.

“Hop in.”

The door clanged behind him and the BV set off down the mountain. The driver wove a path over the rocks and peat hags, choosing his route with care to avoid the wettest areas where the bogs would trap them.

“It’s the only thing that will get you overland in the Falklands,” shouted the driver. “I expect you’ll end up travelling in a few of these before you’re finished.”

Gary didn’t try to reply, his throat was still sore and the grinding noise of the tracks too loud.

The view was bizarre, sometimes they pointed right up at the sky, sometimes down into the ground and he felt slightly sick. A couple of times he thought they would tip over. It took an hour to get down to the new road under construction between Stanley and the new Mount Pleasant Airport.

“Right you are.” The driver stopped by the roadside and was not going to hang around. Gary jumped out with his holdall and watched the BV chew its way back up the slope.

The way was deserted in both directions and the wind pierced his clothes. He started to walk towards Stanley and mulled over the chances of a vehicle’s coming by. The sheer scale of the construction project at Mount Pleasant, in its busiest stage before opening, meant that there must be something soon. He crossed his fingers and stepped up the pace.

After the best part of an hour a Land Rover appeared in the distance ahead, the engine’s noise inaudible above the blasting wind even as it drew closer. He stopped walking, interested to see who it might be. The driver pulled up and wound down his window, releasing loud rock music on a wave of warm air.

“Need a lift, mate?” The man was in civilian worker’s clothing, probably a construction engineer. There was a white hard hat on the passenger seat beside him.

“Yes, but I’m headed for Stanley,” replied Gary.

“I can see that. Listen, I’m going straight back once I’ve dropped this lot off at Mount Pleasant,” he jerked his thumb towards a pile of boxes in the back of the Land Rover. “There won’t be many drivers about today but it’s warm in here if you fancy the ride.”

The lift would involve a round trip of about sixty miles, nevertheless Gary was grateful for the offer so he walked around to the passenger side and wrenched the door open against the pressure of the wind. He threw the hard hat and his bag over to the back seat and climbed in.

Despite the newness of the gravel surface the road was rough and the Land Rover’s tyres thundered along, compounding the noise of thumping rock music and the blasting gusts that hurtled down from the hills. Any conversation was impossible. Gary relaxed into the seat, accepting that his day off was lost but glad to be out of the gale.

It was five o’clock before he arrived back at the coastel, with time only to sort out his kit, eat tea and write home. He grabbed a drink from the machine where a few of the lads spotted him and gathered around.

“What happened to you?”

“We thought you’d escaped.”

“Or got a shag with some slapper.”

“No such luck,” replied Gary, feeling cheated.

They thumped him on the back and commiserated. He went back to the room to write a report on Mount Kent in his green book, which took up two pages. At the end he gave Food 8½ and Relations 9½ but was so fed up he only put 5 for Generally. He pressed the rubber stamp firmly into the inkpad and then onto the page. He signed at the bottom, G. Shewan. Then just as he was putting the diary away and thinking about whether to have a shower now or in the morning, he reconsidered. The outstation itself had been pretty good, it was missing his day off that was irritating and that was due to the weather, not the station. He reopened the pages and took the lid off his pen again. By joining up the curve of the five he could increase it to a six.

The thought of having to work in the morning without a break was sickening.

Now that Gary was managing the whole workload single-handed, the demand for haircuts at the Kelper Store simply accumulated while he was working off site, making his days there even busier than before. The men who worked at the store were worked off their feet most of the time, too, so if he could have taken a break, there was little chance of any banter to brighten the dreariness. There was no canteen in the building and he could only get lunch if he walked down to the warehouses, which he rarely had time to do. He was now averaging fifty haircuts a day. Gary never minded working hard but he resented working on an empty stomach and would return to the coastel tired and grumpy of an evening. Many of his customers didn't even say thank you.

In the green diary he gave the Kelper Store:

Food	0/10
Relations	5/10
Generally	5/10

Total	10/30

He preferred to work anywhere else.

BET

Spring sunshine spread its optimistic light over the north east, nonetheless Bet pulled on her warm coat and laced up her thick, brown outdoor shoes because it was still chilly. She looked at her wristwatch – half past nine. There was just enough time to pop out the back and check the cauliflowers, to see if any more were ready. Even without the allotment there was plenty of produce in the garden and Bet was pleased with Elizabeth's reaction when she had handed over a couple of prize specimens on Saturday. "They'll make a nice cauliflower cheese," she had said. Which of course was why Bet grew them in the first place, because cauliflower cheese was everyone's favourite, especially Tom's.

With the old kitchen knife and a carrier bag in hand, she walked down the wheelchair ramp and stepped along the fragments of broken paving stone which provided a rudimentary pathway through the vegetable patch. The plant in the centre of the row looked magnificent. She bent down and sawed at the stalk with the knife, feet wide apart, knees slightly bent. It was inelegant but this was the best way to preserve your back and she had learnt long ago that looking after yourself was far more important than adopting airs and graces. She turned the cauliflower the right way up in her hand, parting the leaves to look at its whiteness.

“That’s lovely,” she said out loud and hacked off most of the green before popping the cauliflower into the bag. She took the leaves over to the compost heap and threw them onto the top. A tiny slug stuck to her finger.

She would give the cauliflower to her neighbours in the afternoon but now it was about time she set off for the bus. Back indoors she fetched the letter she had spent last evening writing to Gary. She had forgotten yet again to ask for a free airmail form but never mind, using a few stamps on Gary was money well spent. She tucked the envelope into her handbag and made for the front door.

Through the frosted glass a disjointed but familiar shape approached.

“Hello,” she said, opening the door to the postman. “What have you got for me today?”

“Morning, Bet,” he replied, tipping his hat. “Looks like something from that grandson of yours.”

“Oh good!” said Bet. The blue airmail envelope felt stiffer than usual, as if there were a card inside. She opened it hurriedly; eager to see what he had to say, all the while keeping an eye on the time and mindful of the certainty that if she was late the bus would be on time for once.

“Oh, Gary! How smashing!”

She pulled out not just a letter but a photograph of her grandson, hands on hips, grinning proudly for the camera, somehow older looking in his uniform. A beret sat squarely on his forehead and was that a hint of a moustache shadowing his top lip? He looked so handsome.

All of a-dither she made to leave, starting to pull the front door shut behind her before she remembered the key was on the hall table inside.

"Silly me," she grumbled, "Gary, you've got me all in a tizz."

Tom had been moved overnight back to the Sunderland General. The doctors were concerned about a bedsore that wouldn't heal. Bet was unsure how to interpret their cryptic observations but she felt anxious that it was a bad sign. Nonetheless, Tom would be happier on a ward with activity going on around him rather than in that solitary room.

At the hospital she made her way up the stairs to the third floor, distrusting the lift and preferring to walk. Nurses and cleaners bustled along the corridors in silent shoes and a woman pushed a trolley of magazines and sweets, small purchases that might brighten the day of bored patients.

Bet made her way to the stroke ward and scanned the beds for Tom, her gaze alighting on his unmistakeable figure over in the corner, propped up on a mountain of pillows.

"Look at you in your new surroundings, love!" she worked her way over to him, smiling left and right at the other patients as she went. "This is better."

She bent over to kiss his grizzled face, rough stubble grazing her skin.

"Haven't they shaved you? That's no good. I'll have words. Or I'll do it for you myself."

He smiled at her with watery eyes and rasped an incomprehensible welcome. A jolly nurse waddled over to check his notes.

"Mrs Davison? Your husband's doing quite well, he ate some breakfast this morning. We'll give him a shave later and take him into the day room, once the doctors have done their round."

She measured out two tablets and a beaker of water.

"Now, Tom, can you manage by yourself?"

Tom nodded and extended a shaky hand towards the table. Bet could hardly bear to watch but it was better that he struggled to do what he could alone. There was so little independence left, even taking a pill was important.

"We've heard from our Gary," she said as soon as the medication had gone down and Tom had balanced the empty beaker unsteadily back on the table. She rummaged in her bag and pulled out the envelope. "I'll read it to you in a minute but, look, here he is." She pulled out the photo and held it for Tom to see.

Tom's glazed eyes moved from Bet's face to the picture. He leant forward and slowly extended his hand to take it from her, holding the photograph in front of his face and studying it hard. A twitch pulled at the skin of his cheek then the corner of his mouth, lips parted and the widest smile Bet had seen for months spread across his face. It was like the sun breaking through on a winter's day.

"Who's that, then?" The nurse had reappeared at Tom's bedside, curious to join in.

"That's our grandson, Gary. He's in the Falklands."

Tom held fast to the photograph, his grip tight and a Cheshire cat grin fixed on his face. He waved the photo around.

"Hey, girls!" called the nurse to two of her colleagues who were settling an old man back into bed at the other end of the ward. "Come and have a look at Tom's grandson!"

The girls bustled over and held Tom's hand steady so that they could see Gary properly.

"He's a good-looking one!" they exclaimed. "I imagine he's a right one with the girls, especially in that uniform."

Bet sat back, pleased as punch.

After the excitement had died down and the nurses went back to work she read the letter to Tom, who still held fast to the photo. She read about the food and the changeable weather and it sounded as though Gary was having a good time but she was a bit concerned that he was the only hairdresser for all the troops out there.

Tom's energy soon flagged and Bet decided to let him rest. She put on her coat and found her bag which had worked its way under the bed. Then she put her hand out for the letter and photograph which lay on the table. Tom made a whining sound, shaking his head furiously.

"I thought you might like me to get a frame so that we can stand it on your bedside locker. Then you can see Gary even though he can't come in to see you."

Tom nodded, a thin drool of saliva running from the corner of his mouth and down his chin, where it formed a droplet. Bet got out her hankie and wiped it away.

"There you go, love. Rest well and get rid of that sore. I'll bring the photo back tomorrow."

GARY

Gary's weeks now always included visits to other locations away from the Kelper Store. Mondays were often spent at RAF Stanley. On Wednesday this week he had a morning at Falklands Interim Port and Storage System. FIPASS was the floating harbour facility where the Keren had tied up. It was a short walk from the coastel, on the way to the town. It was made of six huge oil-rig barges, moored where the water was deep enough for navy ships and submarines to dock, connected to the shore by a floating roadway. Two of the barges provided jetty space while the remaining four were the base for massive warehouses filled with ordnance and military supplies. The only place for Gary to cut hair was in the toilets.

He grabbed a single tatty plastic stacking chair and placed it in the middle of the tiled floor between the basins, the urinals and the cubicles. There was no table for his equipment so he balanced his tools on a high window ledge behind him. The pane was of that textured glass with lines and dots, the same as in the toilets at school. The room was painted in the same nondescript shade of cream, too, with shiny steel separating the privies.

Gary waited for something to happen. He kicked his heels for half an hour, staring at the tiling and peering outside from time to time, wondering why no-one had turned up. Then his first customer appeared.

"Why didn't you tell us you was comin'?" the man asked in a surly voice. "Some of us 'as been waitin' for weeks an' it would've been useful to know you was 'ere."

Gary felt his collar tighten. He had no control over his schedule nor any advance contact with the locations, so no way of making sure that they put the word out. Everything was organised from Dita's office at FILOG. He felt indignation rise in his throat and swallowed it back down again hard.

"Do people know I'm here now?" he managed to ask.

"Yeah, staff sergeant's just put the word about. You'll get a rush now, most likely."

Gary started on the man with the clippers and sure enough a line of stevedores, warehousemen and engineers soon formed up outside.

"Morning, how are you?" he asked each one as they sat down.

"Piss awful," was the typical reply.

"Crap."

"Shite."

After several times through this routine, Gary gave up. It was impossible to share any conversation with the men. Gary could hear them outside the door discussing the latest ships to come and go, who was arriving and leaving, what supplies were coming ashore, what happened in the bar last night, who beat who at pool, but in the ten minutes he had with each of them he never got past the sneering toilet jibes.

Every now and then someone would come in to relieve themselves.

“Do us a favour,” he would say, “Go in the cubicle, would you?” and the sound of bodily functions would accompany the buzz of the clippers. More than once he broke into loud humming to drown the sounds. He made a mental note to bring the tape player from the Kelper Store the next time.

After lunch he walked across to the shore, relishing the fresh air, and made his way to Falkland Islands Logistic Battalion, the huge warehouse operated by EFI. The staff there worked on dealing with consignments of supplies for the NAAFI shops and facilities around the islands. Rob, Steve and Shaun all worked at FILOG, along with quite a number of men from their floor on the coastel, and Dita, who was their supervisor as well as his. It was good to see friendly faces and even more of a relief to be invited to set up shop in a corner of the warehouse rather than to be sidelined into another toilet. People soon turned up, the pace was steady and the conversations easy.

“Hey, Gaz, fancy a cuppa?” asked Steve, who called by on his break.

Gary was delighted to take a short rest.

“You’ll never guess what the latest supplies from England include,” said Steve, one eyebrow raised in disbelief.

Gary couldn’t think where to start. “Blow-up dolls?” he proffered, shrugging his shoulders.

“They would be useful but no, it’s penguins. Six-foot penguins. Fluffy toy ones. Can you believe it?” Steve was shaking his head and tapping his temple with his forefinger. “They send them out from England because all the wives and girlfriends say to their blokes, Ooh, when you get there, you must send me a penguin from the Falkland Islands. And when the men do get here, they discover that no-one on the Falklands makes anything like that and there aren’t any penguins to send. So the NAAFI get them made God knows where, ship them out here, the men buy them and send them all the way back again. Apparently Interflora delivers them home with a personal message.”

“You are joking.”

“I’m not, mate. There’s loads of them and they’re bloody huge. It would be great if we could smuggle one out to that Argie plane. We could take a great photo of it sitting in the cockpit!”

Gary grinned. “You are mad. Maybe I’ll buy one for Mam.”

“Would she like it?”

“No, but she’d laugh.”

*

One day he went to the British Forces Falkland Islands headquarters, which was located along the sea front beyond Government House. He collected his bag of equipment early from the Kelper Store then walked down Dean Street to the harbour. There was no traffic, just the occasional old Land Rover parked on the pot-holed road. He passed traditional houses clad in clapboard and tin, their white walls, coloured roofs and brightly painted woodwork all cheerful in the autumnal April sunshine. Picket fences or sheets of rusting corrugated iron marked the dividing lines between the properties. Some had low hedges surrounding long, narrow gardens littered with children's swings and toys. The roof lines were crisp against a blue sky, unsullied by television aerials. Peat smoke hung in the air.

He reached the T-junction with the sea front. On his right stood the grandly named Christ Church Cathedral, tiny compared to the one in Durham, a modest building of stone and red brick with a squat tower capped by a pyramidal roof. Gary was less interested in the church than in the whalebone arch that stood as a monument this side of it, its four majestic bones reaching to a point more than twice his height.

Out in the harbour two Royal Navy ships rode at anchor and across the water he could make out the enormous tanks of the naval station. He turned left into a cool breeze, blinking in the bright light. The air was crystal clear and in the distance Mount Kent stood sentinel, benign in the sunshine. Passing the 1982 war memorial, Gary slowed his pace and automatically bowed his head. It was hard to imagine this unassuming place as a field of war with the seas burning. He recovered his gaze and speed and soon came to Government House, its Union Jack flying proudly in the garden. The sun reflected off the glass panes of the conservatory that flanked this side of the property. Gary squinted to see if there was anyone that he recognised but there was no movement. Just in case, he raised his hand to his forehead in salute and gave them a jaunty wave.

On the water near the shore a scattering of flightless ducks was paddling around, bobbing up and down beneath the surface to feed. This was the quietest rush hour he had ever experienced. Less than half a mile further on he turned left and soon arrived at Britannia House, a single-storey, wood-clad building painted brown with white window frames and shutters. Several Land Rovers were parked outside. Gary walked up the steps to the front door and into a small reception area where an army sergeant sat at the front desk.

"Morning," the man said in a no-nonsense voice. "Are we expecting you?"

"I hope so," said Gary, "I'm the barber, Corporal Shewan."

"Ah, yes," the sergeant checked a diary and a list.

He busied himself for a few moments then handed Gary an official card which he had to sign.

"Keep this pass with you at all times. You may be asked for it. Hand it back in again when you leave."

Gary had never had a security pass before. The sergeant checked the list again and picked up the telephone.

"The barber's here." There was a brief pause. "Dining hall. Fine." The sergeant replaced the receiver and pointed at a door.

"Go through there, along to the end of the corridor, turn right and you'll be in the dining hall. I'll let people know you're here. The boss wants to see you, too."

Gary wondered who the boss was but thought better than to ask. He followed the instructions, surprised at how large the building was inside. The corridor went a long way back. He found the hall easily and set himself up at a table where a large window gave good natural light. Within minutes his first customers started to arrive. They all spoke well and looked immaculate in their uniforms, which although the same as his own, fitted these men better than they did the average EFI lad. He recognised a number of people who had sailed on the Keren at the same time as him. There was very little chat but one corporal said, "Hey, you're the kid who beat me at darts," although for all he tried to remember, Gary couldn't place him at all.

Mid-morning, an officer came in to interrupt the flow.

"The boss would like you to come through."

Gary brushed the hairs from the collar of the man sitting in front of him and stood back to let him leave then picked up his tools. He followed the officer to a large meeting room with a polished boardroom table and chairs that occupied most of the space. There were three men at the head of the table, bending over a large map. They looked up as he walked in.

"Aha," said the one in the middle, and Gary recognised him immediately.

It was Major General Peter de la Billière, who had welcomed them to the Falklands on their arrival.

"If you will excuse me, gentlemen."

The two men rolled up the map and made their exit.

"Are you happy to give me a trim in here?" asked the Commander of British Forces Falkland Islands, indicating the room with a general wave of his hand.

Gary checked to see if the floor was carpeted. "Yes, Sir, of course. As long as your cleaners don't mind. I haven't got a hoover."

The Commander sat down in one of the chairs, Gary placed the gown around his shoulders and ran a comb through his hair. Although receding, it was thick and strong and lay close to his head. In amongst the silver was a lot of dark brown, nearly black, indicating his true colouring. Blue eyes looked out steadily under powerful brows, unblinking, enquiring.

“How would you like it, Sir?”

“Short but no clippers.”

Gary started work and the Major General quizzed him gently about life in EFI. Gary sprayed and snipped and trimmed and told him about the Kelper Store and the outstations and how his work was organised.

His customer listened quietly with lips pursed together in a thin line, occasionally uttering the odd, “Hmm, hmm.”

Gary was generous about the people he had met and glossed over the difficulties and frustrations. The Major General said it sounded as though he was doing a good job. The man was charming; not at all the hard-nut Steve would have him be. When the meticulous haircut was finished Gary brushed the back of de la Billière’s collar.

“That’s you done, Sir. I’ll just tidy up.”

The Major General got up from the chair and pulled it out of the way as Gary did his best with the dustpan and brush on the floor. “Can you find your way to the dining hall?”

Gary could feel himself colour up, fearful that the story of his mortifying humiliation in the night exercise had reached as far as the ears of the Big Boss. “Yes, Sir.”

“Make sure you come back regularly.”

“Thank you, Sir, I will.”

Gary accepted payment and reversed out of the room, not out of subservience but because it was easier to push the door with his backside while he held all the equipment in one hand and the dustpan in the other.

After a mediocre lunch during which nobody spoke to him, Gary walked back to the Kelper Store. It was 18th April - he hadn't been here five weeks yet. He totted up the morning's customers in his head and worked out that he had passed one thousand. He didn't mind the milestone; in fact he was quite proud of it and he certainly didn't mind the way that the money was mounting up. He didn't mind the hard work, really he enjoyed it, although at times it could be extreme. But some things he did mind. He minded when people didn't say thank you. He minded that customers ignored him or treated him like a slave (the Major General had been rare in showing any interest). He minded cutting hair in toilets and forgotten corners that smelled foul and had no decent light. He minded when the food was poor and he minded even more when he went hungry. Above all he minded working in the gloomy little room at the back of the Kelper Store.

He turned into John Street and viewed the shop with a sinking heart. It would be so much better if his base could be somewhere else, in a room with light and space and decent music. It would also be better if he could manage his own schedule and communications so that he could ensure people had proper notice of when he was coming. In fact, it would be altogether better if he could run the business, just like he did at home.

He steeled himself, determined to focus on remaining positive, to make the most of this thing that he had started. To help his mood he invested a precious £80 on a personal stereo from the store and chose a selection of tapes. It was a relief to lie on his bunk with the headphones on and block out the confinement of the coastel and its piped radio broadcasts. A driving beat and favourite romantic melodies transported him home, helped him to fill his empty longing with dreams of the people he loved. He was desperate for Lesley both physically and emotionally, unsatisfied with fantasy and furtive masturbation. He had never known that he could miss someone so much.

Just over a fortnight since he had last dialled her number, he waited impatiently for the click of the receiver at the other end.

"Hey, Gary, what's up?"

"Oh, nothing, I was missing you."

"Did you get my letters?"

"I think I've learned them off by heart. Sounds like you are keeping busy, Les."

"I decided there's no point moping around. At least doing stuff with friends takes my mind off things."

Gary realised that he didn't have much idea who her friends were, they had only ever spent time with each other or their families.

"Anyone I know?"

"Oh, Brian and Pete and, well, people like that."

"Brian and Pete?"

"You know, some of the lads from the pub."

The adrenalin rush was instant.

"Doing what?"

"Just the usual, out for a drink or to the pictures. I'm trying not to spend too much money. I'm saving for the train fare so I can come and meet you in London when you get back."

Her voice sang to him across half the world. He couldn't wait to have her arms around him and her breath on his cheek. That night he was lulled to sleep by the music on his stereo and he dreamed of a railway station. He stepped out of an old, dirty carriage with a heavy rucksack in each hand, searching the platform with eager eyes. There maybe fifteen yards away she stood, in red, perfect, her eyes glistening. She rushed towards him. He dropped the two bags and held out his arms, unable to lift his feet, waiting, waiting for what seemed an age, until she flew into his embrace and he was holding her, squeezing her tight, never to let her go.

He awoke with a jolt as a door clanged in the corridor. The room was pitch dark and the gentle breathing of his roommates filled the space. He felt the identification tag around his neck, put the headphones back on and turned his face towards the wall.

In early May Gary made his first journeys of any significant distance to visit the two radar stations on the island of West Falkland: Mount Alice in the south and Byron Heights in the north. The neat grid pattern of Stanley soon disappeared behind them they flew over the expansive construction site at Mount Pleasant, looking for all he knew like Heathrow airport. Gary whistled at the sheer length of the runway and the size of the complex. Then they passed mile after mile of empty, pool-strewn flatlands before the helicopter swooped joyfully west over the wide ribbon of Falkland Sound, its shadow distinct on the glinting sea below, and dipped a salute as it skimmed in over the camps and settlements of Fox Bay. Another twenty minutes on, gaining height all the way as they overflew rounded hills, they arrived at Mount Alice, the southernmost peak on the islands.

Gary relished this trip away, not just because it provided a welcome change from the Kelper Store but because of the chance to see more of the Falklands. Until now his radius had extended no more than forty miles, not much more than the distance from home to his Gran's.

His day at Mount Alice passed without incident. The onward flight was originally planned for the following morning but was delayed for over twenty-four hours by bad weather, so there was nothing for it but to keep cutting hair or kick his heels. When eventually they took off for Byron Heights, it was a clear day with only solitary clouds. They traversed the knobbles and inlets of West Falkland, passing isolated farms and silken threads of fencing that divided the land not into fields but into great tracts of sheep grazing. Here and there random vehicle tracks hinted at connections between the far-flung settlements but there was not a surfaced road in sight. He had never seen a landscape so untouched.

Gary spotted Byron Heights from afar, a long, straight finger of land that pointed like a gun barrel north-eastward towards Argentina. Beyond the mainland, a line of jagged islands stretched ahead into the blue of the ocean like tracer bullets.

He leaned his forehead against the porthole for a better view of the wild outcrops. "What are they called?" he pointed a finger, twisting in his seat and shouting to the passenger behind him.

"Jason Islands," was the yelled reply.

He fixed his eyes on the sharp ridges where skeins of sea birds wheeled, drifting free on the wind like spray. I'd like to go there, he thought, his breath steaming the pane.

Gary was sitting at the front of the Bristow, wedged in by crates of cola and cartons marked fragile. Above the noise of the engines he could hear the squeak of the nylon netting that held everything down tight. Boxes and their contents vibrated and shuddered; his head reeled as they turned in sharply to land. He leapt up to open the door and be the first out. Full of confidence he dropped to the ground and, ducking his head instinctively, checked the buildings to see where he should go. He spotted the office beyond the back of the Eric and set off towards it. The noise of the engines was deafening.

“Oi!” shrieked a voice close to his ear and he felt himself pulled violently back by the fabric of his flak jacket. He missed his footing and his head jerked upwards to see a transparent disk revolving against the sky, only a blur hinting at its existence. He was pulled again and spun into the arms of the passenger who had been sitting behind him.

“You got a death wish?” the man yelled, barely audible above the thwack of the rotors, his wavy hair curling and flattening in the turbulence, then he dragged Gary three steps backwards.

“Bloody hell!” exclaimed Gary, momentarily winded, beginning to register how close he had come to walking into the steering rotor on the tail of the Bristow.

“Come on!” the man shouted, pulling him away around the front of the helicopter and into the Portakabin. Gary felt weak, slightly sick, mesmerised by the near miss. Others were looking at him, their faces floating surreal and disconnected. Gary leaned against the wall of the office and the man finally let go the pincer grip on his arm.

“That was close,” Gary exhaled. “Thanks very much.”

“I can’t imagine you’ll do that again,” the man said.

All day Gary had flashbacks of the spinning blades. Every time his scissors moved near to his fingers he remembered the time Glenn slammed the front door on him in anger and nearly sliced off most of his left thumb. He couldn’t get over the horrible sight of that little cube of meat hanging from his hand. A neighbour had called Elizabeth at work and she had rushed home and driven him to hospital, tight-lipped, her face grey with anger and anxiety. Strangely, he couldn’t remember the pain, although he knew that he had screamed and screamed and couldn’t bear to look at it again. The doctors stitched the piece back on and the blood vessels and nerves mended, but his thumb never healed fully and would forever remain a funny shape. So much drama and all because he had refused to wash the dishes and Glenn had been angry with him and for some incomprehensible reason Gary would not step down.

Elizabeth

Elizabeth was pleased at how her fund-raising event was going. Apart from Lesley and Lesley's mother and grandmother, everyone had turned up and now forty women sat or perched around the sitting and dining rooms, some finding space on the stairs with teacups and slices of cake in hand, while Paula circulated with plates of sandwiches. It had been worth spending all of Monday baking and borrowing china from the neighbours.

Upstairs, the two girls from across the street who had volunteered to act as models were doing a quick change into their next outfits while their mother, Hazel, was passing out order forms and explaining how quickly the dresses would be delivered and who to make cheques out to. Elizabeth liked the last outfit paraded, a green evening dress with a pretty neck, but spending that much money was unthinkable, even though there were plenty of events coming up for which it would be perfect. Cashflow was getting so tight that she might have to sell her car, which would make visiting her Dad more difficult.

"Mam, the milk's run out," Paula pushed through the throng with the blue jug. "What shall I do?"

"Ask Margaret, she's bound to have some in her fridge," Elizabeth replied, and Paula went off to find their next-door neighbour in amongst the gaggle. Elizabeth surveyed peoples' plates. "Heavens!" she sniffed the air. "The sausage rolls!"

She worked her way through to the kitchen and grabbed the oven gloves.

"Stand back!" she warned, opening the door to a blast of heat. The women laughed and flapped their hands and someone opened the kitchen window.

That was close, she thought. She couldn't bear it if she'd burned them. She straightened up and looked around, pushing back a strand of hair from her forehead. No-one really cared about the food, they were all having a great time catching up on gossip, enjoying a few hours' escape from their homes and lives and families. She turned the oven off and put the last offerings out on trays.

High-pitched conversation swelled like the chatter from a swirling flock of starlings coming in to roost. The women who had found seats were immovable now, whilst others ambulated amongst them, hopeful of an armrest or a bit of wall to lean their backsides against, all the while nodding and exclaiming and sharing pleasantries. The girls sashayed down the stairs in their final frocks, one an elegant black cocktail dress, the other a frightful creation in purple. Elizabeth stifled a laugh.

"Ooh, I like that," said a rather large lady anchored in Mattie's armchair. "It's just my colour. Give us a twirl, there." The model obligingly found a space in the middle of the sitting room to turn full circle and pose ironically. The others tittered.

"Do they make it in my size?" asked the interested customer, oblivious to the reactions of her friends. Hazel appeared as if by magic at the woman's elbow, pen and forms at the ready.

Elizabeth decided to go and talk to a new neighbour standing by the window, to ask how the children were settling in to school and her husband into his job.

"Excuse me," she said as she worked her way through the women.

Above the noise and the chatter another sound started to burn into her consciousness, insistent, repeating, like the buzzer on the oven.

"Elizabeth, I think it's the telephone," a voice shrilled across the room.

"Oh bother," said Elizabeth, turning round and ploughing back into the hall. She grabbed the receiver.

"Hello?"

The line crackled and a voice echoed faintly in the distance. Elizabeth put her finger in her other ear.

"Hello? Sorry, you'll have to speak up. I can't hear you."

The voice came back, louder, a voice bringing a rolling wave of maternal nostalgia for its absence these last six weeks.

"Mam, it's me. Can you hear me?"

"Gary? Hang on!" She put her hand over the receiver and turned around to the gaggling throng. She took a deep breath and bellowed as loudly as she could.

"SHUSH, EVERYBODY, IT'S GARY ON THE PHONE!"

For a split second there was silence, then excited twittering stilled by "Ssssshhh!" as forty pairs of ears all strained to listen in on the conversation.

"Gary! You've just caught me in the middle of my Lions do!"

"Sorry, Mam. Shall I get off the line?"

Her head whirled.

"No! Stay and talk to me. It's lovely to hear you. Is everything all right?"

"Everything's great."

"What are you up to?"

"I've seen some penguins at last. We went for a walk yesterday, me and the lads; it was my first real day off – after five weeks, can you imagine? We went to this beach called Gypsy Cove and it was beautiful, with white sand like at Whitburn, you'd have loved it, except we couldn't actually go on the beach because there's a minefield but there were all these penguins. I think they were called Magellanic penguins or something although I'm no good at the names, and when they saw us they ran about. It was amazing. And there were dolphins out in the water."

"It sounds fantastic, love. We're so enjoying your letters." A buzz of conversation started up quietly in the background. Elizabeth relaxed. "Are you eating well?"

"I'm putting on pounds. It's the three-course meals at the coastel and I've been doing weights in the gym to build myself up. I'm missing Lesley a lot. Actually, I'm missing all of you but I wouldn't tell you that."

Elizabeth laughed.

"Well, we're missing you, Gary. You're OK though?"

"Yeah, honestly. Working hard but I'm learning a lot and getting to travel now – I go everywhere by helicopter, it's great. Tell Dad thank you for sorting out my emergency tax, the pay will be a lot better! Anyway, how are you? Have you sold the shop?"

"No, love, not yet. We're still hopeful."

"Oh. Fingers crossed then. How's Grandad?"

"He's OK; not brilliant. He loves hearing from you."

"Oh no, there's the pips."

"Gary," Elizabeth hurried, "Love you, son. Take care now."

"Yes, Mam, love you too." And he was gone.

Elizabeth looked around at the expectant faces, feeling slightly dazed.

"Well?" said Margaret.

Paula came rushing in with the blue jug. "Did I miss him?" she cried. "No! How is he?"

"He's just fine," said Elizabeth, giving her daughter an enormous hug. "He's seen some penguins at last."

GARY

After his precious day off when at last he had got out and been to Gypsy Cove, the schedule was as full as ever. It was always exciting to travel by helicopter to the different parts of the islands but although the scenery was fascinating it was not as dramatic as some of the names would lead you to expect. For example, he felt that Falklands mountains would more accurately be described as hills while the roads quite honestly were nothing better than rough tracks. When he saw that he was to go to an outstation called Kelly's Garden, Gary knew full well that it was unlikely to be a horticultural masterpiece.

Nonetheless, as the Bristow came in to land, he couldn't help but feel dismayed at the muddy mess that was the station. It faced the settlement of San Carlos across the greasy water of Bonners Bay, bounded behind by rock-strewn hills and enclosed still further by a uniformly low layer of cloud. At some time in recent years bulldozers had scraped away squares of earth to create hard standings for a fleet of Chinooks. Between the helicopters, the site was scattered with oil drums, lumps of concrete, rusting metal and a makeshift array of temporary buildings. It was anything but a garden.

Landing demurely on the helipad next to the Chinooks, the chunky Bristow looked puny, a welterweight amongst heavyweights.

Gary was ready for lunch and glad to be shown straight to the NAAFI canteen where a hot meal set him up for the afternoon. Then it was straight down to work. A flight sergeant showed him to a room where a line of jumpsuit-clad men were already standing in wait, their names inscribed on a list taped to the door. Gary was glad of the appointment system but could see that he was going to have to work fast.

He unpacked his equipment and with clippers in hand, comb and scissors lined up on the table, he squared up his first customer on the chair.

"Right, then, let's get started," he said, as much to himself as to his client. "Any requests?"

He tried to keep the options as wide as possible but with only a few minutes allowed per haircut, choice was not really part of the package.

"Just cut it short, anyway you like," said the willing victim, apparently happy to leave the barber to it.

"Number two for you and everyone else, I reckon," said Gary, turning the switch on and feeling the trimmers vibrate in his hand. "What's it like working here, then?"

The patter was the same all day as Gary worked his way through a sea of heads while in the background the familiar *wok-wok-wok* of double rotors rose and fell as helicopters came and went past the window.

The pale grey of the day turned to the charcoal of evening and soon the klaxon was sounding the evening blackout.

One of the waiting customers pulled down the blind. "It's getting earlier every day."

Gary looked at his watch – it wasn't six o'clock yet and still only the end of April. He was just two thirds of the way through today's list.

At 8.30 he finally finished and swept up for the night. It was too late for a proper meal and he had no idea where he was going to sleep.

"You all right?" asked the mess sergeant from behind his desk. Gary had groped his way around the camp in the dark, grabbing a sandwich from the NAAFI bar before he found the sergeant in one of the far-flung offices. "You look all washed out."

"Yeah, just tired," said Gary. "Could you tell me where I'm to sleep?"

"No-one showed you?" asked the man, as if someone else was responsible. He called in a junior rating. "Show the barber to D-13."

Gary plodded along muddy duckboards behind the serviceman, who looked even younger than he was. "You enjoying yourself here, then?" Gary asked, always anxious to break a silence.

"It's OK," replied the youth, clearly uninterested in conversation. "This is it. You've got the place to yourself."

He showed Gary into a container dormitory, similar to the ones he had slept in at the other outstations except that this one was larger and empty of occupants. It was freezing.

Gary shook his sleeping bag out to help it loft before laying it on the furthest bunk from the door. The silence in the room was disarming, as alienating as the chilly temperature. He went over to feel the heater – cold – then fiddled with the control but it just went round and round without actually turning the valve. Normally he would do something practical such as go and find help, search for a spare bunk in a warmer room or return to the bar for music and conversation, but tonight he felt too weary to bother. He splashed his face with icy water and cleaned his teeth then clambered into the sleeping bag fully clothed and with his stereo for company.

It was an uncomfortable experience for Gary to lie alone in silence. Even at home after Glenn had moved out of their shared room, there were always the sounds of his parents and Paula in their rooms across the landing or making bathroom noises through the wall by his bed. He was not used to solitude. This isolation was alarming and made worse by the brutal cold. Gary turned up the volume through the headphones and shivered in his bag, arms wrapped around his curled body, head immersed inside the quilting.

Predictably, his thoughts soon turned to Lesley. What would she be doing on a Monday night, after a day on reception at Henderson's Door Systems where her Dad worked? Gary had never seen her working, although she had shown him the place once, sat down for him at her desk behind reception and put her hands on the keyboard. God, she looked good, in a striped blouse with a Lady Diana collar. He wanted her here in this bed with him now, her warmth and the comfort of her body.

With music still playing he fell into a troubled sleep fuelled by physical and emotional fatigue, huddled on the hard bunk. In jumbled dreams he imagined himself back home in Durham. It was the morning after his return. He left the house and walked down the familiar route to Claypath, let himself into Upstairs Downstairs, turned on the lights, made the coffee and started work just as if he had never been away. With rising panic, he broke out of the sleeping bag and sat up in the freezing dark, hitting his head on the bunk above. He was drenched in sweat.

"Welcome back, Gaz," said Rob, stepping into their room in the coastel on Thursday evening. "Had a nice time?"

Gary was writing in the green book, relating his woes at Kelly's Garden over three days and nights.

"Crap, thanks. I did over 130 haircuts, worked really hard. It's a horrible place, muddy and unbelievably cold. I nearly froze to death on Monday night. On Tuesday thank goodness I went and found the EFI lads who run the bar. They were a great bunch. They told me to move into the NAAFI club on a camp bed, so I did and slept in the kitchen for the other two nights."

"Sounds par for the course. Gave the place a good score then, did you?"

Gary laughed.

"I'm just doing it now. Excluding the EFI guys, food was four, relations were five and generally was five. Maybe I'm being a bit generous. Anyway, that's it. Fourteen."

"You'll be keen to get back there, obviously," Rob nodded his head sarcastically. "Anyway, I've booked the squash court, and you're needed."

As April gave way to May Gary's work grew yet more demanding, so that he wished even more fervently he could manage his own schedule. His colleagues at the coastel, who had no opportunity to travel beyond Stanley, were always intrigued to hear his adventures, what was going on where and how the conditions compared with where they were. Because his job gave him unique access to operations on the islands he always had stories to tell. From his point of view, it was therapeutic to talk about his experiences, to relive the fun bits and put the harsher incidents into perspective.

There were notable trips that gave him plenty of kudos in the retelling; some were amusing although more often than not they had tested his courage. At Goose Green he worked for thirteen hours without a break only to be threatened with a beating from two drunks when he refused them a late-night haircut after he had finished.

Another day he cut hair in the interview room next to the cells at the police station, where a local man was serving a year's sentence for stealing two crates of Penguin Ale. There was a visit to Murray Heights overlooking the southern approaches to Stanley where the Army Air Corps had nicknamed their camp Red Zero One. He even cut hair on a submarine moored briefly at FIPASS, entering through the conning tower and working in a tiny room where the only sound was the quiet hiss of air conditioning.

In the week before the official opening of Mount Pleasant Airport, Prince Andrew, himself a Sea King helicopter pilot, veteran of the Falklands War and still on active service, landed on the islands to perform a few engagements. Gary was surprised when someone from HQ rang to ask if he would cut the Prince's hair but he had to say no, because his schedule was full and there wasn't any free time to offer. He felt compromised to be put in such a position and frustrated because it would have been great to meet a member of the royal family but as far as he could see it was not up to him to cancel any of his arrangements. The man at the other end of the line pushed him hard but there was no option, Gary couldn't let everyone else down for the sake of one VIP, even a royal one.

For the last two days before the airport opening, Gary's schedule had him at Mount Pleasant to make sure that the garrison looked spruce for the Prince and the parades and the world's press. A cheery driver, Rick, came and found him at the Kelper Store, stopping to buy a couple of those big chocolate Wagon Wheel biscuits and a can of cola before they set off.

The 28-mile grit road was familiar from his Mount Kent adventure and Gary noticed that although it was still new, with the amount of traffic and the ever-changing weather it was already showing signs of wear, with ruts and potholes forming just as they seemed to on every little bit of road on the islands. The journey would take them nearly two hours.

It was another dark and gloomy day, with a whistling wind and intermittent rain. Occasionally a break in the clouds allowed through a blinding ray of sun which sparkled on the sodden landscape before the curtains closed again.

They were making reasonable progress when ahead on the gravel surface a dark shape came into focus as a stranded Land Rover, with a couple of figures next to it in an attitude of despair. Rick pulled up alongside. "You all right, mate?" he called out of the window to the nearest man.

"Thank God," the man said.

"We need help," said the other.

They were civilians, wrapped in thick anoraks. Gary thought one of them looked vaguely familiar but of course he saw so many faces that happened quite frequently.

Rick continued. "What's up?" It was quite evident what had happened – the Land Rover had blown a tyre. "Having trouble changing the wheel?"

The familiar-looking man looked up and exclaimed impatiently, "This bloody hire car hasn't got a jack. Can we use yours?"

Rick switched off the ignition and gave Gary a glance with eyebrows raised. "We'd better see what we can do."

The two of them clambered out, Gary wrapped his coat tightly around him and pulled his beret down. He wished he had brought his gloves. While Rick fiddled about in the back, Gary walked to the stranded vehicle to have a look at the problem. He kept glancing at the familiar figure, trying to work out where he could have seen him before.

"I'm sure I know you. Have we met?"

"I don't think so," replied the man flatly.

"No, really, I know your face."

"Look, I'm here to cover the opening of Mount Pleasant. I'm a correspondent for BBC News. You've probably seen me on TV. I am late for an interview so can we get a move on?"

Gary pictured him on the television at home, in the sitting room. "Oh, yes, of course. Right, well, don't worry, we'll get you sorted out."

The man only scowled, turned his back and headed to the other vehicle, where his colleague was watching Rick rummage. “How are you getting on, have you found the damned thing yet?”

Rick straightened up, hands held out empty. He shrugged his shoulders.

“Really sorry, mate, I’ve drawn a blank.”

The journalist drew his head into his shoulders and he swelled with anger.

“What the hell do you two idiots think are you doing, driving about without a fucking jack?”

Gary could feel his own indignation rising but he held his tongue and looked across at Rick. Rick caught his eye, tipped his head towards the front of their own vehicle and without a word they turned their backs on the beleaguered men and walked away. Gary swung himself into the passenger seat and Rick turned on the ignition.

“Hey!” shouted the newsman. “Come back! What about a lift?”

“I don’t think so,” said Rick, pushing the gearstick into first and slamming his foot on the accelerator. “We’ve got more important things to do than look after rude bastards like you.”

Gary looked out at the newsman’s colleague, who had been perfectly polite and now stood by the roadside in a daze. It seemed unfair so he tipped his fingers to his forehead in a sympathetic salute. The vehicle accelerated away while Rick muttered expletives under his breath.

Gary chuckled, “Did you see his face?”

“Serve him right.”

“I thought you might offer them a lift.”

“I was going to.” He pushed the Land Rover into top gear.

“Fancy a Wagon Wheel?” asked Rick and they roared with laughter.

The Royal Welch Fusiliers’ camp was a sea of mud and flapping green canvas about a mile from the new airstrip, their tents lined up in orderly rows until such time as they would move into permanent accommodation. Gary shivered at the sight. The coastel was basic but these poor guys had far worse.

“Come on, Gary, there’ll be some lunch for you. I said we’d wait by the kitchen until someone comes to take you to where you’re going to work.” Rick led him over to a large tent where pots and kettles sizzled on gas burners. Gary sloshed after him through watery mud up to his ankles. The hot food was welcome, even if they did have to eat it standing around in the howling wind. Rain soon turned to sleet and then to snow. Gary handed back his plate and accepted mug after mug of steaming coffee, dancing on the spot to keep warm and chatting with the kitchen lads through the tent flap. He dived for cover when a brief hailstorm hurled stinging ice pellets into his face. The men said they were looking forward to their move into fixed accommodation sometime in the coming weeks and Gary could see why.

They told him there was a bunk for him in one of the tents overnight but Gary had brought no warmer clothing and was already half frozen. "Thanks, but I'll take my things with me and see if I can kip where I cut hair."

Damp and chilled, he was glad when at last a khaki-clad figure appeared to collect him. The rain had stopped and they walked for more than half a mile across the site in the wind, which for all its bitterness at least blew his coat dry. They made their way past building after building: the massive TriStar hangar, fuelling points, customs offices, warehouses, lounges, all the paraphernalia of an international airport. The site was frantically busy with vehicles and men tidying the place up for its showpiece event in two days' time. The white concrete runway seemed to stretch for miles.

They entered an office Portakabin next to the control tower. It was warm and dry and there were a few officers at desks behind the partition, where charts of the site showed just how massive the project was. Gary heaved a huge sigh of relief and set about thawing his hands so that he could start work. It was already going dark. Soon an intermittent flow of customers appeared and Gary began the sheep-shearing routine of short all over and a few minutes of chat. Everyone was excited about the opening on Sunday.

Gary worked solidly for a couple of hours until the trickle dried up. It was 8.30 p.m. and the office was empty. He hung around waiting for more customers, expecting a flood at any moment, but by 10.30 p.m. still no-one had shown up. Outside, there was no sign of life. Feeling disconsolate and forgotten, he thought he might as well unroll his sleeping bag on the floor and make the best of the warmth.

The next morning he was woken at 8.00 a.m. by officers barging in through the door to their workspace. They let him use their kettle and offered their jar of instant coffee for a welcome hot drink. Someone turned up a few minutes later for a haircut.

"Hi," he said, "I hope you can fit me in. I imagined there would be a bit of a queue today."

"No worries," said Gary, still coming to. "There's no rush yet, I just hope everyone doesn't arrive at the last minute, I'm only here for the morning." Apart from the Army unit, there were over two thousand construction workers on the site and no other hairdresser that he knew of; he was sure to be busy. He cut the man's hair then waited. Chewing his fingernails, he wondered what was going on. He sauntered through to the office. They were friendly and didn't seem to mind him taking another coffee and sitting down. None of them could work out why no-one seemed to want a haircut.

"Maybe everyone's just too busy with last-minute preparations for the big event," said one of the men. "Never mind, you're welcome to hang around here."

After taking him to a central canteen for some lunch the same officer went to find out about Gary's lift back to Stanley. It was bad news.

"I'm afraid no-one can take you until after the opening tomorrow morning," the officer said. "They're all required for other duties."

"But that's no good," said Gary, dismayed, "This afternoon is my time off and then I've arranged to come back tomorrow with my mates for the opening. I haven't brought my camera with me or anything."

There was nothing he could do. A few customers appeared so he cut their hair, though officially he should have left. The hours dragged by. By four o'clock he had resigned himself to a boring evening with nothing to do but write up an entry in the green book which fortunately he had brought with him. It was utterly frustrating to waste his rare free time in such a place.

Three hours later he heard a vehicle pull up outside. He rushed next door to the office. A junior rank was driving to the airstrip in Stanley to collect the mail that had come in by Hercules and would be happy to give him a lift.

"Hallelujah!" whooped Gary.

Back at the coastel, Gary made sure that the lads he was due to share a Land Rover with for the opening the next day knew that he was back.

“Let’s leave early,” said the Army corporal who had organised the transport and would drive them. “The whole of Stanley is bound to be going as well as all the military and we want to beat the traffic. Let’s get away by seven.”

“Are you sure that’s early enough?” Gary asked, anxious not to miss the occasion.

“Yeah, plenty. The plane’s not due in until noon and the ceremony will be after that.”

Gary wanted to get a good view, see the plane come in, maybe catch sight of the Governor, Sir Rex Hunt and of course Lady Hunt and Major General Peter de la Billière, who would all be in the reception committee for the politicians and dignitaries from England. He wondered how ungroomed Prince Andrew would look and if anyone else would notice the hair over his collar.

12th May dawned but the morning was barely perceptible, the sky was heavy with dark grey clouds like wet coal-sacks. A sprinkling of snow marbled the ground.

The dimmed lights from another vehicle could be seen pulling away ahead, joined after a few minutes by several private four-wheel drives from the town. The corporal drove the Land Rover hard on the gravel surface, more than once dropping into a pothole which jolted the suspension and made the passengers hit their heads.

"Take it easy," said Rob, "There's no real hurry. We're well ahead of the crowd."

"God knows what parking's going to be like," said the driver. "Everyone will be going." The vehicle spat stones into the deep ditch beside the road.

"Put this cassette on, will you," said Gary from the back, handing his favourite tape to the boys in the front seat. They fed it in and turned the volume up. Everyone grinned.

They made good time for twelve miles until suddenly the vehicle swerved and the driver pulled it to a halt.

"What's going on?" cried voices from the back.

"I think we've got a puncture."

They all piled out to look. Sure enough, the nearside front wheel was completely flat.

"Right," said the driver. "Someone get the spare and the jack."

Gary went round to the back of the vehicle and looked into the well in the floor where the spare wheel lay, its old treads worn down.

"Here's the jack!" Steve pulled it out from behind the seats and brandished it in the air.

"I don't think this is going to be much use," said Gary, prodding the spare. "It's as flat as a pancake."

"Shit," said Steve, echoed by the rest of the group as they looked over Gary's shoulders.

They weighed up what to do, standing around the deflated front tyre, trying to come up with good ideas. After ten minutes or so it was obvious that they had no better option than to abandon the Land Rover and start walking, and as they were less than halfway to their destination, the only sensible direction was towards Stanley where they just might get their hands on another vehicle.

"Do you think someone might give us a lift?" said Steve.

"Start praying," answered Gary, as the road stretched before them.

Reluctantly they began to walk. It was cold and grey, with just a strip of blue sky starting to clear on the far horizon over the sea. From time to time other vehicles would approach, only to pass with a hoot or a jeer as the wheels crunched through the chippings. Every car was full, military and civilian alike, and none slowed down more than to look at them. His fellow castaways were wearing their uniform boots and they strode out ahead. Gary however had put on ordinary shoes to give his feet a change for the day and the gravel pressed sharply through the thin soles. His jeans were no protection against the biting wind and his legs soon felt stiff with cold.

*

By eleven they had covered a lot of ground. The sky had cleared and it was obvious from the familiar shape of the land that they were within a couple of miles of Port Stanley. The number of vehicles passing them had increased to an extraordinary volume: dozens every minute, all of them hell bent on their journey.

“Shit, even if we can find a spare Land Rover we'll never get there in time,” said the Army corporal, looking at his watch.

“Shall we go to the pub instead?” suggested one of the lads as they approached the town.

“There's no point trying,” replied Rob. “Everything is closed. All the islanders will have gone to the airport.”

They dragged their weary feet through the deserted streets, where not a person was to be seen. It was eerie, like an empty film set.

“If there were any criminals, they could have a field day,” remarked Steve.

“There's only one and he's already in jail,” grumbled Gary.

The road took them down to the waterfront, where they wandered out onto the Government House jetty and sat on its edge with their feet over the side, in no hurry now to do anything.

"What a flipping lovely day it's turned out," said Gary. "Perfect for an airport opening." He felt deeply disappointed to miss the big event.

They sat around, staring into the water where ducks bobbed and seaweed floated amongst the sparkling surface ripples.

In the sky ahead he suddenly spotted two pinpricks of light.

"Lads! Is that the plane?"

"Where?" they chorused.

They all jumped up and shaded their eyes; he grabbed his camera from his pocket.

"Look! You can see the lights! And a jet out to each side."

A Royal Air Force TriStar appeared in the sky, its great body larger than anything they had seen fly over the Falklands before, flanked by two Phantom jets. With a deep-throated roar it approached and flew majestically over their heads.

"Wow!" he exhaled, then without thinking he started waving and cheering and whooping at the tailfin that was disappearing towards Mount Pleasant. The friends clapped each other on the back and hugged unashamedly.

"The most exciting phase of development in Falkland Islands history," quoted Rob.

"And we had to bloody miss it," said Gary, kicking his shoes along the planks of the jetty as they turned to walk back towards the empty coastels. "You know what? I only went and left my favourite cassette in the Land Rover."

Bet

She sat next to her friend Dot on her way home in the bus, glad of the company. Everyone was so kind, they always asked after Tom and offered to help, not that there was anything anyone could do. But she appreciated the support.

"You seem quiet, Bet. Is everything all right?"

Bet pulled herself back from her thoughts, forced a smile. The streets of Sunderland crawled by the window.

"Oh, well, you know. He isn't getting any better. I worry that he seems to be going backwards."

Dot murmured and put her hand on Bet's arm.

"It was hard enough to get him home after his first stroke six years ago. And now? He's weaker, I'm older, who knows. I want him home, Dot, I really do, but I find it hard to believe it's going to happen. The best I can hope for is that he'll end up in a nursing home."

"Come on, Bet love, don't give up just yet. It's only been what? Less than three months?"

Bet nodded glumly. They had been three long, difficult months.

"You're both made of tough stuff. Just keep going. For him. He'll be the first to notice if you give up."

Bet heaved a sigh. "You're right of course. It's just hard to think that this is all his life is going to be from now on."

Dot squeezed her arm.

The bus stopped outside the football ground and twenty or so disconsolate fans filed on board.

"Oh dear," said Dot. "You can see how the match went. Badly."

"Look, there's Tony." Bet had recognised one of the passengers, a thickset middle-aged man from Whitburn. He worked like Tom in the pit until it closed, then he had started his own business as a window cleaner. As he passed, she tapped him on the arm. "No good then, Tony?"

"Oh, hello, love," he said, "Didn't spot you there." He sat down heavily on the seat in front of them, wafting flakes of cigarette ash and a smell of boiled onions. Others found spaces, all downcast and silent.

"Hopeless we were, effing hopeless. Two nil. I despair. Beaten by Stoke City."

"They should have had some women on the team then they would have done all right," said Bet sideways, giving Dot a nudge.

"Old age pensioners would have played better," wheezed Tony.

"Well, Dot," said Bet, "We're in, then."

Dot smiled. “You should watch what you say, Bet, or they’ll sign you up.”

“I wouldn’t mind. I’m quite good in goal.”

“Hey,” Dot leaned forward and poked Tony in his bulging shoulder, “Could you get her a trial?”

Tony half turned in his seat. “Frankly, ladies, having you in goal would be an improvement, even if you just stood there with your handbags.”

The sun pushed its way through the dreary clouds and as the bus turned along the front, Bet watched it illuminate a distant ship which glistened against the blackness of the North Sea.

The next morning Bet was just getting her coat and scarf on when the telephone rang. Although she had been up for two hours, it was still only eight thirty, too early for it to be any of the family. With foreboding she picked up the receiver.

“Morning, Mrs Davison. Doctor Harrison from the hospital. Are you coming in this morning?”

“Yes, Doctor. What is it?”

“It is urgent that I see you. How soon can you get here?” His voice was steady, despite the word urgent.

“I’ll be there as fast as I can.”

She walked down to the bus stop beside the cemetery feeling remarkably calm. A robin hopped along the top of the wall and she wished she had brought some crumbs. When the bus arrived she sat in her normal seat, looking out at the sea and the amusements on the front, open-minded about what the day would bring.

Bet looked at the bespectacled surgeon who sat impassively opposite her at his desk, fingers pressed together.

"Just tell me, Doctor."

"It's really not good news, I'm afraid, Mrs Davison."

He gazed at her calmly with grey-blue eyes unblinking underneath long eyebrows, which rose into tufted points. They would have been comical had the situation not been so serious.

"Your husband has become extremely unwell overnight and is in a lot of pain. The symptoms indicate that gangrene has probably infected the sore on his leg."

Bet was horrified, wasn't sure that she had heard the words right.

"Gangrene? I thought that was something soldiers got in the First World War, in dirty conditions when there wasn't proper medical treatment."

"The bacilli that cause it are very common and enter through a wound. I'm just awaiting the result of some tests from the pathology lab but I am pretty certain of the diagnosis from an examination of your husband this morning. We need to act quickly as gangrene spreads very fast."

"Act quickly?"

"Untreated, it will kill him."

Bet sat unmoving, allowing the words to sink in. She could hear her blood beating in her ears.

"What's the treatment then, Doctor?"

"For gangrene, the only remedy is to cut away the infected tissue and surrounding healthy tissue. In your husband's case, that means we need to amputate the infected leg after which a course of penicillin should help."

Bet felt sick. She looked at the wall with its anatomical posters of the nervous system and muscles. She started to tremble. "Is there any alternative?"

"I'm afraid not. I have talked to your husband about it but he is not in a state to confirm any decision. You will need to sign the consent forms for him."

Tears pushed at Bet's eyes. "Can I go and see him?"

“Of course. As soon as I have the diagnosis confirmed by the lab I’ll need you to give the go ahead and we’ll have him prepared for theatre immediately.”

Her legs felt weak, as though they might give way beneath her. Tom had been moved into an individual room next to the ward and the corridor seemed to grow longer with every step, as if it was taking him further and further away. She put her head around the door. Lying back on the pillows, her husband was yellow faced. She had not realised before just how terribly thin and shrunken he had become. The strong arms that once had wielded a miner’s drill were as thin as straws. His face looked tortured even in semi sleep.

She stood beside the bed, looking down at her man, smoothing the hair back from his forehead.

“Oh, Tom. How could life do this to you?”

GARY

Out in Stanley Harbour an oil-tanker rode at anchor, its upper decks reflecting brilliant white in the sunshine while the black paintwork of its hull was streaked with rust that was visible all the way from FIPASS. It must have discharged its cargo into the tanks at the Navy station, since the load line, a bright red, was a long way above the water. The tanker was so huge it all but blocked the view of the ridge of land behind. Nearer, a Navy frigate was tiny by comparison as it swung with the tide at the same angle as the giant.

Standing on the FIPASS jetty in the breeze, Gary didn't know what type of vessel would take him out to the tanker so when he saw a combat speed boat heading towards him, he assumed it was on some other mission. It roared towards the port, cutting a slice of white foam through the dark water, with two well-wrapped figures in the stern. They pulled up at the quayside where he was standing and hailed him.

"You the barber?"

"Yes."

"Hop aboard, then."

Gary faltered for a moment, unable to believe his luck. One of the FIPASS staff threw down two mailbags marked for the ships.

"You coming or not?" the Navy pilot said.

It would be easier to climb down the ladder without a holdall over his shoulder. He motioned to the pilot to catch the bag rather than just drop it, mindful of damaging any of his tools and especially his precious scissors. Doing his jacket up, he stepped on to the ladder, clambered down and into the rocking boat.

"Get this on you." The second in command handed him a dark-blue life jacket. "Just in case."

Gary wasn't sure how much use a buoyancy aid would be in the freezing water. You might float but what was the point if the cold was going to kill you in seconds?

"Sit down there." The pilot motioned to one of the forward seats.

Gary settled himself obediently and they cast off. They pulled out quietly from the quay, passed a flock of gulls that were screaming and diving onto the surface of the harbour then suddenly the engine roared, the boat surged forward and its prow lifted. They drove at full throttle through the scattering sea birds. The wind whipped Gary's face; he caught his beret and stuffed it into his pocket. His hair was flattened against his head. With the other hand he gripped tightly to a handle on the side of the boat as they accelerated over the waves, his fingers gradually losing all sensation. Spray flew up from the hull, drenching him. He whooped and laughed with excitement.

They pulled in for a moment at the rear of the frigate, HMS Avenger, where eager arms reached down for the mail sack. Then they were off again, bouncing across the water for the tanker. The ship towered above them like a skyscraper. The crew threw out fenders to protect the tiny shell of the speed boat from the rusting monster and Gary eyed the rope ladders nervously.

"Is this it?" he asked, looking up for what seemed like miles.

"Don't worry, your bag can follow on a rope once you're up there safely," the pilot replied. "Keep the life-jacket on until you're on board – someone will lower it back down to us from the top. Just take it steady and don't rush."

Gary stood up and grabbed the ladder which swung free in mid-air, clear of the concave ship's side. At least they were in the lee of the wind and the movement of the water was not too dizzying. He took a deep breath.

"Right. Here goes."

Tentatively he put a foot on the wooden rung and, holding on for dear life, put his full weight on it. The ladder swung inwards. An involuntarily gasp escaped him.

"Don't worry. I've got this end," said the crewman, holding fast to the ladder a little below Gary's foot. "You won't go anywhere. Trust me. Just climb."

Gary exhaled and looked up. "Right." Hand over hand: one nervous foot at a time, he pulled his way up the ladder. Once he got into the feel of it, it wasn't too bad; in fact it was quite exhilarating, working his way up the giant ship's flank like an insect. When the wind suddenly picked up, he felt confident enough to carry on. Up above him, smiling faces leaned out and made signs of encouragement. Gary concentrated hard on the job in hand and steadfastly did not look down. He noticed the blistering of the ship's side, the knocks and the scratches, the way that the black paint was dull with all the weather and the salt. When his eyes finally came to the level of the deck, strong hands tucked into his armpits and he was manhandled over the top of the railing. He spluttered, breathless from the exertion, pulling his coat back down and glad to be on his feet. "Thanks."

After they had pulled up his bag one of the crewmen took him inside the white stack at the stern of the ship that provided living accommodation and, at the top, the bridge. They went up a couple of flights of stairs. It was impressive how clean and shiny everything was. A few crew members passed on the stairs looking immaculate, just as smart as their Royal Navy counterparts if not better, and they all wished him a good morning. He followed into an office where a chair and table and mirror had been set up. There was a broom in the corner and a large bin.

"This all right for you?" his guide asked.

"Yes, it looks great. Thanks."

"Good. Well, it's after eleven o'clock already. I'll send along the first men."

Gary took off his coat and moved the furniture around. His first customer appeared through the door, smart in a crisp white shirt, and the day's work started.

At midday Gary finished his fourth cut and the customer checked himself in the mirror.

"It's lunch soon. Fancy coming to the bar for a drink? It's a tradition when we're in harbour. You'll have plenty of time to finish afterwards."

Gary followed the officer along the corridor to a small bar, stacked with a selection of spirits and bottled beers, presided over by a smiling crewman who polished glasses with a tea-towel.

"What will it be? Gin and tonic? Brandy and ginger?"

Gary was not used to spirits or any kind of alcohol at midday. "I'll just have an orange juice, if that's OK."

"Orange juice for our visitor, please, Ray."

Other men began to fill the small space and each in their turn ordered a drink and raised their glasses in a toast. They were a friendly bunch. The Captain came in wearing a broad grin and a discreet amount of gold braid.

"Aha! You must be Corporal Shewan! Glad to meet you," he shook Gary's hand jovially and Gary was glad of all those years when his Dad taught him the importance of first impressions and a firm handshake, nothing like a wet kipper.

“Welcome aboard the Lumiere. I hope you’ll have some lunch with us.”

Gary felt a little dazed. He followed the Captain through to the dining room next to the bar and looked around for a servery or a hatch where he could pick up a tray but there was nothing like that.

“Come and sit down.” The Captain motioned Gary to sit next to him at the table, which was laid out with a cloth and starched napkins, heavy cutlery and wine glasses. The bar steward appeared through a swing door, balancing a tray of steaming plates on his shoulder. One by one, he placed them in front of the men.

“This smells good,” Gary said.

“We have an excellent cook,” said the Captain. “And it’s always a pleasure to get to port and have fresh produce. Now, don’t hold back.”

The conversation was pleasant and Gary munched, managing to smile and be polite, but mostly he was just enjoying the unaccustomed luxury of waiter service and a five-course meal. None of it was fancy, in fact it was good home cooking, but he felt like a king. He sipped water from his wineglass.

Gary returned to work feeling full and soporific as one by one the rest of the crew appeared for their haircuts. One of the men who had helped haul him aboard came to tell him that the tug Beaulieu was on its way to pick him up. Gary packed his things, swept the last trimmings into the bin, left the room exactly as he had found it and headed for the outside. All in all it had been his best day so far and when he got back to the coastel he would enjoy writing his report in the green book. Gary thought about scores. They were going to be high for the tanker on every count. The only things that could have improved the day were music and a beautiful woman, but he had to remain realistic. Yes, this was about as good as it could get.

"Gaz! You walking in?" It was the start of another week and Rob caught up with him on the causeway where he had stopped as was customary to tip their hats to Sammy the seal who, even when they were early like today, was already sitting on a pile of palettes at the land end.

"Hobbling, more like," replied Gary, whose knee felt stiff and sore for no particular reason. "My knee's shot. Maybe it was climbing that ladder or maybe it's because I've put on so much weight."

"You look as skinny as ever to me."

"Hah! I'm bursting out of my shirts. Had to sew two buttons back on yesterday."

Rob clapped him on the back. "What will Lesley think?"

Their footsteps crunched along the gravel in the dawn greyness. Gary dug his hands deep into his pockets.

"Hopefully she'll approve. Always gives me a hard time about my skinny ribs. She never stops going on about who she fancies on television, how fit they are and well-built."

"Let's go by the coast path," said Rob.

Tracing the waterfront was their preferred route except in wet weather, when the ground would turn into a quagmire and splash mud over the ankles of their boots and up the backs of their legs. The two friends walked along easily, quoting jokes they could recall from Friday night's comedy show in the gym, sharing ten weeks' worth of ritual banter and mutual experience.

"D'you know I've done two thousand two hundred haircuts."

"Bloody hell!" whistled Rob.

"I know. It's all that extra time I've been putting in. I wonder if it's a record."

"No wonder your knee hurts."

Rob stopped as usual at FILOG and Gary headed on up the hill to the Kelper Store. It was the same grim place as always, with piles of flattened cardboard boxes stacked up outside against the wooden side wall and functional displays of goods inside. He found the supervisor behind a pyramid of marmalade. "Did the office phone through with my schedule? It wasn't ready when I left."

"Morning, Gary. Let's have a look." The man headed for the desk out the back and grabbed a clipboard off the top, where someone had written the telephone message. He tapped it with his biro. "You're here until Wednesday. The guys at Fox Bay are due a visit on Thursday, with a Bristow coming back to Stanley at three-twenty on Friday afternoon."

"Fox Bay. Sounds good." Gary was always pleased for any trip away.

"Has your boss told you that you might be moving?" enquired the supervisor.

"Moving? Where to?" It was the first Gary had heard of it.

"Apparently, they're planning to set up a shop for you on the coastel, seeing as so many people come from over there anyway. This store is going to be closed down, at least for EFI use, and will be handed back to the islanders. Everything's moving to Mount Pleasant, bit by bit."

"No, I didn't know."

"You'll be sorry to leave us," teased the supervisor.

Gary walked through to the horrible little room beside the store, bending and rubbing his sore knee as he went. It hurt to put his weight on it.

During the morning the usual stream of customers flowed through, some of them EFI lads, some military. Gary's knee grew more and more painful and he started to find it difficult to bend. Eventually he couldn't put his weight on it at all and then his other leg started to hurt, too, taking the full load all the time.

"You'd better get that seen to," said a shorn customer after Gary had hissed and groaned his way through an agonising ten minutes with the clippers. "I'm driving back to the Canache. I'll take you to the doctor, if you like."

Gary was grateful to shut up shop. "Sorry, gents," he said to two beefy servicemen who stood waiting. "You'll have to try again tomorrow. I can't do any more today."

At the military hospital, housed in temporary buildings opposite the coastels, the doctor told him to sit up on the bed and felt his good knee first. "How's this one?"

"All right."

"Any injury to the bad knee? Have you knocked it recently?"

"Not recently. I did have an old injury, a few years back, when I was learning to dance rock'n'roll and doing the splits, but that got better and hasn't been any trouble. I suppose I might have hit it last week when I was climbing on board a tanker but I think I would have noticed."

"Hmmm. Been working hard, have you? On your feet a lot?" The doctor moved his hands to the sore knee and started to feel it. Gary winced.

"Yeah, long hours, sometimes twelve hours, officially six days a week. Sometimes seven. My schedule's a nightmare and I get hardly any free time."

The doctor manipulated his leg. Gary sucked air in through his teeth.

"Hmmm. Well there's no evidence of ligament damage. And there doesn't appear to be much swelling. It could be a cartilage problem. Sometimes the inside surface of the kneecap can get roughed up and feel very sore. Sounds like you might have been overdoing it."

There was nothing to say.

"I'll prescribe you some anti-inflammatories, they should help. In the meantime, take twenty-four hours bed rest, lying down. Give it a chance to settle. One of these, three times a day, for a week," he handed Gary a packet, "And if that doesn't do the trick, come back and see me again."

"OK."

"Do what you can to get a bit more rest. Your schedule sounds punishing. I know you're young and fit but you do need to look after yourself. Have a word with your boss. Doctor's orders."

Gary couldn't see how having a word with anybody would make any difference.

"Do you think you can make it back to the coastel?"

Gary looked out of the Portakabin window. The coastel was only a few hundred yards away. "Yeah, I should manage. If you look out in ten minutes and see a lump that's not moving, it's me. Send out the rescue nurses."

He enjoyed the enforced bed rest, listening to tapes on his personal stereo, catching up on letters to family and friends. He couldn't remember when he had last spent a whole day in bed. Shame Lesley wasn't here with him.

He went straight back to work the following afternoon, his knee still hurt but at least he could stand up and he knew that the longer he lay in bed daydreaming, the bigger the queue for haircuts would grow. Dita had been concerned about the doctor's assessment and wanted Gary to take another day off but he didn't think it was worth the hassle.

On Thursday morning he was on the Bristow for Fox Bay. He craned his neck to see out of the window during the flight even though he had travelled the route before. Below, the winter landscape was washed-out and windswept with pools and lagoons spreading as far as the eye could see. The bleakness was desolate but somehow beautiful.

They swept in over a destroyer in Falkland Sound which trailed two white wake-ribbons across the satin water, then rose over a low line of hills towards the village of Fox

Bay East. The helicopter banked and turned above the red roof of an enormous woollen mill. Gary had read about it in the local paper and grinned to himself at the thought of Prince Andrew on his recent visit, declaring it open with his hair all scruffy.

The helicopter took them upriver to Doctor's Creek where it alighted at the camp of the Royal Hampshires. Gary ducked around the front of the Bristow and headed straight for the NAAFI building, made up of the usual Portakabins. The bar smelled faintly of stale beer and cigarette smoke but when a smiling corporal suggested this might be the best place to work Gary was happy because there was a good music system with decent speakers.

"Right, when do I start?"

"Relax," said the EFI corporal, who introduced himself while he continued to bottle up behind the bar. "There'll be some lunch in the canteen next door in about half an hour. People won't turn up for you until afterwards. Go and have a look around."

Gary took a short stroll along the water's edge, where thick kelp beds stilled the waves so that the water licked *flop-flop-flop* against the shore. Pairs of white and brown geese flew overhead while far out, a pod of dolphins played in the weed.

He took a great lungful of tangy air, gathering up his energy for the afternoon. His knee felt a lot better.

Work started as soon as lunch was over and the hours passed quickly until half past seven in the evening, with just a few minutes' break for tea. The bar opened, he packed away his clippers and a steady stream of men turned up to swill pints and feed money into the insistent slot machine. The music was turned up loud and a fug of cigarette smoke started to rise and gather in a brown pall under the ceiling. The corporal worked single-handed behind the bar. The poor man was finding it impossible to keep pace with customers and empties.

"Is it always like this?" shouted Gary above the din, pint in hand.

"No but the other barman's having a couple of days' R and R in Stanley."

"R and R?" Gary scratched his head.

"Rest and…"

"I know what it is; I was just thinking how nice it would be to have some myself. You look like you could do with a hand." He set off around the room collecting up the empties, piling stacks of pint glasses on the bar. "Do you want me to wash up?"

"That would be great, cheers," called the flustered corporal, who was scurrying back and forth, trying to serve three servicemen at once, selling cigarettes and dispensing change for the fruit machine as well as pulling pints.

The bar closed promptly at eleven and the good-humoured Hampshires dispersed without a murmur of discontent.

"That's another hectic night done," said the corporal, locking the grille over the servery. "Thanks for your help, you're a pal."

"No worries," said Gary. "Would it be OK if I kipped at the back of the bar on that padded bench?"

"Help yourself. See you tomorrow."

With his headphones on, Gary slept well.

He worked steadily again the next morning, looking forward to the afternoon flight, and made sure he was at the office by the helipad with twenty minutes in hand. Nobody was gathering, which was unusual as the seats were always filled.

"Is no-one else going back?" he enquired of a sergeant who was working behind a battered desk. The man looked up at him, surprised, and then carried on searching for whatever he was looking for amongst his papers.

"Back?" He lifted documents from a plastic stacking tray and rifled through them.

"To Stanley," said Gary. "On the Bristow."

"Not expecting any flights today, mate." The sergeant put his hands on a manila file. "Aha!"

"You're joking," said Gary. "I thought one was coming in at twenty past three."

"Wrong info, sorry. Maybe tomorrow."

Gary let out a sigh of frustration. "I'd better do a few more haircuts, then. Could you phone around and let people know I'm still here?"

"No worries."

Gary tramped back across the camp to the NAAFI bar and unpacked his bag. Within minutes the Hampshires were taking advantage of his delay. He did another fifty-six haircuts that afternoon and evening. He carried on working even when the bar was in full flow, reckoning he might as well keep busy and pocket the extra cash. The customers were all delighted.

He slept well again in the bar for a second night, woke early on Saturday morning and packed ready to go. He wolfed down some breakfast and dashed over to the office, eager to secure a seat on the Bristow. The sergeant shook his head.

"Don't think one's coming today."

"What? Can't you radio them? Surely someone else on West Falkland must want to go to Stanley."

The sergeant was sympathetic but there was nothing Gary could do.

All day he darted between the bar and the office, convinced that at some point matters would be resolved. There was a lot of to-ing and fro-ing at the camp, including other helicopters, but no offers of help. The sergeant held up his hands, powerless. Gary fumed and cursed and eventually went to the gym to sweat out his anger.

On Sunday morning he woke early, packed his bag yet again, stuffed down another breakfast and made his way across to the office. The weather was still the same, crystal clear, breezy.

"You're in luck," said the sergeant. "There's a Bristow coming mid-morning."

"Thank God for that."

With nothing better to do, Gary hung around the office while other people came and went. A pile of boxes and mailbags grew beside the helipad and other passengers gathered piecemeal. He went to watch the S-61 come in, its red and white body visible from miles away, like a dragonfly whirring in across the water. It touched down lightly on the pad and disgorged half a dozen laughing servicemen. The ground crew jumped on board and started to lift out crates and boxes and mailbags, replacing them with the ones Gary had seen stockpiled, whilst two others fed a long hose into the helicopter's fuel tanks. "OK, lads, all done," they shouted to the waiting passengers once they had withdrawn the nozzle.

Gary was at the front of the line to get in and he threw himself down gratefully onto the rearmost seat. Others followed after him, gradually filling the places going forwards. He was impatient to get to the letters that would be waiting at the coastel and to enjoy at least a little bit of his weekend. Then he became aware of consternation at the front. The flight crewman disappeared into the cockpit and returned with a tattered clipboard, from which he started reeling off names. Gary listened as one by one, each of the men raised a hand or grunted acknowledgement. The crewman came down the narrow gangway towards him.

“Sorry, laddie. It’s the barber isn’t it?”

Gary nodded, a sick feeling in the pit of his stomach.

“Thought I recognised you. I’m afraid we’re fully booked. You’re going to have to get off.”

Gary protested feebly but knew it was useless. He could see the last serviceman standing at the door, waiting for his seat.

When the Bristow lifted off, firing a blast of turbulence downwards and a scattering of grit upwards, Gary watched it forlornly, burning in the face, his head exploding. He had never felt so exasperated. It turned and swept away, disappearing eastwards over the sea. He kicked his holdall, too frustrated to care about his precious tools. Across the other side of the helipad the two fuel operatives were throwing sand on spilled oil.

“Hi, guys.” He recognised them both or at least their neat haircuts.

“Hi, what’s up?”

Gary walked over to them and gritted his teeth. “Long story. Look, do me a favour, would you?”

“Sure.”

“If anything comes in, anything at all, will you ask the pilot if he will give me a lift back to Stanley?”

“OK. Where will you be?”

“Over there in the NAAFI.”

Gary grabbed his bag and walked back to the bar. He banged in through the door, glad that no-one was there to sympathise. He might have been rude. He kicked the dormant fruit machine, threw his bag down on a chair and stared out of the picture window towards the helipad.

The next forty minutes passed more slowly than any minutes he had ever been aware of. He was used to waiting, but two whole days had already been a long time and he didn’t know when help would come. A Gazelle flew in – a tiny, black wasp, the sky visible through its bubble windscreen, its tail long and pointed with a great sting at the end. It was the Ferrari of helicopters. He watched, filled with envy. One of the refuellers ducked in under the rotor-blades for a couple of seconds then ran out again, waving, towards him.

Gary looked around, failing to register immediately that here was help at last.

"Bloody hell!" he exclaimed, grabbing his bag and running out.

A crewman jumped out of the Gazelle with an armful of kit. "All right, mate?" Cool as you like.

Gary nodded breathlessly, his heart thumping and eyes taking in the streamlined machine.

"Put this lot on."

The crewman strapped him in to a waterproof oversuit, a life jacket, headphones and microphone. Gary felt floppy as a doll, bemused by what was happening and needing help to do up the fastenings. A firm hand on his shoulder propelled him towards the beast.

"Right, in you get!"

He clambered into a tiny seat in the back and his holdall was pushed in behind him. In front, the pilot turned round and gave him a wave. Hands pulled the seatbelt tight around him, the crewman jumped aboard the other front seat, the door was pulled to and the engine roared.

Gary heard a smooth voice through his earphones. "You all right in the back there?"

"Yeah, thanks!"

"Just sit tight, we'll have you back in no time."

The rotor turned transparently, the machine lifted, and suddenly they were moving forward and up over the ground, twisting and banking and leaning and Gary felt a surge of exhilaration shoot from his toes to his stomach to his fingers to the top of his head.

The pilots were talking a language Gary didn't understand, a sort of flying code, checking their instruments, speaking on the radio to base, checking in with other pilots. "We've got a special delivery for Stanley, about ninety minutes' round trip." At least that much was comprehensible. They skimmed low over Falkland Sound; Gary wondered if they might dip down to touch the water but all they did was frighten some sea birds. It was fantastic, so fast and so smooth. His head reeled. The brown swamplands of Lafonia sped towards them, flat, wet, glinting in the low sunshine. They followed a river then a vehicle track that wound its way across the featureless landscape.

"Hey! There's Goose Green!" said Gary, suddenly recognising buildings he had visited only a few weeks ago. They cut across Darwin Harbour. To their left the hills of Wickham Heights filled his view, the highest point passing behind his shoulder, its rocky top kissed by cloud. The pilots spoke to air traffic control at Mount Pleasant and it hove into view, the shining runway stretching like a bandage, the mass of buildings an ugly wound in an empty landscape.

"Wow!" shouted Gary as they dipped over Fitzroy and Bluff Cove, then followed the familiar road towards

Stanley. He would never have imagined travelling it at this speed. He could see the harbour and the little town and at the far end, the coastels. They flew in low, skimming the tops of the accommodation blocks and the hospital Portakabins, past Surf Bay and its white rollers on their right, and on to the helipad at RAF Stanley.

"Wow!" he exclaimed again as they peeled him out of all the straps and webbing. "That was amazing!"

"Happy to help," the crewman remarked and tipped his forehead, jumping back in. The Gazelle lifted off and Gary waved manically.

He hoped fervently to find his friends at the coastel, although chances were that they'd all be out enjoying the Sunday afternoon sunshine. He skipped along the road, buzzing with excitement and ready to relate his best story so far. He was eager to collect the post which he knew would be waiting.

He trotted along the causeway, whistling to himself, swinging his bag, glad to be back. He found the pigeon-holes all picked clean except for the letter S. Five letters awaited him. Gary said hello to the duty sergeant, scooped the envelopes into his hand, waved at a couple of lads he recognised, and ran up the stairs looking at the handwriting. The pale blue envelope was from his Gran, the blue one from his Mam, the green one from Lesley, another green one from Lesley, and one with writing he wasn't sure he recognised. The address on the back told him it was from one of his old schoolmates, which was a nice surprise.

His fingers itched to open them all. He hurried down the corridor to their room, pushed in through the door – no-one in – and dropped his bag on the floor. "Bloody hell! What a day!" He wrenched his beret off his head and threw it down on the table.

His thumb was already under the flap of the first envelope, the one from his Gran, and he pulled out the letter, eager to read all her news. His eyes scanned her familiar handwriting, all loops and odd capital letters in the middle of sentences and a slight shakiness.

Well son or should I say Grandson, I expect by now you will have received Mam and Dad's letter telling you about Grandad.

Gary's heart stood still.

I didn't write last week as I wanted you to get Dad's letter first. It has worried us all having to tell you when you are so far away, but Gary don't grieve son Grandad is at rest now and free from pain mentally and physically…

Gary landed heavily on the chair in the middle of the room.

… and you know it was no life for him, just lying in a hospital bed and no hope of ever coming out.

Gary's chest heaved.

He is still with us in spirit Gary and I still read your letters to him. Forget him as he was these last six years and just remember him as he was playing on the beach with you all, gathering whelks, playing crazy golf, football and taking you down the allotment to see the hens and rabbits, taking us to the fair ground and the pictures…

Gary could read no more. His breath came in short, stabbing gulps, up from his stomach, stifling him. Grandad. Grandad. He looked back at Gran's first lines and broke into an animal wail, his head tipped back to the ceiling, eyes squeezed in agony. He held the pages to his face, gasping for air.

He abandoned Gran's letter without finishing it, throwing himself on to his bunk and tearing open the envelope from home, desperate to know what had happened. His Dad's writing greeted him.

Dear Gary. We are writing to let you know that Grandad Davison passed away this morning.

He died peacefully in his sleep. Sorry we had to give you this news but we were sure you would wish to know. He has been poorly for some months as you know, so it is a relief for everyone to know his suffering is all over. Gran has decided to have him cremated on Thursday. Everyone thought this would be best. Lesley has sent flowers from you and her and she will attend the cremation on your behalf.

Gary gasped again; eyes wet, cheeks trembling and hot. He read on, past his Dad's kisses and on to his Mam's handwriting.

Hello Son. It really was for the best. He didn't always know us when we went to visit. Your photo was on the windowsill in his room. So although you were so far away you were the last person he would see.

He felt despair overwhelm him. How could Grandad be dead? How could his hero not be there anymore? Gary visualised the strong arms, the steely eyes, remembered the humour, the temper – and felt his own resolve ebb away. He turned to the pillow and buried his face, wracked with uncontrollable misery.

When he heard the door click he had no idea how much time had passed: minutes or hours. The tenor of their voices told him that they had had a good day, whatever they had been doing.

"Hey, Gary! You're back," said Shaun, who must have been the first in through the door. "Had a nice time?"

"Get off, you bugger!" Rob laughed, to the sound of scuffling and Steve's unmistakeable giggle.

"What's up, Gaz?" Shaun drew nearer.

Gary dragged his head up from the pillow and turned towards them, not wanting to look, eyes still closed, the corners of his mouth twitching.

“Oh shit, what happened?” Rob’s voice pushed through. Gary knew they would see the letters scattered all over the place. “Bad news?”

Gary nodded and breathed in with a series of shuddering gulps.

“Hey, lads,” said Rob, “Give us a few minutes, eh?” and the other two backed out of the room, looking embarrassed and concerned. The bunk dipped as Rob sat down next to him. “Come on, Gary, what’s up?”

Warmth emanated from Rob’s body but Gary was glad he just sat there without trying to comfort him. He took a deep breath and cleared his throat, opening his eyes and focusing on the brown carpet.

“My Grandad. He died.”

“Oh.”

The two of them sat in silence. After a while Gary felt he could say a bit more.

“I never thought it would happen but maybe it’s for the best. He’s been through hell. They all have, especially my Gran.”

Rob said nothing.

“It’s just that I would have liked to see him.” Gary felt another tear trickle down his cheek. “He’s being cremated on Thursday. I’ve got to go.”

“What happened?”

Gary snivelled. “I think he just faded away in that hospital.” He heaved a huge sigh. “I need to talk to Dita, see if I can go to the funeral. How on earth will Gran manage?”

Gary felt Rob’s hand on his shoulder, firm, calming. “Listen, Gary, your family will look after your Gran.”

Gary gathered up the letters and rubbed the back of his hand across his face, spreading tears and snot. He wiped his nose on his cuff. “I still want to go.”

“Shall I fetch you a coffee?”

Gary nodded.

When Rob disappeared out of the door Gary breathed hard and looked at the letters in his hand. The one from his Gran was five pages long. He had only read the first two. He started again, teeth gnawing at his fingernails. He got past the bad news to where she thanked him for the beautiful flowers that Lesley had sent for them both.

They were lovely and Lesley came to the funeral. It was great seeing her, she is a smashing lass.

Gary looked to the postmark on the envelope – first of June. Yesterday. That was quick. Then at the letter from his parents – twenty-sixth of May. Last Sunday. The cremation was over already. He gulped, feeling the fluttering in his chest and stomach start again. He fought back more tears.

You are moving in select circles, aren't you? Dinner with the Captain and five-course meal, ha! Don't expect that when you come to see me – you will be lucky if you get pie and five chips. Will I have to pay to speak to you?

He laughed despite himself. Inimitable Gran.

Weather has been lovely today. I went down Marsden beach with Alan and Nancy and children. Guess what? I was chasing Paul in the shallow water with a pail of water and I fell in. Don't you dare laugh. And Paul finished the job and threw his pail of water over me, so I didn't need a bath when I came home.

Rob was right. Maybe it was a release for her as well as for Grandad.

Rob appeared at the door with a steaming beaker of coffee from the machine. "Here you go." He put it on the table. "How's things?"

Gary looked up at the sympathetic face of his friend. "There's no point going home. He's cremated already."

"Oh."

"Gran seems OK. She's as daft as ever. The family's taking her out and spending time with her."

"Good. What about you?"

"I'll write. That's the most important thing."

"Yes."

"I suppose I'd better just get on with the job. I can't tell you what it's been like." He heaved another sigh. "Bloody hell, Rob, I nearly forgot. I came back from Fox Bay in a Gazelle!"

Rob whistled through his teeth. "Really?"

"Yeah. I'll tell you and the others about it over tea. I had a terrible time for a couple of days but the ride back was fantastic. Honestly, what a day. You couldn't make it up."

He got the green diary out of his locker.

"When the new shop opens in the coastel next week things are going to change. I'm not just some stupid kid who's come out here to get pushed around. I'm going to persuade Dita to let me take control of things, manage it all myself like a proper business."

"Watch out, Gaz, you're sounding far too grown up."

"I'll make Grandad proud of me."

By the time he had read all the letters right through he felt calmer. He sat down to write to Gran but the words were hesitant and slow to come, as if they would rather stay in the pen than risk crying all over the open page.

I could never have had a more caring Grandad and I will never forget the good times we had together. He would not have wanted me to get too upset and I always felt as if he was proud of me coming over here. I have always been proud of Grandad. He is the kind of Grandad everyone would love and you are the perfect Gran. So please take care of yourself and don't worry about me, I will be back soon and I really look forward to seeing you again.

It was not much of a letter but he hoped that she would understand how difficult it was to find the right-sounding words. He wondered how she was coping. Not just with her grief but with being alone in that empty house and no Grandad to look after. What would she do with herself now?

The next day Gary went to see Dita in his office in the Portakabin adjoining FILOG. It was a characterless space, painted in the ubiquitous shade of cream that graced every NAAFI room, with a board covered in lists, timetables and notes. There were two desks, one for Dita, as head of security, and, opposite, one for the warehouse manager. Dita's desk was piled high with papers, stacked up against his blotter and phone.

"Sorry about your bad news," he said as soon as Gary walked in the door, standing up to hold out a hand, sandy moustache twitching and eyes pale behind transparent eyelashes.

Gary shook the proffered hand across the desk. "Thanks. It was an awful shock but I'm trying to keep positive."

"Good man. Is there anything I can do?"

Gary shook his head but tears welled up without permission. He drew a deep breath and pulled the emotion back in. “I just want to get on with my work.”

His boss gave him an appraising look. “Well, there’s a few things to talk about, let’s sit down, shall we?” Dita motioned that he should pull across the plastic chair from beside the other desk.

“There’s a couple of bits of good news that might cheer you up.” Dita’s face did a little twitch of a smile. “Number one, we’re going to close the Kelper Store barber’s as of tomorrow.”

A triumphant “Yessss!” escaped from Gary’s lips.

“One of the offices on the sea-deck corridor of the coastel has been cleared for you as your new shop. You can have a word with the chippy as soon as we’ve finished, he’ll do the work to fit it out while you are off site this week, so you can open next Monday. I’ve told him you’re on your way.”

This news was sooner than he expected and all the sweeter for it.

“Number two, it’s obvious that we need a second barber, there’s far too much work for one person to do on their own.”

Gary rocked the chair slightly and couldn’t help responding. “You’re telling me! Have you done the maths? I would have to do at least seventy-five haircuts every single day without a break to keep two thousand men tidy. It's just not possible."

"Well, help is on the way. There's a new barber called Wayne arriving next week on the SS Uganda. He's a few years older than you but less experienced so he'll be your junior. You'll need to show him how things work."

"Great."

"And by the way, I've been letting you get away with it up to now but as soon as Wayne gets here, you're to have your hair cut. You're a bad advertisement."

"Just when I thought things were going well."

"Actually, there's some more good news. Your hard work and all the extra time you've put in haven't gone unnoticed. I expect you know that Major Stevens is handing over to Major Hill in a fortnight?"

Major Stevens was the boss of FILOG who everyone including Dita reported to. Gary had checked in with Stevens on a regular basis to report his activities and had cut his hair a couple of times.

"I didn't know he was leaving already."

"Stevens has put you in for a commendation. Commendations usually go up to the Colonel but this one's gone further, in fact all the way to the very top – to the Major General himself."

"De la Billière?"

"The very man. Well done, Gary, it's a credit to you. He's awarded you an extra four days' holiday."

"What, on top of the double holidays I've already earned?"

"On top."

Recognition at last; a warm glow rose from his stomach to his chest. He sat for a minute savouring the feeling before he realised that the meeting was over. On the other side of the desk Dita stood up, hand outstretched again. He stood up himself, took it and held on for a moment, thinking fast. There would never be a better moment to tackle the question of his schedule.

"Actually, Dita, there's something I wanted to ask you."

Dita let go of his hand and motioned to him to sit down again.

"When I'm based at the coastel, who's going to run my schedule?"

Dita's eyes narrowed. "The guys in the office here, of course. Why?"

"What if I did it myself?" He looked at his boss intently, watching for his reaction.

Dita twitched his nose and sniffed. "Don't you think you've got enough to do, especially with the new barber arriving?"

"The thing is, Dita, no offence or anything but it's all a bit hit and miss. I never know if I'm booked or not for a return flight and nor do the outstations. It would be so much more efficient if I made all the arrangements and if I spoke to all the locations, I could make sure they knew when I was coming and were putting the word out. If there's going to be two of us cutting hair, I'll have time to manage it all. What do you say?"

Dita raised one eyebrow, pursed his lips and put his hands to them as if in prayer but not really, he was just thinking.

"Well, it's a fair point. But it's not up to me. You'd have to ask the Major."

"Would you ask for me?"

Dita sucked his teeth and paused to think. "You know, it's not very good timing, what with the changeover and everything. Leave it a couple of weeks while the new barber settles in and the new Major gets his feet under the desk, then let's think about it again, eh?"

Dita's eyes were as pale as a winter sky.

Gary got up disconsolately and headed for the door. He turned in the doorway, biting his lip.

"I've got something to ask that you could say yes to."

His boss raised his eyes to the ceiling although Gary was sure it was in jest rather than genuine impatience.

"What would be the chance of borrowing a Land Rover some time? One weekend, I mean. To get out and see some of the place. It's frustrating being stuck here."

"You'd need an Army driving licence."

"How do I get one of those?"

"You'll have to take a test with one of the transport guys. To show you're a competent driver and can deal with things like changing a wheel."

"Would that be with or without a jack and a spare?"

"Haha, very good." The lads had told Dita about their mishaps, which he appeared to enjoy.

"Seriously, could you organise it for me?"

"Don't see why not."

"This week?"

"Check in with me tomorrow evening."

"Brilliant. Thanks."

He turned to the door again.

"There's one more thing…"

"Don't push your luck, Shewan," Dita snarled, grinning. Gary gave him a wink and dodged out of the door. A ball of paper hit him on squarely the back of the head.

Elizabeth

Elizabeth was roasting chicken thighs for supper and she had taken them out of the oven to turn them over and pour off the spitting fat. The smell wafted through the house while out of the corner of her eye she could see Schweppes watching her every move, drooling for a chance morsel that might just drop to the floor. Upstairs, Paula was revising for her exams, at least she hoped that was what Paula was doing, although it was equally likely she would be knitting or writing love letters to that Spanish lad from last summer's holiday despite having a so-called boyfriend locally.

The sound of the car in the drive was followed by the click of the front door and jangle of keys on the hall table.

"Hello, pet." Familiar arms encircled her waist from behind. She breathed in his smell, a woody mix of bees-wax polish and pine furniture.

"Hello, Mattie love," she replied.

"How are you?"

"Oh, you know. Missing Dad. Keeping busy."

He kissed her behind the ear.

Mattie subsided into his armchair at the far end of the dining room, kicked off his shoes and grabbed the newspaper.

"Smells great. By the way, I've got good news," he said.

"That's a relief," she replied. "I've got bad news. Well, go on."

Mattie was leafing through the paper. "Remember I went for an interview to be manager of that furniture shop?"

"The one in Billingham? That was weeks ago."

"I know. I thought they must have given it to someone else but they phoned me at work today and offered me the job!"

"Mattie! That's brilliant, love. When do you start?"

"Monday. I've just got to see this week through. What a relief. And it will mean quite a bit more money."

She went over with her padded green oven gloves on and pressed her lips to his forehead. "Thank God. There's nothing left in the bank. Even after selling my car I've spent every penny and another bill has arrived this morning."

Mattie hugged her around the hips. "So, what's the bad news, then?"

She pulled away and returned to the hob, where she turned the heat up under a pan of water.

"You mean that's not enough already?" She couldn't help laughing then sighed. "It's our Julie. She's handed her notice in. She's going to work with her Mam and Dad at the garage."

"You're joking." Mattie closed the paper and dropped it on the floor. "She always swore she wouldn't work for them."

"Well, she is. I phoned Glenn to see if anything was wrong but he says it's just the money. I can't blame her but I don't know how I'm going to replace her." She pulled a packet of frozen peas and carrots out of the freezer compartment of the fridge. A teaspoon of salt made the boiling water bubble feverishly. "I thought my own salon was ticking over quite nicely but now it's turning into a disaster, too. I can't believe how everything is going wrong."

Mattie ran his hands through his hair. "Hold on a minute, pet, you've got way too much on your plate. Let's put Upstairs Downstairs with an estate agent. I know it won't help you replace Julie but it will be one less thing for you to do and it might help get rid of the place sooner. They can show people round, which will save you a bit of trouble. You're wearing yourself out keeping both businesses going."

"But what about the cost? They'll take a good few percent."

"It will be worth it to get that shop off our hands."

He got up to lay the table, setting mats and cutlery in their usual places, reaching up into the cupboard for glasses, running a jug of water from the tap.

Elizabeth started to make gravy, thought about the shops, thought about her father. She thought about him most of the time. It had been ghastly watching him turn into a skeleton so depressed in that hospital bed. When they had to amputate his leg, she imagined he might die on the operating table but because he was a pitman through and through he kept right on fighting, like those strikers who had stayed out doggedly even after the cause was lost. It was awful, but a part of her had hoped that he wouldn't wake up from the anaesthetic to battle on. It broke her heart to see him and her Mam together afterwards, holding hands for hours in pitiful silence, with that terrifying flat space in the bedclothes where his leg used to be and nothing to be said that could make things better. His brother came down from Scotland to see him and it was one of the rare times she ever saw her father cry.

Things had got worse very quickly. Just days after the operation she, Mam, Alan and Roy gathered at the hospital to be told that the gangrene had spread. Now the doctors urgently needed to amputate his arm but he was so confused that he couldn't possibly know what was going on let alone make a decision for himself. He hardly recognised them anymore. She looked at the others, recoiling from the decision they were being asked to make.

"He'll die if we say no," said Roy.

"What's left for him if we say yes?" said Alan, who could always be relied on to take the opposite standpoint from his brother.

"He can't use that arm anyway so he won't miss it," replied Roy.

"That's not the point," said Alan and they all knew he was right.

"What shall we do?" her Mam said. "How much more hell should we put him through? It's no life."

"Can't they put him to sleep? Please, God, why can't they let the poor man out of his misery," she heard herself praying aloud.

They shook their heads and refused to sign the consent forms. Her Dad died in terrible pain two days later and with him went a piece of her, the girl that was his daughter.

She felt Mattie's warm hands on her shoulders and his lips on the back of her head.

"Things will get better, pet."

She sniffed back a tear. "I know, they will. And I think that's a great idea about using an agent for the shop."

"It's either that or sell Paula into slavery to cover the bills. I did try raiding Gary's bank account, but no luck." That was just like Mattie, to lighten the mood.

She drained the vegetables; steam clouding the kitchen window, then added a generous knob of butter.

"Give our girl a shout, would you," she said, "Food's nearly ready."

Mattie headed for the bottom of the stairs. "Paula! Dinner's on the table!"

She dished the meal out on to plates and put the jug of gravy in the middle. Poor man, she was so caught up with her own troubles that she had hardly considered what he had been going through these past few months, hating his work as he did.

"Mattie, do we still have that bottle of wine I won at the raffle?" She was sure it was in the larder somewhere, a good bottle of something white with a picture of a château on the label.

"The one we said we'd save for a special occasion?"

"That's the one. Come on, let's open it. I think we should drink a toast to you and your new job."

GARY

Even though it was only mid-afternoon, the dusk of southern winter started to draw its veil over Stanley Harbour, painting the hills purple like a bruise. Clouds blew in across the stars and threatened another snow flurry, hanging as heavily as washing over sagging lines. Officially Gary's day had finished when the helicopter landed at Stanley Airport but, a week on from his conversation with Dita, he felt that if he couldn't sort out this business of managing his own scheduling, he would go mad. He barely broke step as he passed the coastels, sticking instead to the path and continuing his determined pace towards Stanley.

In the dim light, a crane on the FIPASS floating harbour was unloading supplies from a naval auxiliary ship while tiny fork-lift trucks twirled and lifted the loads high, like children who had won a party game, circling with their prizes held in up-stretched hands. Where the ebb tide had exposed wet mud, silhouettes of tiny wading birds scuttled about, feeding before dark. Warehouses on the shore had faded to a muted dullness.

Gary tapped nervously on the open door of Major Hill's office. The new Major looked up from a mountain of paperwork, strands in his thinning hair highlighted by a desk lamp.

"Ah, the barber, Corporal… "

"Shewan, Sir. Gary Shewan."

"Gary, ah that's right."

"Sir, could I have a word?"

The Major said nothing but methodically folded his papers into a neat pile. Gary stood on one foot at the threshold, watching the square hands move, the gold wedding ring catching the light.

"You'd better come in."

He put his bag down just inside the door and walked the few paces towards the desk, pulling his beret off as he did so, turning it around in his hands.

"How's your new salon, Gary?"

"Good, Sir, thanks. The chippy did a great job setting it up. It's much better than the Kelper Store."

"Excellent. And the new barber?"

He had to think quickly, Wayne was about as stupid as was conceivable for a human being to be and he had given Gary a terrible haircut, too. "It's early days yet. I hope he'll settle in, there's a lot of work."

"Do sit down, Gary." The small talk was over and the Major leaned back in his chair with his hands clasped. "Now, fire away."

Gary took a deep breath. "I don't quite know how to start, but I've had a ridiculous day and I've come straight here to tell you about it because it happens all the time and I want to ask you if I could please organise my own schedule from now on." He wasn't sure if what he had said made any sense but it felt good to have got it out.

The major's lips pressed into a thin line and his eyes narrowed.

"This sounds serious but I don't entirely understand. What do you mean when you say you've had a ridiculous day?"

Gary stopped turning the beret and marshalled his thoughts into some kind of order. "Right, well, do you know that ship the Alwin in San Carlos Waters?"

"Not really but carry on."

"The thing is, the office organised for me to go to cut hair. It's a small ship, not big enough to have a helipad, so the Bristow landed on another ship, HMS Diligence. So far so good. Except the Alwin wasn't alongside as expected and it didn't have a boat to come and get me."

"Oh."

"And I wasn't going to swim a quarter of a mile." Gary got up and started pacing the floor, unable to keep still as the frustrations of his day unfolded. "So I thought I would do a few haircuts on the Diligence." He turned round. "Only there weren't any to do."

"Oh?"

"It's an unusual ship, the Diligence, you might not have heard of it yet. It does repairs to all the other ships. It's got a helicopter pad on the top of its bridge like a great mortar board sticking out. The crew are skilled blokes and you wouldn't believe the number of trades they've got between them."

The major sucked in his cheeks.

"And one of them knows how to cut hair. Quite well, actually. They all looked smart."

"Ah."

"So for over three hours I had nothing to do there but sit in the mess-room looking out of the window at the Chinooks in Kelly's Garden, thinking what a total waste of time while just across the water on the Alwin there was a load of men wanting to have their hairs cut."

"Hmm."

"And then I realised that another ship had turned up on the other side. It was the Guardian, one of the patrol ships. I asked if I could cross over to it, I mean, I needed to do something useful with my day. But because they come alongside the Diligence so often, most of them had already had their hairs cut by this engineer bloke, too. In the end do you know how many haircuts I did?"

The Major shrugged his shoulders.

"Six. And then guess what, as if it wasn't bad enough already? There was a snowstorm. The Bristow that was supposed to arrive at one couldn't come until three. If you add it all together, my day was made up of two hours' travelling, five and a half hours' doing absolutely nothing on a repair ship and half an hour's work on a patrol ship. Eight hours to do six haircuts, none done on the Alwin and the queue at the salon just getting longer and longer."

"Hmm."

"So you see it would be so much better if you would let me organise my own itinerary and transport and communications because then I could get the details right as well as making sure there are contingency plans."

Now that he had got his speech out of the way, there didn't seem to be a reason to be standing up so he sat heavily on the chair.

It was the major's turn to get up and go for a little walk around the office.

"What does Dita say about this?"

"I think he's worried about adding to my workload. But I can manage, honestly; I'm always up to date with my paperwork and stuff and the new barber ought to make things easier."

"Right, Gary. It seems pretty simple to me. We should let you have a go."

Gary closed his eyes and tipped his head and the chair back in gratitude.

"Thank you," he said.

"Let's give it three weeks to start with. I'll check in with Dita, make sure he supports the decision."

"Thank you, Sir. You won't regret it."

"I'd better not."

The walk back to the coastel was so familiar that the darkness didn't bother him at all. With his bag slung over his shoulder and bouncing gently against his back he felt excited by the opportunity to take control of his work and optimistic for the first time in a while.

As soon as he got in, he would write to Paula and thank her for being nice to Lesley at the funeral. He had phoned Lesley and heard all about it. It sounded as though everyone was OK and Gran seemed to be coping well. Paula had been a real star, not just making space on the pew but treating Lesley like a friend, including her in everything and introducing her to people at the wake.

Lesley. She would be looking fantastic as the days at home grew warmer and sunnier, a hint of tan in her cheeks, enjoying the lighter evenings. Here, a keen wind blew from the south, a glacial breath from the Antarctic, and in places the gravel under his feet was lifted on stalks of ice from the wet path. The heavy clouds gradually disappeared to leave a sparkling starlit evening, with a narrow sliver of moon that threw a brittle light over the sea. Despite the ugliness of the military buildings he found the scene hauntingly beautiful.

*

There was something about Lesley going to Grandad's funeral and representing him that had changed his feelings, made Gary surer of her than before. In her latest letter she had enclosed a photo.

Look at me in my new glasses, she wrote. *I bet you won't fancy me anymore.* The stupid thing was that when he looked, he thought she was even more attractive than ever. There was no question about it; his feelings for her were deepening. He would never leave her again.

When he got back to the coastel he found Rob in their room.

"You look like the cat that got the cream," said his friend.

"Yeah, Major Hill has agreed that I can organise my own schedule."

"That's worrying. He should know better than to trust anyone from the north east." Rob had been giving him stick for days because the referee at the FA Cup final, Peter Willis, who was from the Durham County Football Association, had sent off a Manchester United player for a foul and there was a lot of argument about whether he was right or not.

"For God's sake, Rob, you're not still going on about that, are you?"

"Well, honestly, it was a crap decision."

“It was a good decision. You’re just sore because your team was rubbish.”

“And you only support the ref because you’re a Geordie git like him.”

Gary grabbed his pillow and started hitting Rob with it. “Wrong! How many times do I have to tell you? I’m a Mackam not a Geordie, I’m Sunderland. Learn some geography!”

“Right! You’re in trouble, Shewan!”

Rob yanked his own pillow off his bunk and piled into Gary, hitting him blithely over the head, the two of them laughing like schoolboys.

“Stop, stop! Enough!” Gary emerged hot and breathless from the fight. “I’ve got to cut hair later in the shop and I don’t want to be all sweaty.”

“Can’t the new barber do it? How’s he getting on?” asked Rob, blowing into his moustache where a piece of feather had got stuck.

“He’s totally thick and he makes a right mess of everything. I hope it’s just him getting used to things. It will be great once I can get rid of him to the outstations.”

Rob had put his pillow back in place and was looking at the photos of his wife and children on the wall by his bunk.

“You heard from Lesley this week?”

“Yeah, she’s got glasses. Looks fantastic. Here.” Gary found the photo and held it out proudly.

Rob made an appreciative sound, halfway to a whistle. “You’ve got one hot bird there, Gaz. I’m dying to meet her when we get back.”

“Hands off! You’re married!”

“I’m sure I could show her a good time.”

“She only wants me.”

“You think? Girl like that, I can’t believe it. She’ll be after a man who can really look after her.”

“Shut up. You’re as bad as Steve, sex mad the both of you.” He was always pleased at his friends’ reactions, although he pretended not to be. “She’s been fantastic, especially over Grandad. Listen, Rob,” he said more seriously, respecting the older man’s experience and sure enough of the friendship to confide in him, “Can I ask you something? When you decided Susan was the one for you, how did you know?”

“I was drunk.”

“No, be serious.”

Rob gave him a sideways look, eyebrows raised.

“Hmm. That’s a hard one to answer. I suppose I’d have to say I just knew. It felt right. You know, here.” He tapped his diaphragm with his fist.

"Yeah, like hell." said Gary, not because he didn't believe Rob, but because he wasn't sure whether the feeling he had for Lesley was that feeling or not. "Come on, how do you know?"

"Like I said, you just do. And I reckoned Susan felt the same about me."

Gary wasn't any clearer. The trouble was, not seeing Lesley for so long, he didn't have any idea how she really felt about him. He was sure she would like the new Gary, the more confident, surer Gary. Physically, she was bound to approve. He had bulked out so that his clothes were snug and when he lay down on his bunk the waist of his trousers felt tight, the belt pinched just a bit so that his belly hung over. It was amazing; he had never properly filled his clothes before nor been in such good shape, fit rather than fat.

Just before seven o'clock that evening he opened up his shop on the coastel's sea-deck for an evening shift, hit play on the tape player and sang along, making the words his own.

The cream colour on the walls still retained the freshness and heady smell of the paint brush, while the wooden worktops were clean in a way that only new surfaces could be, as yet unscathed by scratches or dents. Wayne had done a reasonable job of sweeping up yesterday's mess and had had a try at completing the books, although he couldn't add up properly.

Gary took his scissors out of his bag and sat himself down in front of the mirror, snipping to even up the ragged lines over his ears, humming along until a deep voice broke his reverie.

"Barber." He looked up from where he was to see one of the paratroopers from Coastel One standing at the door like a mountain, eyes glowering beneath heavy eyebrows.

"Yes?"

The man had a look on his face that meant trouble, a broken front tooth serving to accentuate the threatening expression.

"The other bloke did this today and it's crap." He turned around so that Gary could see the back of his head.

Gary motioned for him to sit down and looked the haircut over. The man was right, it was terrible. All Wayne had done was skim unevenly with the clippers. The top and the back were ragged. "I'm sorry you're not happy with it. I'll do it again if you want but I'll have to charge you."

"You what?" The man's voice was like the rumble of a train.

"I'm happy to recut it but you'll have to pay. It's your choice."

The Para grunted his assent. "Fucking hell."

Gary set to work with the clippers, so that the hair was even all over. It only took a few minutes.

“That looks better. Listen, it only needed a bit of tidying up. How about if I charge you just half?” He brushed the man’s collar before the giant stood up again to tower over him.

“I’ll warn my lot not to come to that useless lump of shite,” the paratrooper said, handing over the money.

“I’m sure he’ll get into the swing of things soon enough.”

“He’d bloody well better, or the only thing swinging will be him. Tell him to keep out of my way.”

There were two more complaints that evening. Although Gary’s personal reputation was sky high, if the new barber was useless it could only lead to trouble and it would be better to avoid that here on home turf. The sooner he could get rid of Wayne to the outstations, the better.

Over the next few days Gary had to repair a lot of Wayne’s handiwork but he was glad of the extra activity as he grew bored so easily. It seemed ironic that the second barber had arrived just when the demand for haircuts had dropped off a cliff. The lead-up to the opening of the new airport had created a massive peak in demand but now they would have to wait for everyone’s hair to regrow before trade would rise again to a steady level.

He started to liaise with Bristow Helicopters and the outstations to organise itineraries and hair-cutting schedules, enjoying the telephone contact with people and places he knew, but he still found that he had time on his hands. Nonetheless he decided to send Wayne on his first trips alone. It would be better to have the idiot out of the way so that Gary could have some breathing space and get into a new routine at the shop.

He had taken to bringing his writing pad with him so that he could scribble long letters home during quiet spells, of which there were plenty. Although he was no penman, he found the process a good way of expressing his thoughts and of sharing his ideas.

Dear all, it's your good-looking son again. At the minute I am absolutely bored stiff. It is 2 p.m. and since 10 a.m. I have only done two haircuts so you can imagine how bored and p____d off I am.

I have written for a reason but I hope you are not getting sick of me asking you to do this and that. But I know how much you love me and you enjoy doing things for me (haha!).

Anyway, one good thing about me not being so busy is I have had time to sit and think (yes, think!) about what I am going to do when I return. I have thought a lot, but all I can think of so far is to be a rep for a hairdressing wholesaler as I may as well use my qualifications. Is it possible for you to send me addresses of any local wholesalers? As I have plenty of time, I can write and see if they have any jobs going. Because I am definitely packing in cutting hair when I return.

I am quite looking forward to looking for a new job. I know there isn't much going at the minute but a rep is a start. It is not my idea of an ideal job but it is a start.

I was thinking of taking singing lessons and becoming a pop star, or an actor. With my looks how could I fail??!!!

Sorry, I'm in one of those moods.

Yes, I'm going to start thinking seriously about what I want to do. Even if it means learning another trade. But one thing is for certain, I am NOT joining the Army, RAF or Navy. No way!!

It's amazing the amount of people out here who are in their late twenties or early thirties and all they do is clean toilets, answer phones and have no trade and are as thick as two short planks. I have realised I do not want to be like that when I get to that age.

So as I have said I will have to have a good think about what I want to do although I have always got my hair-dressing to fall back on.

Well, I think I have gone on enough for today so I will go for now.

By the way, you might be getting my letters a while after I have written them as they only send the mail off the island twice a week.

So see ya!

Look forward to hearing from you.

Bye

Gary (CPL. DON'T FORGET!)

As Dad always says, "Won't be long" – about 83 days!!

The shortest days of the year. Outside it was mostly dark and there was often a layer of snow on the ground. The lights in the coastels remained on pretty much all the time.

"Hey, Gary." Rob stuck his head around the salon door late one afternoon to find him looking through a magazine. "Busy doing nothing again?"

"Hey, Rob. Yeah, it's gone quiet. What are you doing here at the coastel, shouldn't you be at work?"

"The bosses want everyone up at the gym for some announcement at five, remember?"

"I'm glad you've reminded me. Any idea what it's about?"

"Nah."

Gary tidied everything away and grabbed his cash box. "I need to take this to our room first."

He followed Rob up the stairs and took a detour down their corridor to hide the box away in his locker. By the time he re-emerged the stairwell was full of EFI lads, a khaki and denim snake that wove its way to the top floor and through the swing doors into the gym. Major Hill was there, standing at the far end where visiting comedians and singers performed the monthly entertainment. Gary shuffled in behind the lads from his corridor and joined Rob who was waiting cross-legged on the floor. It was like being at school again for morning assembly. As he put his hands down he could feel gritty motes of dirt that had been walked in on dozens of pairs of boots.

Hill was pacing up and down, nodding to people he knew. Gary gave him a look and received an acknowledgement. He noticed that the major had a slight twitch in his cheek, as if a tiny thread was being pulled from the inside.

He looked around to see if he could spot Steve and Shaun only to see them come in through the swing door, Steve giggling as usual and doubtless making some joke. He lifted his hand in a wave. They made their way over and sat next to Gary and Rob.

“What’s it all about, lads?” said Shaun.

“No idea,” he replied.

“Must be important. Do you reckon we’ve been invaded?” said Steve.

Dita and the other bosses were standing at the back just like the teachers used to stand, keeping an eye on everybody and making sure there was no larking around. Gary wondered if they knew what this was about. The only time they had been called to the gym before was when they had night exercise. He hoped he wouldn't be made to go through that humiliation all over again.

The Major looked at his watch and then at the bosses, who checked their own wrists and nodded. They came and sat down and a hush fell upon the room.

"Good evening, men, I expect you're wondering what this is all about," Hill started. There was a ripple through the audience and Gary couldn't help feeling it was going to be bad.

"I won't beat about the bush. This is the news. There's going to be a change to your contracts of employment. The Ministry of Defence has decided that EFI personnel, who as you know provide NAAFI facilities in war zones, should operate under the same rules as the Army, Navy and Air Force, that is to say, under military law. They have decided that everyone in the war zone should operate on an equal basis and this will simplify procedures, including disciplinary procedures. Well, I'm bound to say it does make a lot of sense but anyway, it is not up for discussion. What it means for you, or should I say all of us, is that we are formally required to enlist into the Army."

A gasp went around the room and Gary felt quite sick. A buzz of under-the-breath expletives could be heard all around him.

"Be quiet, please. Let me finish. You are required to enlist into the regular army but it is on a special "type S" engagement, the same that they use for the Territorials. Your pay and conditions as well as your working arrangements will all be identical to those under which you are operating now. Your contracts are still short-term contracts. So don't react or worry; nothing will change that will make any practical difference. The only thing required is that you swear in."

There was shuffling and grumbling. Gary shook his head. "There's no way I'm joining the Army."

"There's only one kind of swearing I'm fucking prepared to do," hissed Steve next to him.

The major continued his speech. "Frankly it's just a paper exercise, everyone, you don't literally have to go through any swearing in. The process is a formality, there's just a new contract to sign. There's a copy here for each of you to look at." He waved a document in the air. "Copies will be posted on the noticeboards as well. You're to sign up individually with your manager by Saturday."

There was a pause. Gary wondered if the major was going to invite questions but he didn't.

"That's it. Pick up a copy of the standard contract on your way out. If you have any questions, talk to your next in command, they can make any representations to me. Thank you and have a good evening."

He nodded to the bosses, who all stood up. Gary found himself getting up from the floor, on automatic pilot. When everyone was on their feet, Major Hill left the room.

The silence was short-lived but palpable.

"No way!" exclaimed Gary again. "I am never, ever going to swear in, not to the Army."

"I did my EFI training with them in Germany and it was the worst week of my life," agreed Rob. "They can't make us do this."

"It looks like they are going to," said Shaun.

"I don't trust them," said Gary. "If it makes no difference, why do we have change?"

"Let's go and find Dita. I am not happy," said Rob.

"Nor me," said Steve and Shaun in unison.

"Come on then, let's go."

The four of them joined the throng of men leaving through the swing doors and, with a copy of the new contract each in their hands, clattered down the stairs.

In between floors Gary looked at the small print and scratched his head. "God knows what this is all about."

"Where do you reckon Dita might be?" asked Steve.

"He's bound to have headed to the offices," said Gary. "I bet they've all taken cover."

They carried on down to the sea deck and through to the office corridor, where the darkened barber's shop was locked up for the night. Further along Dita stood in a doorway, chatting to colleagues inside.

"Here comes trouble," their boss said amiably as the four of them approached. "You look like you mean business. I imagine you are here to see me?"

"Right as always, Mr Wearing," said Steve. "It's funny how you always know what's going on. Must be those security devices you've planted everywhere."

"Haha," said Dita, and turning to the men in the office, "Right, guys, looks like I'd better sort this lot out. I'll be back in a minute."

He swung out of the doorway and pointed down the corridor to where another door was open and lights on. "Go down to that spare office at the end."

Gary followed the others, hard on the heels of Steve, who was humming a theme from a spy movie. He turned in to the office, which was just the same as every other office on the coastel, cream-painted, square, with two army surplus issue desks, a couple of stacking chairs and grey filing cabinets.

"Right. What's up?" asked Dita.

"We don't want to join the Army," said Rob, taking the lead. "It's not right, Dita. We should have some say in it, don't you think?"

Dita looked them in the eye, from one to the next, pale eyes watery. He sniffed with a twitch of his nose.

"Sorry, lads. The orders have come from the Ministry of Defence; it's not a consultation. You're in or you're out."

"What would happen if I chose out?" asked Gary.

"You'd be on the next plane home, Sunny Jim. Finished. No bonus. Tail between your legs. Listen, I know it's being imposed on you, but if you want to stay on you don't have a choice. It's that simple."

"It's bloody unfair," grumbled Steve.

There was a bit of Gary that would quite like to be on the next plane home. "It's tempting," he muttered but there was no way he was about to give up on the job and the money and the experience and the adventure, not least because Grandad would never have thrown in the towel.

"Listen, lads," said Dita, "Sleep on it overnight then get your arses over to my office at FILOG tomorrow and sign on the dotted line, OK? As Major Hill said, it's not actually going to make any difference. And don't forget, I've got to do the same so you're in good company."

Gary stood looking at the others for a moment, then at Dita. "Enough said. But you should know it's under protest."

Dita shrugged his shoulders.

“Is this office bugged then, Dita?” said Steve. “You know, you could be Q in the James Bond films. With all that security stuff.”

“Haha,” said Dita. “Right you lot, get out of my hair. See you tomorrow.”

Gary trooped out behind the others, distrusting what was happening and deeply uneasy that the Army would take advantage of them. At the end of the corridor they came to the arrival hall with the kiosk and the pigeonholes.

“Shall we go and get a pint, lads?” Rob had turned around to face them all. The friends never went to the pub of an evening, it was too far to go to Stanley in the dark and too frightening to go to the bar on the next coastel. They were all saving money anyway. “We could take our darts over to Coastel One.”

“But what about the Paras?” said Shaun. “I thought you were all scared of them, especially Gary.”

“Me?” Gary replied, managing not to rise to the jibe. “I reckon they’re mostly all right; just keep a low profile. I must have cut all of their hair by now and they’re OK as long as you don’t answer back.”

“I’m up for it,” chimed Steve.

“Right,” said Rob, “Let’s go. I reckon we should celebrate our last night as civilians.”

BET

For six years Bet had spent every waking moment thinking about Tom's needs. She had washed and shaved him, dressed him, fed him, told him the news, pushed him about, listened to him, interpreted for him, cried with frustration with him, kept things going, smiled, did everything to make his life worthwhile. In short, she always saw the man as he was before he had turned into a helpless creature in a wheelchair. Even after his second stroke, when he was in hospital and the nursing staff took on most of the load, every moment of her days revolved around Tom; she stuck close by his side and endured the journey hand in hand with the love of her life.

And now what? No more trips on the bus to Sunderland, no more dominoes, no more washing and ironing his pyjamas. In the mornings she would come down to the kitchen in her dressing gown and slippers and be surprised by how large the room was without his bed and the hoist.

Days after the funeral, Elizabeth had come over to help sort out his things, bagging everything up into bin liners. The two of them set about the job with a fierce practicality.

"Right, Mum, how do you want to do this? Some things could go to Oxfam."

They both knew it would be better done quickly but Bet found herself holding each item to her face, trying to inhale the essence of him. There was the old-feet smell of his tan leather lace-ups, the ones that, in those days when he could still walk, he would polish to a gleam before going out. She breathed in the worsted tweed of his best suit and the soft cotton freshness of his favourite shirts.

When they had bagged everything up, they lugged half the precious cargo down the street to the charity shop and left the remaining bags outside the back door for the dustmen. All that was left were a few personal items, the framed photo of Gary, a watch and fifty years of memories.

“It’s not much to show for a life, is it?” she said as they sat down over a cup of tea in the front room, looking at the pathetic relics.

“No, well, he never was one for material things. He made us all happy and that’s what counts.” Elizabeth sounded a little short, which was out of character. Bet knew she was struggling with her own grief.

“Aye, he was a good man. Even the children in the street loved him, the way he sat outside waving to them on their way to school.”

“There, you see.”

“Mind, but he had a temper on him.”

A hint of a smile crinkled around Elizabeth's eyes. "Yes, he had a temper all right."

"Terrifying he was, sometimes. He'd rant and rave."

"He certainly would. He was no saint." Elizabeth looked at her watch. "Well, Mam, I'd better get going. I've got loads to sort out at home."

"All right, love," she stood up to collect the cups onto the tray and felt a sharp twinge in her arm.

"Something wrong, Mam? You're wincing."

Bet put the tray down and rubbed the joint where it hurt. "It's my shoulder. I fell on it a few days ago, not a proper fall but I slipped and hit it against the wall, and I think I have pulled it now, lifting those bags. I was moving the furniture around earlier this week which probably wasn't such a good idea."

"Mam, you're to look after yourself, you hear me? If you need things moved, you're to let me and Mattie know. We'll come and do it for you, or we'll get Glenn to help." Elizabeth eyed her with concern. "You should get it seen to. Would you like me to make a doctor's appointment for you?"

Elizabeth always looked after everyone else, especially the family. She never had time for herself but always made time for others. She was one of life's true givers.

Bet laughed. "I think I can manage to make a phone call, love. Don't worry, I'll do it as soon as you're gone. I promise. Do you know, I've started to notice how threadbare this carpet is with your Dad's stuff out of the way." There were bald patches where his wheelchair used to stand.

Elizabeth scuffed the patches with her shoe. "You're right. Mattie wants to take us all to see his new shop on Sunday. Perhaps you should let him help you choose a new carpet."

Bet thought about it. Her daughter was right, it would be nice to freshen the place up, give it a bit of a lift. Maybe it would make it easier to start facing her new life without Tom. "That's a good idea, love. I'll catch the bus to yours, save Mattie driving over."

"Don't be silly."

"I'm not being silly. I'm perfectly capable."

"I know you're capable. We'd like to come and get you." Elizabeth picked up her handbag and car keys off the table. "I worry about you, Mam. Have you thought about joining the Women's Institute? It would do you good to get out and about a bit."

"I know, love. All in good time." It was so difficult. She wasn't ready for life without Tom even though she had been expecting it these last years. It was disorientating to have choices about what to do and when. Elizabeth was right, she should go to the WI with one of her neighbours but perhaps not quite yet. "Have you heard from our Gary?"

Elizabeth stopped mid-step, fingers on the door handle. “Yes, a gap and then four letters at once. He says he’s well and truly a soldier now, they made him sign up.”

Bet thought her daughter looked tired, quite pale. If only they could sell that blessed shop, it would make such a difference. “Do you think he’s enjoying himself? He sent me a lovely letter after your Dad died. I hope it didn’t spoil things for him, I know he would have been very upset.”

Elizabeth smiled. “Oh, you know Gary. He takes things hard but then he finds a way of bouncing back. I’m sure he’ll be fine. He’s been thinking about his future. Imagine - our Gary thinking! God only knows what ideas he’ll come up with and then in the end it will be like flipping a coin.”

Bet pictured her grandson in his uniform, his bright smile and those flashing eyes. “He’s a good lad. I can’t wait to see him again.”

“Not long to go now, Mam, three months.” Elizabeth rattled the car keys. “I need to be off. Sure you’ll be all right?”

It was amusing to hear her daughter fuss – of course she was all right. She had managed all these years, hadn’t she? “Don’t worry about me, pet. Go along with you now. See you at the weekend.”

“All right.” Elizabeth gave her a warm kiss on the cheek. “I’ll tell Mattie about your new carpet.”

“Bye, love. Thank you.”

The door clicked to and she turned back to face the room. The house had very little of Tom left in it. She took his few things upstairs and put them on her dressing table, alongside her hairbrush and face cream. There was nothing wrong with wanting to keep his memory alive and this way she would look at them every morning and every evening. Gary's latest letter was sitting refolded into its airmail envelope on her bedside table, next to the telephone. She picked up the receiver and dialled.

"Hello? Could I make an appointment to see Dr Roberts, please?" Shooting pains ran up into her neck from her shoulder. She didn't think she would be writing any letters this week. "Yes, it's Mrs Davison."

Gary

"Steve, Rob, stand over there so I can get you in the shot." He pressed the record button and the video camera hissed into life, the viewfinder pressed into his eyebrow.

"These are two of the lads, Rob and Steve, in front of our coastel, Coastel Two," he narrated. Rob waved and Steve grinned, making a V-sign with two fingers above Rob's head.

"Behind them is Coastel One and the other way," he panned the camera towards Stanley, "is Coastel Three and Stanley Harbour, which is the centre of our universe here in the Falklands."

It might be midwinter's day but nature had delivered a surprisingly crisp, bright morning, the air so clear that he felt he could reach out and touch the far hills, their outlines as sharp as a paper cutting against the pale blue of the sky. What a bonus on his full weekend off.

"OK, lads, that's a good start. Let's head for Gypsy Cove."

He had rented the video camera from the EFI store and Dita had been true to his word about enabling him to take the driving test and borrow a Land Rover. "Here you are, Gary," he had said on Friday evening at the coastel, handing over a key. “It’s got a full tank of petrol – fill it up again before you leave it back with me on Sunday.”

“Thanks, Dita, you are a superstar.”

The lads had spent time on Friday evening looking at the map and planning their day out. Gary felt like a film director, with imaginary storyboards ready in his head. Rob and Steve would be his co-stars.

They set off up the road to Stanley Airport, quiet now that Mount Pleasant had opened. Many of the temporary buildings were part dismantled. Until the middle of May the air had shuddered with the coming and going of Phantoms and Hercules, but since then only the regular whirr of Bristow helicopters could be heard, indicating the local movement of military personnel and supplies. Every contractor would move to the Mount Pleasant complex eventually, along with the rest of the garrison. When that happened the coastels would be empty and could be redeployed somewhere else in the world. All that would be left at Stanley Airport with its short runway would be the two FIGAS Islander aircraft and the privately-owned planes.

At the wheel of the Land Rover, Gary bypassed the airport around its western perimeter and took a short detour along the edge of a low hill down to a cove where a magnificent wreck stood upright with her keel firmly anchored in the sand, three masts pointing to the sky. He pulled on the handbrake.

“Come on, lads. Someone told me this ship was built in Sunderland.”

He scrambled out of the Land Rover and they slammed the doors behind them, a sharp wind ruffling their hair. The water all the length of Stanley Harbour sparkled turquoise in the winter sunshine, with Tumbledown, the Two Sisters and Mount Harriet a dull brown in the distance. At low tide it might be possible to climb aboard the abandoned schooner, but not today.

“It’s amazing, it looks like it’s just waiting to be loaded,” said Rob.

“Here, let’s have a go with that thing,” said Steve, making a grab for the video camera.

“OK,” said Gary, handing it over, “You can film me talking about the view. Just keep the camera still and I’ll point out all the places.”

He took a few paces forward and half turned towards the camera.

“Recording? OK. Hi, folks, here I am in Whalebone Cove in front of a beautiful ship called the Lady Liz, that was built in the yards of Sunderland. Sadly I don’t think she’s ever going to make it back there again. Behind it you get a great view of Stanley Harbour and Port Stanley, the capital of the Falkland Islands. It’s called the capital but it’s more like a village. That huge construction out in the water is FIPASS, the floating jetty where our boat came in when we arrived here. Up behind are the hills, the highest one is Mount Kent with a radar station on the top, where the wind blows like you could never imagine."

Steve stopped filming. Gary walked over and looked over Steve's shoulder. "Here, press rewind then replay so I can have a look." He squinted into the stamp-sized screen where he could see himself talking to camera.

"Hey, not bad! I was going to be the cameraman but maybe I should be the presenter. I look loads better than you two!"

Steve pressed the stop button and pushed him, knocking him off balance so that he stumbled several paces backwards. Gary made to retaliate with a rugby tackle.

"Watch out for the camera!" shouted Steve, dodging the attack.

"Cheat!" laughed Gary. "Come on, let's find ourselves some penguins."

They piled into the Land Rover and set off again to rejoin the track heading north-eastwards. On the high ground above Gypsy Cove they left the vehicle and wound their way on foot down the narrow path to the cove through low scrub then mounds of a tall grass that grew in great clumps, like pillars.

"Hey, guys, keep quiet on the way down. I want to get some film of the penguins so please don't scare them off."

Rob and Steve crept obediently behind him while he picked his way with care through the grass, making sure not to tread on any of the holes in the ground which were penguin burrows, although at this time of year they would not be occupied, and stopping at the fencing which marked out the area containing mines.

"Sssh! There they are," he whispered, motioning the lads to keep down behind him. They crept forward together, breathing heavily with concentration. Down at the far end of the beach, a small cluster of penguins was swimming in the water. One by one the birds popped up onto the sand, where they gathered in a small huddle a bit like busy women out shopping. As they moved, they held their little flippers out for balance. Gary held the camera up to his eye and pressed record.

"Damn," he said. "There's no zoom on this."

"Can't we get any closer?" said Steve.

"You know the rules. Anyway, there's not much point, we'd just scare them and they'd all head off into the water," whispered Rob.

"Oh well, it's better than nothing. At least I know the dots are penguins."

"Isn't that an albatross?" Rob was pointing into the sky, where an enormous bird skimmed through the air on motionless wings.

"Fantastic!" said Gary, the camera fixed to his eye, following the bird against the blue.

“Wow, that’s huge,” said Steve.

They made their way back up the bank to the Land Rover. Gary pressed the replay button and looked at his work so far.

“None of that has come out, everything’s too far away. The albatross looks like a sparrow.”

“Biggest sparrow I ever saw,” said Rob.

“I’ll film over those bits, there’s no point keeping them. Right, where’s next? Surf Bay and then into town?”

Gary revved the engine and they set off.

“Hey, Gaz, if this movie of yours is any good I’ll have to borrow it off you to show my family,” said Rob.

“Yeah, no worries.”

“I’ll come and fetch it off you. Then I can meet Lesley.”

“Good idea. We’ll all have to meet up when we get back.”

“Definitely.”

“Listen,” Steve piped up, “Why don’t we go out into the camp to see if we can find the only tree on the island?” Steve was always full of ideas.

“Do you know where it is?”

“Not a clue.”

“Haha! Let’s go and find it then!”

*

Gary's muscles were tiring but, with his back steady all along its length against the bench and his eyes staring firmly at the high ceiling of the gym, he decided to try one more set of lifts. In the background, music provided a rhythm that helped to focus his mind on what he was doing. He pushed the weights up, straining his weary arms. By the third lift, his shoulders and biceps were starting to wobble. By the fourth, he wondered if ten was an over-optimistic target. By the fifth he knew it was and at the sixth his strength gave way. He dropped the weights back onto their stand and eased himself up, rubbing the tops of his arms and the muscles of his chest.

"You're not doing badly there, Gary," said the army gym instructor in his strong Glaswegian accent. "Quite an improvement compared with how you were when you first arrived." Scotty gleamed with good health, muscles visible through the thin fabric of his tee-shirt and thighs straining at the brushed cotton of his tracksuit bottoms. He was short but stocky, with a perfect, inverted-triangle body shape.

"Not sure if I should take that as a compliment," Gary puffed. "Trouble is I've put on weight with all this army food and I need to shift it."

"Stop lifting such heavy weights and use up some calories instead. Get your running shoes on and go outside. Ever done any running?"

"Quite a bit."

"So get back out again. Half an hour at a time, minimum. Work up a sweat. And cut down on your food."

Gary rubbed his head and laughed at the irony.

"I can't believe I'm having this conversation. I've looked like a piece of string ever since I was a kid, though I always ate well. In fact I could never get enough food in me. I've always been hungry, even with Mum's cooking and everything. Dad used to say I had hollow legs."

"Well, it looks like they've filled up now."

Scotty moved on to talk to the guy at the next station. Gary grabbed his towel and headed downstairs to the shower room. In through the sprung-loaded door, the atmosphere was hot and steamy, with puddles all over the floor. In the far corner, Rob stood under a stream of hot water, head back, letting it sluice over his face. Gary turned to strip off and a bar of soap hit him squarely on the backside.

"Hey!" He swivelled round to face Rob, who somehow was in exactly same position as before, eyes closed, water cascading over his shoulders, a picture of innocence, except that his stomach was twitching with laughter. Gary grabbed the bar of soap from the floor and threw it squarely to hit him hard in the midriff.

Rob exploded, letting out his tightly held breath and bending to rub the spot the soap had hit.

"Oh, hi, Gary, didn't see you there," he spluttered, "What you been up to this evening?"

Gary chose a shower a safe distance away and turned the water on full. The jets hit the back of his neck and streamed down his body. "God, that feels great," he said. "I've been in the gym, trying to lose a bit of weight."

He pinched the skin of his belly between thumb and forefinger, a good inch separating the two. "Look at this! It's fat! I don't want to get a gut. Anyway, what've you been doing?"

"I challenged one of the lads to a game of squash. Won fair and square. You should run around more if you want to lose weight, it's better than darts and weights." Rob turned off the water and went to pull his towel off its hook. He rubbed his hair until it stood on end, quickly dried off his body then wrapped the towel around his waist.

"Yeah, that's what Scotty said. You're probably right." Gary lathered soap all over his body, inhaling its clean smell. "Truth is, I'm quite glad to have filled out. I must weigh more than my brother Glenn now. That'll make him worried!"

"Yeah, well, never underestimate your big brother, that's my advice," said Rob, grabbing Gary's clothes off the bench and towel off its hook, and making a quick exit.

"Hey!" Gary shouted after his departed friend, "Come back here! Rob!"

There was little point in rushing his shower. He relaxed in the water and luxuriated in the warmth, letting it wash away his day.

After ten minutes he turned off the taps and squeezed as much water as he could off his skin with the palms of his hands. The door opened and Shaun came in, towel tight around his waist.

"Hey, Shaun, do us a favour, would you? Go and get my towel. Rob's nicked it."

"Sorry, mate. You know the game. You're on your own."

"Bastard!"

"Yeah. An' I'm not letting go of my towel till you're out of this place. So you might as well get going."

"You're as bad as him!"

Gary put his hand on the handle, took a deep breath, pulled the door open and hot-footed it down the corridor.

"Hey! Gary!" Laughter followed him as he passed each bedroom door, where the men whiled away their evening.

"Fuck off!" he responded, making it to his own door without being flicked, to crash through. "Bastard!" he said by way of greeting to Rob, who was standing in the middle of the room dangling the towel in one hand and grinning widely.

He grabbed the towel and wrapped it around his damp body, cross for leaving himself open to the trick.

"I'll get you back."

"I'm sure you will," said Rob, laughing and retreating from the game. "Anyway, how's Wayne getting on? Any better?"

Gary massaged his scalp, feeling a sensation close to despair. "Oh God, you have no idea. I've spent all day listening to people whingeing on about how dreadful he is. I mean, as if I didn't know already. What on earth can I do about him?"

"Can't you give him a kick up the arse?"

"Honestly, it wouldn't make any difference. He's so thick he doesn't know how to do anything right. I'll just have to keep sending him off to the outstations. At least that way I won't have to deal with complaints here."

"It's your own bloody fault, mate. You've set a standard he can't match."

"Yeah, more fool me." Gary pulled on his jeans and sweater.

"Heard from Lesley this week?" asked Rob.

"Course. Two letters. Why?"

"Just checking. Hoped she might have forgotten about you by now so that I could look her up when I get home."

"No chance."

"So you're still keen on her then?"

"Course. Stupid question."

Rob was rummaging in his locker but Gary could tell that he was only pretending to be doing something while asking personal questions.

Gary picked up his darts from his locker. “Right, how about a game of darts? Payback for being a bastard.”

He looked Rob in the eye and got a steady stare back.

“Loser buys a pint in Coastel One,” threatened Rob.

“You’ll need your money, then.”

Elizabeth

Her mother settled onto the sofa and raised the mug to her lips one-handed, sipping at the hot tea, her other arm pinned to her chest in a sling. "I'm delighted about my new carpet, Mattie, thanks for taking me round the shop and helping me choose."

"That's all right, Bet," he replied, sitting himself down in the armchair. "I'll get one of the fitters to give you a call this week and they can measure up."

"And it was a lovely lunch. Thank you both."

Elizabeth was concerned that her mother wanted to travel from Whitburn on the bus with her arm so bad but Mam had insisted and had bought a return ticket as she was not going to let Mattie drive her back either.

"What do you think I am, some old cripple?" she had asked.

That was typical of her mother, not wanting to be a bother and not letting anyone help.

"You've got enough on your plate without fussing over me as well."

In fact her mother had arrived rather pleased with herself, saying she had enjoyed the journey. There she sat in her Sunday best, looking better than she had done for ages, pinker in the face, more rested, even though that arm was giving her pain.

"Are those some new fish you've got in the tank there?" Bet asked, pointing with her mug towards the two white fish in the smaller tank.

"Yes, they're kissing fish."

"And they really do kiss," said Paula. "Look." Sure enough, the two fish swam towards each other with protruding lips and locked together mouth-to-mouth to float gently up and down in the water, their tiny fins like the wings of hummingbirds, fluttering so fast that you could only just see them.

"We got them from the garden centre, didn't we, Mattie? They must be about the fourth lot of fish we've bought, what with the ones that died and the others that ate each other."

Mattie laughed. "I never knew why the children bought me those Siamese fighting fish in the first place. They were nothing but trouble. Once they'd finally finished each other off, we thought we'd try something a bit friendlier. Let's hope these ones last longer."

"Right, folks," said Paula, heading for the door, "I'm going to my room to do my last bit of revising."

"How many more exams then, Paula?" asked her Gran.

Paula stuck her bottom lip out and sighed. "Just two, then I'm all finished. Thank goodness."

"How do you think you've done, love?"

"Terrible. But it doesn't matter. I've got my college place already."

"She did really well in her interview," Elizabeth explained. Paula had been offered a place unconditionally and Elizabeth couldn't imagine what her daughter might have said to impress them so. Not that Paula didn't deserve a place, it was just that it was unheard of to get through on an interview alone. "And she's going to help out in Upstairs Downstairs until college starts, aren't you love?"

"Or until you sell it, Mam." Paula turned to leave the room and planted a kiss on her Gran's cheek on the way. "Take care, Gran. See you next week."

"Ta-ta, love," said Bet, with a beaming smile. "Good luck with those exams, now."

Paula groaned and pulled a face then disappeared upstairs.

"Right, Mam, ready for a top up?" Elizabeth stood to take the mug from her mother, who held it out gladly. Beyond the front window, a red car pulled onto the drive.

"Mattie, is that Lesley? Go and open the front door, would you, while I pour Mam another cup of tea." She took her mother's mug out into the kitchen and opened the fridge door for the milk. Schweppes looked up from her basket and gave a little grunt at the sound of the front door.

"You're not on very good form, are you? Anyway, it's only Lesley so you may as well stay put." Schweppes rolled her dark eyes so that the tan eyebrows twitched up and down, then opened her mouth in a big yawn and settled back into her basket. In Elizabeth's hand the quilted tea cosy was warm to the touch and smooth from use, old-fashioned but practical; she had had it for years and the tea was still steaming hot.

Once the tea was poured, Elizabeth went to the hallway where Mattie and Lesley were chatting, Mattie clasping an envelope in his hand, Lesley standing in the open doorway, wearing a red tee-shirt and a pair of long, white shorts. She had good legs on her.

"Hello, Lesley, love. Mattie, show Lesley in, don't keep her standing around on the doorstep."

Mattie looked up at Lesley, "Oh, sorry, pet. Thanks for bringing this. Come on in."

Lesley had on a new pair of glasses, they suited her well. She was perfectly made up, as always, but the impression was less flashy, an improvement. She sat down on the sofa next to Gran and accepted a cup of tea while Mattie ran his thumb under the flap of the envelope and pulled a card out.

"Ah, that's grand," he said, beaming, waving around the card with Happy Father's Day written on the front, "Thanks, love."

"It's from Gary," she said by way of explanation to Elizabeth and her mother, "He sent it last week and asked me to bring it round today." Mattie got up and stood it on the mantelpiece next to the ones from Glenn and Paula.

"Aye, he's a good lad," said Gran.

"Right, while I'm up," said Mattie, "I think I'd better make the most of this fine day to do some work in the garden. I've got paving slabs to lay."

He disappeared upstairs to change out of his good trousers and shirt. It was heartening to see how much happier he was since the new job had started, he'd got all his old energy back.

"Mattie's helped me choose a new carpet," said Bet, turning to Lesley with a look of satisfaction.

"That sounds nice," said Lesley, sipping her tea, which steamed onto the glasses perched on the bridge of her perfect nose.

Elizabeth was glad to let the two of them chat while she looked at the cards on the mantelpiece. It was strange to have this Father's Day without her own father. She was thinking about her Dad more, not less, as the days went by, trying consciously to push aside the images of those ghastly final weeks and to remember him in youthful times, when he had been an anchor in her life. She hoped that Gary was getting over the loss a little bit, better than she was.

Mattie popped his head around the door on his way outside. "I'll be in the garden if anyone wants to come and work off their lunch," he said. "Could always do with a hand."

"Fat lot of use I'd be," said Bet, waving her bad arm and laughing until the movement made her wince. "I'll offer my services in a few weeks' time. Hopefully after you've finished!"

Elizabeth sat herself down in the armchair and drank her tea, feeling the comfortable shape of Mattie in the seat.

"Have you had a nice weekend, Mrs Shewan... Elizabeth?" asked Lesley, polite as ever.

"Oh, not bad," she said, thinking back to the week and how awful it had been. Even selling her car had not made an overall difference to their finances. The additional cash had covered the outstanding bills but costs never stopped piling up. "Mattie loaned us his car so that Paula and I could go to Newcastle yesterday – I wanted a pair of shorts for my holidays and she wanted a couple of tops. Mattie's taking me to Greece in September to celebrate his new job. I know it's ages off yet but we're both really looking forward to the break."

"That sounds nice. Any news on Upstairs Downstairs?"

"Not yet. You know, it's been well over three months since we first advertised and feels like it has been hanging around our necks forever. We get people looking and a few made an offer but so far the deals have fallen through. It's so frustrating. Pat has kept the place going but even she is leaving now. I'm not surprised but it's a disaster."

"Oh dear."

"Yes, the new girl at my own salon up here, Iris, you know, the Irish one, Julie's replacement, she's been coming up with ideas for how to get rid of it. She even offered to get me a bomb made up!"

Her mother laughed, "Oh dear, I hope she isn't in the IRA."

"Anyway," Elizabeth carried on, "We'll just have to keep going somehow. It's great that Paula's going to help out. It would be nice to think we could sell it before we go on holiday, then I could relax about our spending money."

"I'm sure it will sell," said Lesley. "And if it doesn't, you can hand it back to Gary when he gets back." The girl looked sideways from behind her glasses and winked.

Elizabeth couldn't imagine having to tell Gary that he was needed to go back to the shop, they all knew that was the last thing he wanted.

"Ha! I just hope we've got rid of it before then. I've been making enquiries for him about becoming a rep with one of our suppliers. Though why he should ever be interested in doing that I can't imagine."

"Are you coming to the duck race next Sunday, Lesley?" asked Bet, pulling herself forward to deposit her empty mug on the table by the arm of the sofa.

Lesley's face remained a blank although Elizabeth knew she had invited her weeks ago.

"Yes, Lesley's coming with us. You remember, love? You bought some ducks."

"Oh, yes" said Lesley. "Sorry, I had forgotten."

"You can still come, can't you? I've booked lunch for all of us at the Coal Hole first. And afterwards everyone is coming back here for tea. It will be quite a party."

Gran couldn't clap her hands, but she patted her knee with her free palm.

"How will it work?" asked Lesley. "The duck race, I mean."

"Haven't you ever been to one?" asked Elizabeth's mother, as if there was a duck race every other day in Durham. "They use those toy ducks like the ones you get for the bath. The first one to pass the line is the winner."

"It must look weird," said Lesley, her forehead wrinkled.

"It should be good fun," said Elizabeth. "Mattie's quite anxious about it, but if they can sell a few more ducks by the end of the week it will be the biggest fundraiser of his year. Gary's bought two so we'll need to cheer those ones on as well."

"What happens if Gary wins the prize?" said Lesley.

"Well, perhaps you could collect it for him," she replied.

They chatted on until Elizabeth's mother looked at her watch and said it was time she went to catch the bus home, and Lesley offered to drop her off at the stop even though it was only just around the corner. Mattie was still out the back working up a sweat in the late afternoon sunshine. Elizabeth planted kisses on their cheeks, noticing the difference between her mother's lined skin and Lesley's smooth perfection. When she came back in from waving them off, pulling the front door shut behind her, Paula appeared at the top of the stairs.

"Has she gone?" Paula said.

"Gran?"

"No, Lesley."

"Yes, love. Why?" It wasn't like Paula not to be friendly. Of all the family, she was the one who always made the most effort with Lesley, did her very best to make her feel welcome and defended her especially when Glenn and Julie made derisory comments. She turned towards the kitchen and Paula followed down the stairs and through the hall. Poor, listless Schweppes wagged her tail hopefully in her basket, waiting for her tea and walk. "Right, you. Let's sort out your food and take you for a walk."

Paula loitered around the doorway, looking sheepish.

"Is Schweppes OK?"

"I think so, love. She's on heat so I expect she's feeling a little strange."

"Oh." Paula went over and fondled the animal, cupping the soft face between her hands and planting a kiss on the top of the wet nose. "Do you think Lesley really loves Gary?"

She wondered why Paula had thought to ask such a question out of nowhere in particular.

"Well," she chose her words carefully, "She certainly seems to be missing him. Why do you ask?"

Paula pulled one of the chairs out from the table and sat down with one foot underneath her bottom, playing with pretend crumbs on the table.

"It's just I saw her out in Durham with some boys in the week. I can't help wondering about her sometimes." Paula suddenly was avoiding her mother's eyes; in fact she looked troubled.

"Well, love; she still comes to see us. She sounds pleased whenever our Gary has rung and she's obviously missing him as badly as ever. Why do you wonder about her?" She was intrigued now.

"Oh, it's nothing, I'm just being stupid," said her daughter, pushing the tip of a finger around as if to trace the woodgrain, not saying whatever it was she might have seen.

Elizabeth scooped Schweppes's food out of the tin into an enamelled dish and set it in front of the wagging animal. Schweppes started to eat in great gulps, hardly pausing to chew, just grabbing at the food with her teeth and tongue and inhaling it down.

"Hey, Mam?"

"Yes?"

"I'll give you a hand with the wedding you're doing on Saturday if you like."

"Oh, Paula, thanks love. That would be marvellous. There are four bridesmaids. And they're all going to have fresh flowers in their hair."

"I am dying to be a bridesmaid. Do you think it will ever happen to me?" Paula asked, scooping her hair back from her face and holding it up on the top of her head, flouncing up from her chair in a pose, looking over her shoulder.

"I'm sure it will, love. You've got two older brothers."

"Yeah, but I might get married before Glenn or Gary."

"Well, that's up to you. Right. I'm going to take the dog out for a walk. Are you going to do more revising or do you fancy coming with me?"

Paula turned the other way, hair still up, other hand on hip, posing like a model. "I'll come with you. I need to walk off my lunch, I'm still feeling full and I'm determined to lose a few pounds before the holidays."

GARY

Gary sat on his bunk and tore open the purple envelope from Paula, who was a loyal if infrequent correspondent, adding a page of gossip every few weeks with letters from their Mam or Dad. This was the first time she had posted her letter in its own envelope.

Dear Gary,

Hope you're all right, not working too hard. I'm sitting in your shop doing nothing so I decided to write you a letter. Did you know Pat's leaving; she's setting up on her own. So there's only Tina, Melanie and Sue. Tina permed Sue's hair – it's really tight.

Anyway, me and Jacqui went to see Gran and Grandad Shewan yesterday and they said they'd wrote you a letter. We asked them to come to the duck race on Sunday but they said it was too much hassle. Lesley's coming, by the way. She's coming out for dinner to the Coal Hole with us as well. Are you two going to get married when you get back or are you going to call it all off? I hope you get married so I can be a bridesmaid. I'm not courting at the moment, dead boring, eh?

I've finished all my exams: I think I've failed them all but it's too late to revise for them now. Oh, I got a letter off my Spaniard. He says he still loves me.

I'm going to Blackpool on 10th August. I've saved up no money at all yet. You should send me some to go on holiday with, that's what big brothers are for (JOKE).

Glenn's bought himself a motorbike; it's the same age as me. I think it's a 250 but I'm not so sure. Have you got plenty of music to listen to, cos if you haven't I'll send you some tapes. Just tell me what you want.

I've lost four pounds (in weight) and I'm going to continue my super diet and be eight stone, so you'll have a lovely bridesmaid (hint, hint).

Well, I'd better go.

Lots of love,

Paula xxxx

Her writing was neat but spidery so that he had to concentrate hard. Paula made him smile, she wrote just as she talked and he could hear her voice, see her facial expressions.

"What are you grinning at, Gaz?" said Steve from the other side of the room, lying on top of his bunk.

"Oh, nothing. Just my kid sister."

Steve sucked in air between his teeth. "What's she been up to?"

"Well, she says she's not seeing anyone at the moment."

Steve sat up. "I'd better write to her then. See if I can get her interested in me."

"Try if you like. I've sent her a couple of photos. Maybe she'll fancy you back. But you'd better move fast, she's going on holiday soon and she's bound to meet someone."

"I'll write and invite her on my holiday in September. I'm going to book a trip to Greece. You and Lesley and Paula should come."

"I'll think about it. But Paula definitely won't have enough money. She's asked me to send her some for her weekend in Blackpool. The cheek!" His eyes travelled over the page, re-reading.

Are you two going to get married when you get back or are you going to call it all off?

"I could send her some of my tips but I've only got Falkland's pounds so that's no good," he said, distracted.

"You wouldn't send cash, would you?" said Steve, reading his own letters.

"I don't see what I can do, she hasn't got a bank account so there wouldn't be much point sending her a cheque."

I hope you get married… It was ridiculous, or was it? He missed Lesley terribly.

What was he meant to be thinking about? Oh, yes, holiday money for Paula.

“Wait a bit. I could send a cheque to Mam and she could cash it. That would work.”

“Nice of you, big brother. You can make a cheque out to me, too, if you’re that flush.”

Steve swung his legs over the side of his bunk and dropped to the floor, landing with a heavy thud. “It’s Saturday night and I need a drink. How’s about we find Rob and some of the others, then go next door for a few pints? The Paras are out on exercise so we won’t have any trouble. You can tell me all about Paula and how I can win her over.”

“All right, but just the one for me. I’ve got work first thing in the morning and I want to finish the video later on.”

They still weren’t sure about some of the troops in Coastel One but as long as they went in a group Gary felt confident enough and they had taken to going for a pint when they knew the most terrifying of the Army types would be out of the way. Tonight it was smoky and crowded, full of military and EFI lads and even a few EFI women. In the corner two fruit machines blared out repetitive, teasing riffs and their lights flashed up, down and in circles as if to say *come and play, come and play*, greedy for anybody’s money. There was a group of men playing bar billiards and another group using the dartboards.

“Gary and I will get the drinks in,” said Rob, his voice raised above the hubbub. “Pints all round? You guys, go and grab some space somewhere.”

They had pooled their money into a kitty rather than stand each other rounds, it worked out fairer and easier especially when, as this evening, there was a number of them. Rob took charge as usual; he was the oldest, but Gary always found himself looking after the money. The two of them elbowed their way towards the bar, Gary leading with one hand extended, as if to part the waves of bodies. Quite a few of the men said hello as he pushed through, no doubt recognising him. Others ignored him or scowled, resisting his advance into their space.

“Come on, gents,” he said more than once, “Let us through, will you?” Once he felt a foot trip him up but he took it in good humour and refused to feel threatened, although the air was heavy with testosterone.

“Phew,” Rob said when they got to the bar, “Let’s send someone else next time.”

They leaned their forearms against the sticky counter, where glasses were stacked and pools of beer evaporated in a whiff of stale yeast. “Hey, lads, all right?” Gary said to the two EFI colleagues who were working hard to keep the pints moving. “Six pints for us.”

When they headed back with three pints each, he let Rob go first; this time the tide was less resistant, happier to let them out and create more space. They found the others sitting on low stools around a stained table, Shaun dealing out the cards into six hands.

"You in?" he asked.

"Course," said Gary, setting the glasses down then wedging himself onto a seat between Shaun and Steve.

"Cheers."

He raised the glass to his lips and took a long draught, savouring the bitter taste despite the taint of cigarette smoke in his nostrils. Coastel One was better than nothing especially on a night like this when the most frightening of the muscle-bound servicemen were out on exercise.

The beer quickly went to his head and he found it hard to concentrate on the card game but it didn't seem to matter, the others were hopeless.

"Bloody hell," said Steve, getting up. "Gaz, you win yet again. Right, who's for another drink?"

"Not me, I'll quit while I'm ahead," said Gary, all of a sudden weary of beer and male company. He would do anything for the smell and laughter of girls, the lightness and the ease and the flirting. He missed Lesley more than ever. "I'll see you guys later."

He left the noise and smoky atmosphere of Coastel One, walking out along the causeway to the shore in fine sleet that chilled his face. Oily water lapped quietly over the pebble beach of the Canache. Even in blackout conditions, just enough light seeped from the windows of one of the Portakabins to see the path. He tried running a few paces but his stomach felt so full of beer gas it was more comfortable to settle back into a walk.

At the payphone in Coastel Two, he threw off his coat and dug into his pocket for coins. They had spoken only on Wednesday but he needed to hear her voice again. His fingers dialled automatically. *Drrr, drrr. Drrr, drrr.* Ten rings.

Fifteen.

Eighteen.

Twenty.

No reply. In frustration he kicked the steel plate screwed along the base of the cubicle.

Back in the room, he paced the floor with one hand stuffed deeply into a trouser pocket while he chewed at the nails of the other. Rob would be going home in the middle of August. His own departure, a month later, seemed so far in the future it was like being in the longest tunnel in the world with no light at the end yet. He was sick to his stomach with desire for his reunion with Lesley.

The pad and a black biro were on top of all his kit in the locker along with yesterday's letters, including the one from Paula. He grabbed them all and threw himself onto his bunk.

Well hello Paula,

How's life? At the moment I am alright and no, I'm not working too hard.

Steve, one of my roommates, sent you a letter and a photo, he liked the sound of you and he would like a photo. He's 25 years old, tall dark and ~~ugly~~ handsome (isn't my writing terrible?)

You asked if me and Lesley are going to get married. Only if she will have me. But even if she will, it won't be for a few years yet.

Don't bother about failing your exams. You couldn't do much worse than I did.

I would send you some money for your Blackpool holiday but I've only got Falklands money. Tell you what, I'll send you a cheque and you can cash it off Mam. OK?

You say you are on a diet, you should see me. Dad's got nothing on me. As I write this letter, I've got to keep pushing my belly to the side. Hard to believe, isn't it?

What you can do for me is phone Lesley. Ask her if she wants to get married (not for a few years though) and tell her I want to know; and you want to know so you can continue your super diet.

Well, I will go for now, take care and if you offer your body with the shop they might sell it quicker.

Don't work too hard,

Love,

Gary xx

SEE YOU SOON!

Just as he finished writing the door handle rattled and the lads fell in one by one.

"Hey, Gary! Stop wanking!" yelled Steve, coming over and shaking him by the leg.

"Get off," he pulled himself free from Steve's grip and pushed his mate away, turning his face from the beery breath. "Leave me alone."

Steve grinned inanely and launched himself onto his own bunk.

"You in a bad mood, Gary?" asked Rob.

Gary turned around to Rob's penetrating gaze, "No. I'm just jealous of you going home in August. I'm missing Lesley more than ever."

"Yeah, well, lucky me but it's a month's less pay than you and then as soon as I get home, we'll spend it all. By the time you lot get back I'll be thinking about having to come away again," said Rob. "Being married makes things more difficult not easier, you know."

"I don't know, I reckon it might be all right" said Gary, folding the letter for Paula into an envelope.

"Watch out," said Rob, "Sounds like you'll be going down on one knee as soon as you get back."

"I don't think so, but who knows," said Gary. Rob chuckled, then turned to his bunk, while rhythmic snoring vibrated from Steve's wide-open mouth.

Elizabeth

The River Wear twists and pushes its tortuous way through the towns of County Durham, following the contours and meandering in great loops as it heads towards the sea at Sunderland. Beyond Durham and Chester-le-Street it surges under the A1 and into Lambton Park, where the historic Chester New Bridge marks the start of a curving arc around an open space known as the Raceground, finally passing by Washington, under the A19 onto Monkwearmonth.

Five miles upriver, at the family home in Gilesgate, Elizabeth had got up early to prepare for the invasion which would follow at tea-time.

The table was starting to disappear under a mound of mugs, cups and plates that she salvaged from the deep recesses of the kitchen cupboards, polishing each one with a tea-towel to remove the dust that had accumulated since the last party.

On the draining board, four loaves of bread awaited the spread of softened butter and fillings prepared the night before: egg mayonnaise and cress, fish paste, tuna, ham and cheese. Serving plates and a new roll of cling film sat on the worktop, ready to be pressed into service.

“Hi, Mam,” Paula appeared at the door wearing a long blue tee-shirt that Elizabeth was sure was Gary’s, rubbing the sleep from her eyes.

“Hello, love, you’re up early.”

“The light woke me,” said Paula, coaxing her fingers through bed-tangled hair and stifling a yawn. "Do you need a hand?"

“It would be great if you’d take Schweppes out. It’s a nice morning and she’d love a run.” Elizabeth set up a production line on the table, loaves at one end, bread board, knife and butter, fillings, serving plates, cling film. She unfolded a clean apron, put it on over her head and tied the tapes around the back.

“Where’s Dad?”

“He’s gone to make sure the ducks are ready but he’ll be back in time to take us for lunch." The butter was the perfect consistency. "They are so lucky with the weather, there’s not a breath of wind. Mind you, the river’s low at the moment and if there’s no current we could be waiting for hours for those daft ducks. You should put your shorts on so you can get in the river and push them along!”

Paula rolled her eyes. "Right, I’ll go and get dressed.”

After Elizabeth had made, plated and cling-filmed sandwiches and started a letter to Gary, Mattie came back to take them to the pub for lunch. Eleven family members plus Lesley gathered to eat at the Coal Hole, then rather than take time catching up on their news they piled into cars and set off for the park.

The last day of June, it was a glorious afternoon gleaming with soap-powder brightness and saturated with colour.

The roads were busy with Sunday traffic, families going out for the day.

“Here, does anyone want a drop of my suntan lotion?” Elizabeth asked, passing the tube backwards in the car where Paula had squeezed in between Gran and Lesley. “This sun is strong today.”

“You look as though you’ve already got some colour, love” responded Elizabeth's mother, “Have you been lying in the garden?”

Elizabeth laughed. “I’ve been in the sun all right, but not lying down. I took the ironing out to the garden on Monday and did it in my bathing costume. What a sight!”

Mattie shot her a look from behind the steering wheel. “Honestly, pet, what will Lesley think?”

Paula sighed audibly.

“Oh, I don’t mind,” piped Lesley in the voice that Glenn always mocked.

“Lesley, pet, have you heard from our Gary this week?” asked Bet, changing the subject.

“Yes, twice, thanks Gran.” There was a pause, as if she was thinking. “Did he tell you about the video they're making?”

“It sounds like he's got a bit of free time at last,” Elizabeth said, half turning her head so that Lesley could hear her in the back seat. “We’ve been getting more letters, full of

Gary's usual carry-on. Can you do this for me? Can you do that for me? Asking for things for his new shop over there in the coastel. He needed some new scissors; he's worn out the ones he took. But it's good his work seems a bit easier and he's got time to have some fun."

"Right, ladies," said Mattie, who had been concentrating on the road, "Here we are."

They pulled over the bridge and onto the verge where other cars were already parked in a snaking line alongside the park track. Just ahead, Glenn and Julie were dismounting from their motorbike, their hands pulling off the visored helmets. Some of Mattie's committee members had set up stalls selling raffle tickets and home-made jams and cakes. Pushchairs and blankets were dotted here and there, children ran about and adults lounged in the sunshine, enjoying the warmth and treats from their picnic boxes. A crowd was converging on the riverbank close to the bridge, where three huge plastic bins bulged with yellow ducks, ready to be launched onto the river.

Glenn and Julie came and joined them as they walked towards the bridge, where the start was planned for two thirty.

"What numbers have you got?" said Paula to Lesley.

"A hundred and three and a hundred and four," said Lesley.

"I wonder how many they sold. They must've bought every bath duck for miles around and spent all night painting the numbers on. Hey, Mam," Paula continued without pausing for breath, "What numbers have we got?"

"All the ducks between twenty and twenty-nine, that's two each for Gran, you, Gary, your Dad and me. And I think Glenn and Julie have got thirty and thirty-one, haven't you, Glenn?"

"Well I won't cheer for those two, then," said Paula, turning and punching her brother's leather-clad arm, receiving a playful thump back. "Hey!"

"It's nearly two-thirty," said Glenn, digging beneath his cuff for his watch. "Must be about ready to start."

Across the grass Elizabeth spotted various friends. "Oh look, there's Cy and Margaret, and Hazel and Ray." She waved and the neighbours turned to join them. Soon their number swelled as the usual crowd of Keith, Thelma, John, Ellan, Celia, Ralph, Keith and Sheila appeared from their cars just in the nick of time for the beginning of the race. They were such good friends; they supported every event she or Mattie were involved in and they had parties and they loved getting together with all the kids every year for a New Year's dance at a local hotel.

"Mam! Don't miss it! They're about to start!"

Up by the bridge, three of the committee members had waded into the water with the bins of ducks. Mattie stood to the side with a starting pistol. One of the Lions over by the stalls was acting as compere with a microphone, who called everyone to the starting line.

"Ladies and gentlemen, welcome to Lambton Park and we're about ready to start the Lions Club charity fundraising duck race!" he bellowed. "Who's the lucky duck today? First to the finishing line will win a handsome one hundred pounds!"

Some of the audience applauded. It was a good prize, which was why they had sold so many tickets and crowds had turned out in support.

"Second place, twenty-five pounds! Third prize ten pounds! They're under starter's orders. We'll just wait for our President to give the signal…"

Mattie looked at his watch and raised the firing pistol into the air. Paula put her fingers in her ears. At exactly two-thirty he pulled the trigger. The bang made Elizabeth jump, along with many of the people along the bank. There were exclamations of excitement, dogs barked and a baby started crying. A child let go of a silvery balloon, which floated up into the sky and then bobbed along the line of the river, caught in some current of air created by the flowing water.

The committee members upended the bins and suddenly the river was full of yellow ducks, most of them floating drunkenly on their sides. At first they just bobbed about, gathered in a mesmerized huddle, then the flow of the water caught them one by one and they started to head downstream.

Lesley laughed and clapped her hands. “Don’t they look funny!” she squeaked, her mouth open in surprise, relaxing the pensive expression that had clouded her face throughout lunch in the pub.

“Where are ours?” said Bet, peering at the bobbing mass.

“Look! Look! Hey, Gran! You’re out in front!” yelled Paula.

“Am I? Oh, that’s good!” laughed Gran.

People started to disperse along the riverbank, following the progress of their ducks, children splashing the water’s edge with sticks to encourage theirs along. The bobbing flock spread further out along the river, some ducks more streamlined or better moulded than others, or perhaps just caught in the right place in the flow. Unlucky birds were held up in the sluggish water along the banks.

“Hey, look!” exclaimed Lesley, “Which one is that?” She pointed a finger towards a solitary duck that was going round and round in circles alone at the back of the flock, caught in some eddy of its own, twenty-eight painted in red upon its back.

“It’s Gary!” roared Glenn, “Haha! Well, wouldn’t you know!”

“Glenn!” reprimanded Elizabeth, “Some brother you are! Get in there and help him out of his fix!”

Without more ado, Glenn ploughed thigh-deep into the sluggish water, reached the lone duck and tapped it along with the flat of his hand. It jumped several inches and, as if awakened from a dream, set course squarely for the rest of the flock and raced towards them in a strong current of water.

“Glenn, your leathers! You’ll ruin them!” shrieked Julie. “Honestly, he’s mad. Thank God they're third hand.”

“Come on!” shouted Paula, “They’re getting away!” She skipped down the riverbank with Lesley by her side, the two of them pulling off their heeled sandals and running in bare feet, joining small children who shouted encouragement.

“Right, Mam,” said Elizabeth, weak from laughing, “Come on, no need to follow the whole way. We can cut across the race ground in no time and we’ll be ready for those ducks as they come around the bend. I can see some of our friends have already had the same idea.”

While the youngsters walked, ran and yelled beside the river, older supporters chose the easier route directly across the grass, along the back of a fenced patch of scrubland and out to the far side where the river turned back on itself. On the opposite bank woods rose up steeply, their summer leaves a uniform dark green, drinking in every ray of sunshine that fell on them. On this side, the lawns sloped gently to a point in the river where floating planks and a net formed a finishing line, where one of the committee stood with a notebook, ready to log the numbers that arrived first.

"Here's a place," Elizabeth said as they drew alongside her brother Alan and sister-in-law Nancy, who had already found a good spot near the finish. She tested the clover-riddled grass with the palm of her hand to check that it wasn't damp and beckoned to her mother. "We'll get a good view from here and no need to run about."

"That'll do nicely," said Bet, leaning down and lowering herself to the ground carefully, still protective of the arm that had caused so much trouble for a few weeks.

Elizabeth waved to Cy and Margaret and soon a cluster of friends and neighbours gathered around, chattering excitedly.

The progress of the ducks could be followed easily from the left, as committee members and children and dogs progressed along the riverbank towards them, shouting and cheering, mixed in with the occasional expletive and child's wail of anguish. The compere's commentary floated like a murmur on the air and lent an air of officialdom to the afternoon, focusing attention on the race. Occasionally his voice would rise, shouting encouragement to the ducks.

"Is that number twenty-two in the lead now? Come on twenty-two! Oh no, forty-seven and what's that - looks like fifty-nine – have overtaken. Some have got stuck on the bank there, give them a helping hand, go on. Oh! There's a small group making a getaway in the lead. Come on everyone, give them a cheer!" Then the voice would dip again and the noise would waft on the air, floating away to the background, providing only a gentle reminder that the event was still on.

Elizabeth could think of no better way of spending a day out. She was surrounded by her whole community of family and friends, all joining in, all having fun. It was wonderful to see her Mam looking well and even if Bet hadn't got much of a routine going since Tom had died, at least she was coming for a day out once a week with the family. Elizabeth would feel better if only she could persuade her mother to find something to focus on.

Her mind drifted away, thinking about the tea and the order in which everything had to be done: kettle on first, get drinks made, and then Paula could help unwrap the plates of sandwiches. Everyone should find something to sit on outside in the back garden. Mattie could carry his armchair out from the dining room for her mother, although knowing her she would probably insist on sitting on the hardest thing available. Her Mam really did look well, it was quite remarkable.

A figure landed on the grass next to her. It was Lesley, face flushed, the tops of her shoulders pink where the sun had caught them.

"You all right, love?"

"Yes, thanks." Her smile exposed beautiful teeth but there was no crinkling around the eyes.

"Nice to have you sit with us," said Gran.

Lesley played with a piece of clover, tearing the three leaves away one by one, and then picking another piece.

“Everything all right?”

“Yes, fine, thanks,” Lesley said, looking away up the river to where the happy gaggle approached. “Everyone’s having a great time.”

“And you?"

"Oh, well, you know…"

"How are your ducks doing?” Gran asked.

Lesley turned her face, looking brighter. “Hopeless!” she said. “I think they got left behind somewhere. Actually, it’s impossible to see the numbers on most of them. I thought I saw Gary’s doing quite well but I lost track of him. I think one of mine’s going along upside-down!”

“Well, they’re coming down the straight now. Someone’s got to win,” said Elizabeth, feeling sorry for Lesley. If Gary had been here, he and Lesley would be running along hand in hand, or he would pretend to throw her in until she screamed and then, like as not, she would unbalance him and he would be the one that ended up in the water.

“Here they come,” said Alan, as the ducks approached the finishing line in a long mass of yellow, funnelling between the planks like cars getting into lane for the roadworks. Glenn and Julie were way behind, too hot in their motorcycle leathers to run, but Paula and the cousins were screaming encouragement at the ducks with the lad from next door, the two girls from opposite, and a mass of children. Lesley jumped up and went to join them, all leaning forward to see which numbers had got through first.

None of the family won anything, but it didn't matter. Someone had brought a football and a spontaneous game started up, with the two motorcycle jackets as a goal at one end and piles of sweatshirts at the other, while the adults chatted and wandered back to the stalls at the start line or bought ice-creams from the van that had pulled up across the grass, following the crowd and jangling the tune of Greensleeves loudly enough to drown out conversation.

Committee members were in the river again, scooping dripping ducks into sacks. The last stragglers were coaxed through by enthusiastic supporters. Mattie left the team dismantling the finish and came over to join Elizabeth and the crowd of friends.

"Well done, Mattie, that was brilliant!" she exclaimed, giving him a kiss on his shining cheek.

"How much money do you reckon you made, then?" asked her brother Alan, looking pinker in the face than usual and really quite well considering his health was so poor.

Mattie scratched his head, a smile beaming from ear to ear. "Reckon it'll be more than a thousand pounds by the time the stalls have totted up," he said. "Looks like it's been a big success all round."

"Hey, well done," said Cy from next door. "Shame it's not going into your own pocket, eh?"

"Cy!" said Margaret in a reproving tone of voice, at which Cy turned around and said, "What?" She muttered and tutted at him while he looked for support from the men in the group with his hands held out in supplication.

"Come on," said Mattie, "I need you lot to dig into your pockets and make sure every last raffle ticket is bought before we do the draw. Get over there and make sure you've got a few each."

The group ebbed and flowed, formed and re-formed as individuals joined friends amongst the crowd. When every last item was sold and prizes were collected the event was finally over; Elizabeth looked across the scene and waved at family and friends, the signal that it was time to head home for tea.

Despite their pub lunch, everyone seemed glad of the sandwiches, which Paula and Lesley carried out from the kitchen and offered round. Gran eventually accepted Mattie's armchair but insisted on sharing it with Hazel's two girls from across the street, who perched on an arm each, like winged dragons at a baronial gateway, keeping still lest they should fall off.

Paula had got onto her favourite topic, being a bridesmaid. Lesley's face had settled back into that distracted expression. Poor girl, she would be so much happier with Gary here. Still, not too long to go now, he was well past the halfway mark.

GARY

With his focus on setting up the new barber's shop at the coastel, it had been more than a few days since Gary had walked down the causeway at dawn and it was going to make a welcome change this Wednesday. His destination was HQ BFFI where the officers would need proficient cutting. He couldn't trust Wayne to trim the top men's hair properly.

Gary pulled up the zip on his windcheater and pushed the door open to a frosty morning. Dawn was happening just a fraction earlier now that they were into July. A weak sunrise filtered through the sky from the east, as pale and as grey as a ghost, casting dull light over the Canache.

Two thirds of the way down the causeway there was a knot of people, dark shapes huddled together to one side, and an excited buzz of voices. Out on the water the scene was far from normal. Two black inflatables had secured a CSB between them. In each boat there was busy activity. A geyser of bubbles heralded a diver who appeared from beneath the surface shaking his neoprene-clad head.

"What's going on?" Gary asked as he approached several familiar figures who had clustered to watch. The water near the boats was an unusual colour, a kind of pink.

"There's been an accident," replied one of the EFI lads. "Sailor's been beheaded."

"You what?" He felt slightly nauseous. "What happened?"

Another of the men turned round, one of the lads from FILOG.

"We think two navy guys borrowed that CSB for a bit of a joy-ride. Only they didn't see the cables in the dark, ran straight into that one. It sliced the head off the bloke in the front, just like a cheese-wire."

"Oh God, that's revolting," said Gary, fascinated and repulsed, staring at the blood. "What are they diving for, the head?"

"God knows."

"What about the other bloke?"

"Dunno. He'll be in some big shit, that much is certain."

A military police Land Rover beetled between the Portakabins and down to the shore. Other vehicles appeared behind. It was obvious that the incident would kick off a whole series of procedures and investigations. Two armed policemen started towards them down the causeway.

"Looks like it's time to make a move," Gary said.

"OK, now, break it up." The approaching voice was stern. "Come on, guys, move along now. There's nothing to see."

The men started to peel away, heading on towards the road or down the footpath towards Stanley, but Gary found it hard to tear himself from the scene. He hung back, watching the blood slowly disperse in the still water.

"Come on, barber, move it." The voice was insistent. He looked into the face of the military policeman, a total stranger. It was funny how people recognised him now.

He spotted Rob and Steve walking towards them from the coastel.

"I'm just hanging on for my mates," he said, the excuse sounding spurious even to his own ears.

"Yeah, well, wait for them at the end of the causeway. We need to keep this area moving."

Gary tore himself away, dragging his feet and looking over his shoulder at the diver and the boats. Behind him, he saw Rob and Steve slow down but the police wouldn't let them stop. They soon caught him up.

"What's the story, Gaz?" Rob asked, his voice a little breathless.

Gary summed up the situation.

"Bloody hell." Rob's face paled.

Steve stuck his tongue out to one side and drew his hand across his neck.

"You lads walking in along the shore?" Gary asked.

“Reckon so,” said Rob. They turned hard right to follow the footpath into Stanley. Behind them, others were emerging from the coastel on their way to work. The low, watery sun started to break through the misty cloud.

Staring into that bloody water had shaken Gary up. It was surprising to see that the surroundings on the way in looked just the same as usual.

“They must’ve been going at one hell of a speed,” said Rob, who was equally thoughtful.

Gary couldn’t help remembering his own trip in a CSB across Stanley Harbour on the way to the Lumiere. “What I can’t understand,” he said, “is how anyone could be so stupid. I mean, to take one of those boats and drive it into the Canache in the dark and between the coastels. It must be obvious there’d be cables in the way. What the hell were they up to?”

The others were losing interest already but Gary couldn’t stop turning it over in his head. “The thing is, I thought they were meant to be the smart ones, the Navy guys who get to drive the boats and stuff. If they can be that stupid, what hope is there for anybody?”

“Maybe they were on some secret mission,” said Steve.

“Yeah, a mission to be complete tossers. I probably cut that guy’s hair.”

“He’s had the ultimate cut now!”

"What about his family? Imagine having to tell them what happened. It wasn't exactly a hero's death, was it?"

Under their boots the ground crunched and squelched, in a half-frozen state between ice and mud. The air was dry and their breath steamed. People could be seen moving about in the town and on the bridge out to FIPASS.

"So, what's in store for you today, Gaz?" asked Rob. "You don't often go this way anymore."

"HQ," he replied.

"Back to see the Big Boss?"

"Yeah. And anyone else who turns up." Major General Peter De la Billière was by a long margin his favourite client, but he wasn't going to say so, though everyone admired the man.

"Ask him if we can all have a pay rise," joked Steve. "And a few days' extra holiday."

Steve's finger poked Gary's ribs, hurting and tickling at the same time so that he twisted away, laughing. "Oh, I forgot, you already got the extra holiday."

After the others had turned off to FILOG, he settled back into his thoughts and a more relaxed pace along the front. The incident with the CSB was bothering him, so much so that he moved on autopilot, focused inwardly rather than on his surroundings. The walk to Britannia House passed without further incident and he arrived in good time, pulling himself together as he walked in through the front door.

“Morning, Gary. Here’s your pass. You know the routine.”

Everything ran so much smoother now that he was organising his own schedule and phoning ahead to confirm the arrangements.

“Dining room?” he asked.

“Remember where it is?”

“Course.”

The first appointment on the list was for the Major General, only this time the assistant said that de la Billière would come to Gary in the dining room. Perhaps he was less busy, too, now that Mount Pleasant was open, though Gary couldn’t quite believe that.

He set himself up in his usual place, where the natural light from the windows was best, although today it was so weak that more shadow was cast by the strip-lighting from above. A few crumbs were left on the corner of the table where the wipe of a dishcloth had missed them; he brushed his hand over the surface to sweep them away. The dark-stained door swung open and Major General Peter de la Billière strode in, looking relaxed in regulation army shirt and sweater, not much different from any other officer except for the badges on his epaulettes and the seniority that he exuded in his bearing.

“Morning, Corporal. Gary Shewan, isn’t it?”

"Yes, Sir. Morning." He was surprised and impressed that the Commander BFFI remembered his name. "Short as possible, no clippers?"

De la Billière sat himself down and Gary set to work with gown, spray gun, comb and scissors.

"Well then, Gary, how's it all going in the world of haircutting?"

"Fine, Sir. A bit easier now with the second barber here."

"Hmm. How far into your tour are you?"

He resisted the temptation to say one hundred and six days out of one hundred and eighty-two. Instead he said, "It's been over three months now, Sir."

"Ha. Counting down the days by any chance?"

"Yes, Sir." The new scissors sliced cleanly with a delicious sound and feel; he had been waiting to use them for the first time with this customer.

"Know what awaits you when you go back home?"

"Not really, sir, though I've been thinking about it quite a bit."

The finest trimmings of silver and dark brown fell to the floor, some landing on the lip of the chair back.

"I expect you'll be glad to get back to proper haircutting."

"Actually, I dread having to go back to it. I just hope my parents can sell the salon they bought for me to run. The thought of doing this job all my life is horrible."

It had come out without thinking and Gary stopped. The major general said nothing and Gary was left with the clear impression that he could confide in the senior officer.

"I've only just started to realise what a problem I left them with, my Mam and Dad. I feel terrible about how much it must be costing. Mam is working at my salon on her days off but money is still so tight that she had to sell her car. My parents have never criticised me or complained and that just makes it worse."

"Well, if you're feeling bad then it might be a good idea to say all of that to them." The Commander sat stock still. When he spoke, he kept his head absolutely motionless. Impressive. He let Gary absorb the advice for a few minutes. "Did you get to the opening of the new airport?"

It was a relief to have a change of subject, even though this one brought its own sense of frustration. "Yes, sir, we tried but we had a puncture so we didn't get there. I was really disappointed." Gary focused on getting a clean line over the Commander's ear.

"Shame. Important day for the Falklands. Still, you have the knowledge that you were here and part of making the islands a safer place to live."

"Yes, Sir. At least we saw that first TriStar go over."

Gary cut carefully around the other ear, a precise line with the points of the scissors. This new pair really was excellent. He could throw the old ones away; they were as blunted as rusting hay-cutters. He brushed the hair off the Commander's collar and shoulders and whisked the gown away.

"There you are, Sir."

De la Billière stood up and put his hand in his pocket for his wallet.

"Thank you. Good job."

When the Major General started to walk towards the door he turned on his heel.

"Shewan?"

"Sir?"

"Well done on your commendation, you can be proud of that. Keep up the good work while you're here." He acknowledged another officer who held the door open for him. "I hope your parents have better luck with that salon."

Gary realised he was holding his breath. A feeling of warmth rose from the pit of his stomach, up through his chest and behind his face, pushing his mouth into a wide grin. He would write home as soon as he got back to the coastel.

That first week of July the levels of business continued to grow. Gary was sending his hapless second-in-command to the outstations while he preferred to pick up the regular custom at the coastel and around the military and EFI facilities of Stanley. There was an incessant demand for haircuts and he wished he could have a holiday. This morning he was in the barber's shop, where a long queue was forming.

Although he was happy that the scheduling experiment had proved successful and he was going to be allowed to continue to manage the itineraries and communications, the telephone would ring every few minutes to interrupt the practical work of shearing.

“Look, we can't wait another two weeks, we need you sooner not later.”

“When can you get here?”

“Don't send that useless sidekick of yours.”

"Major Hill here, I'm sending out a memo to everyone with a new outstation schedule that will start on Monday. I'm committing you or Wayne to get around the outstations every fortnight, all right?"

Gary found it difficult to get his work done between all the calls and had to apologise not only to the customer whose haircut had been interrupted but also to those in the queue whose patience was frayed by the lack of progress.

“Sorry, gents, let’s hope the phone stops ringing for a bit." He trimmed the last stray hairs then undid the gown and brushed off the man’s collar, “Hope that’s all right for you.” He accepted payment and a meagre tip, made a note in his notebook and turned to the next customer. “Ready?” He shook the gown out, wrapped it around the broad shoulders as soon as the next customer sat down and looked at the face in the mirror. “Any requests?”

“Don't get funny. I’ve heard about poofs like you.”

He skimmed the man’s scalp as quickly as he could with the clippers without sacrificing attention or care. He didn’t want to waste the crisp sharpness of the new scissors on routine cuts, they needed to last. In the background, his music provided a strong rhythm that helped to keep his pace going and his morale intact. He found himself humming along, eyes focused firmly on his subject, hands moving swiftly and expertly. He felt good; confident of what he was doing, certain of his ground, the equal of any serviceman or EFI employee. The job was done in only five minutes but there was no tip.

The next man sat down, a familiar face from the coastel. A thickset, swarthy man from Gateshead, it was one of Dita's security team who always exchanged jokes and banter. A bull neck pushed his head forwards and the arms were too thick to lie flat against his sides, his frame bulged out of the chair, wide hips swelling under the metal arms.

“What fettle, Gary?” he said.

"I can't keep up today." Gary glanced at the queue and sensed mounting irritation. "I don't know why it's so frantic."

He started on the hair that was as black and shiny as Tyne coal.

"Did you hear there's a new regiment just come in today, the First Light Infantry?" The man twisted round to make eye contact as he spoke and Gary had to turn the great face back, holding the head firmly for a moment to make sure his customer stayed still.

"Yeah, know anything about them?"

"Aye. Geordies apparently, from Newcastle, South Shields and Sunderland. Maybe some of them are from your way, like. Some are based at Whitburn."

"Whitburn, really?" said Gary, clipping as fast as he could go, tipping the head the other way. "Must be from the base over by the allotments, near my Gran's. I just hope they all had their hairs cut before they came out."

"You'll meet them all soon enough, no doubt."

Just at that moment, the telephone rang again. Gary groaned.

"Sorry, back with you in a sec," he said, heading across the room to the beige plastic monster that demanded his attention so persistently.

"Barber's shop. Shewan here."

"Gary? It's Major Hill again. We've had HMS Avenger telephone us. They're coming into Stanley Harbour and want a barber at 8.30 on Sunday morning. There's about a hundred and fifty men on board, they've got just one day."

"OK," his mind was racing, Sunday was his day off. Saying no was not an option.

"I presume you can sort it out?" said the Major down the line.

"Yeah, just tell them it's fine," said Gary, noting the details on the jotter pad. He would send Wayne and hope the idiot could handle the pace.

He put down the receiver and stopped for a moment, blowing out his cheeks. Waiting patiently in the chair, the customer watched him eagerly, jet-dark eyes following every move.

"Problem?" he said as Gary returned, settling himself to start again but distracted by the latest call.

"No problem," Gary flexed his arms, "Just more work."

The telephone rang again.

"This is ridiculous!" Gary slammed the clippers down, stamped across the room and yanked the receiver off its hook. "What?" he snapped, patience exhausted.

"Gary? Hill again."

The Major. Just his luck. He felt the blood rush into his whole face as he cringed an apology.

“I need urgently to speak to Wayne, where is he?”

Taken aback, Gary couldn't respond; no-one had ever asked to speak to Wayne before, least of all the Major, whose voice sounded gruffer than usual. Absent-mindedly he rubbed at a rough patch of the new paint on the wall above the telephone, which shed flakes like dandruff onto his fingertip and the wooden worktop.

“He’s over in Fox Bay today, Sir. He’s not flying back until tomorrow.” He was sure he heard the Major swear under his breath. “Can I help?”

“As soon as he gets back, send him over to the office immediately to see me. No delay.” The Major’s voice sounded stressed.

“Is there a problem, Major Hill?”

The Major let out a sigh of exasperation down the line.

“I’ve just had a call from the officer commanding Byron Heights.”

Gary’s heartbeat quickened; Wayne had been there yesterday. Hill’s voice rasped down the phone line.

“Apparently Wayne had a few too many in the bar and got completely out of control. The idiot pissed all over the room he was put in - his bunk, the next bunk, all over the floor. They’ve banned him from going back.”

“Shit.” It wasn’t the ideal response to his senior commanding officer but he was lost for words; Wayne had behaved like an even worse prat than usual.

“I’ve been getting calls all week complaining about his haircutting anyway, so this just confirms that we’ve got a problem. I’m afraid it’s bad news for you, Gary. All the outstations insist on having you, not him. You’re going to have to look at swapping over the roster, get yourself out a bit more and let him work at the coastel for a bit, where we can keep an eye on him and see what we can do by way of damage limitation. I’m sorry if it means you’re going to have to pick up more work again.”

Gary's heart sank. Just when he thought he was getting things under control. “OK,” he responded, half swallowing the words.

“Send Wayne over to me as soon as you see him,” said Major Hill. “Let’s have another conversation after that.”

“OK, Sir,” said Gary, feeling anything but positive. “Speak to you tomorrow, then.”

“God help me,” he said, walking back to his customer and feeling suddenly heavy in his arms and legs, looking at a queue that now extended out of the door and down the corridor. “You know, all I really want is a few weeks at home with my family and my girlfriend.” His head was hammering.

“Ah,” said the coal-headed man, “Join the club, fella. Join the club.”

Gary lined himself up again with the clippers.

“Shit!”

“What’s up?”

“There’s no way the Major will let me send Wayne to HMS Avenger on Sunday. I’ll have to do it myself. There goes my weekend.”

SCISSORS

JULY 1985

GARY

It usually took a few hours before the post arrived at the coastels from the airport. This evening all the pigeon-holes bulged and the "S" slot was especially full. Gary grabbed the whole pile and sorted through, forming a kind of shelf against his chest with his left hand, using the fingers of his right to flip the envelopes forward, pulling out the ones addressed to him and holding them in his teeth. As usual, there were letters from Lesley, his parents and Gran. It was the best moment of the week, the moment when home came to the Falklands.

He raced up to the room and threw his bag down, expecting the other lads to follow at any time, keen to read in peace before they interrupted.

First he opened Mam's letter, full of sunshine and duck-race day, so that he could almost smell the grass and hear the excited laughter, picture them all back at home for tea, his Mam saying, "If only Gary was here, it would be perfect." She wrote: Your duck's still swimming, to make sure he didn't get too cocky. He laughed and kissed the page.

"Thanks, Mam!"

It sounded as though they had had a great time. It was hard to imagine their midsummer warmth while it was so cold and brittle here.

Next, Lesley's letter. He wondered if Paula had said anything to her about wanting to be a bridesmaid or whether Lesley would want to marry him. His thumb found a gap on the upper edge of the gummed flap and worked its way in, impatient but tearing carefully so as to preserve the envelope. He pulled out the pages of lime green paper and settled back to read, holding the I Love You bear under his chin to bring her closer, as if he could smell her, imagining the station platform, dropping his bags, her running into his arms.

Dear Gary,

Sorry I haven't written for over a week. Actually, I have written quite a few times but I tore the letters up. I'm not sure how to tell you this Gary, but I'm going out with someone else. I wanted to wait till you got home to tell you but I can't keep pretending. The chances are I would bump into Paula or one of your friends when I was with my new boyfriend and they would tell you, which would be worse. I'm really, really sorry to do this in a letter while you're in the Falklands, but at least this way you've got a chance to get used to the idea before you get home.

Today I met up with all your family and we had a good time at the duck race. Your Dad was proud of how it all turned out. I felt terrible because I knew I was going to write this after. Your Mam passed on to me those t-shirts you sent home – thanks.

Anyway, Gary, better go now. I hope you're all right and I'll write again soon.

Lesley x

He stared at the paper and right through it into nothingness with eyes that felt as though they had lost the power of sight. Everything in his world slowed to half speed. He could hear the blood pumping in his temples, feel the bellows movement of his ribcage and lungs as he became acutely conscious of his breathing. It must be a mistake.

Lesley's handwriting swam in and out of focus, her words drifting about like seaweed on the lime-green tide of the page. Gary's eyes ran down the letter again, his heart hammering so hard that it hurt. A fine sweat broke along his hair line and his lip and he felt slightly faint.

Could she have meant anything else? He paused on each word, testing its meaning, checking and rechecking for alternative interpretations.

He wanted to stop the clock, to turn back time to those minutes of anticipation before he opened the letter. He wanted to reverse the last week, rewind the last months, go back all the way to that day in January when he answered the advertisement in the Hairdressers Journal.

A disembodied howl filled the air. It appeared to come from another mouth, a tortured animal wailing in despair. In his hands the green pages were ripped unrecognisably, as if in destroying them he could deny their message, while a hot burning rose in his chest and his face, making him as breathless as if there was a fire inside him.

The door smacked open and Rob sauntered into the room, brandishing a handful of envelopes.

“Ta-dah!” he hooted, “Fan mail!”

Gary couldn’t pull his eyes away from a fixed spot somewhere the other side of the wall. He realised that he was standing in the middle of the room surrounded by green confetti, rooted to the floor and looking idiotic, but there was nothing he could do. It was as if his brain had become disconnected from his body so that all motor function was lost.

“Heard from Lesley?” asked Rob, distracted by his own letters which he was ripping open with enthusiastic haste. “Looks like my older one is learning to hold a crayon.”

Gary struggled to regain his composure, face smarting, hands shaking. He was aware of his roommate on the outside of his consciousness, floating like a distant bird on a breeze.

“Gary, you ignoring me?”

Concerned now, the voice came clearer across the room. Gary could not speak. Rob came and waved a hand in front of his face.

“Gaz! Snap out of it, man!”

"She's dumped me." He heard the words tumbling heavily out of his mouth.

"You what?" His friend backed off a few paces and looked him in the eyes. "Lesley? Shit, Gary, you were only just talking about marrying the girl. What happened?"

Gary felt suddenly weary, leaden to the last fibre of his body. All the energy drained from his limbs, seeping out through his feet into the rough-carpeted floor, leaving his body like jelly. He staggered over to the table and pulled a chair out, landing on it heavily and burying his face in his hands. The heat from his face radiated into his palms.

"What did she say?" Rob had come over and was hovering somewhere behind his shoulder.

"I can't remember. She's found someone else." His voice stuck thick and nasal in the back of his throat. His eyes were filling with tears and his nose with snot. His whole head felt as though it might explode.

Rob sat down next to him, close but not touching.

"Jesus, Gaz. What can I say?"

"Shit, Rob! How could she do that to me? How could she? How…" he trailed off, unable to finish, his world crashing in about him in a chaos of jumbled emotions, all of them unbearable. He leaned his forehead on the cool table and wrapped his head in his arms, a stream of hot tears gushing down his nose in a hell of burning pain.

*

“Don’t worry, Gary, we’ll see you right.” Dita had never looked so paternal, his faced creased into a kindly expression of concern that betrayed genuine affection for the miserable heap that stood in front of him.

“Thanks, Dita. This is the end of the line for me.”

Gary felt washed up, all his energy swept away by that piercing bolt from Lesley. He hadn’t slept, too afraid of dreams in which he might see her, equally dreading that he might not.

“I’ll have to get on the phone to the Major and clear it with him. We should be able to put you on Tuesday’s flight out, there’s bound to be a seat. Come and check in with me in the office first thing on Tuesday morning.”

“I wanted to see it through but it’s been hard, harder than I could ever imagine.”

“I know, Gary. You’ve done a great job. You deserve to go home.”

“I’m sorry, especially leaving you with that idiot Wayne.”

“Yes, well, you let me worry about him. He’ll just have to do what he can until we get another barber sent out. Now you head back to the coastel and get on with your work while I organise a seat for you on that plane.”

Dita really wasn’t at all bad. In fact he had been so decent throughout that Gary thought of him as a kind of father figure. “Thanks, Dita. You're the best boss I've ever had.”

"I'm the only boss you've ever had. Now fuck off out of here before I change my mind." Dita gave him a huge wink and a thumbs up.

Gary turned to the door and felt the sharp flick of a rubber against his ear. As if in confirmation. That was it, he was going home. He only had to get through the weekend, pack, work on Monday, then it was over.

As soon as he was home he would go and see Lesley. If he could get there quickly, there might be a chance she would change her mind. It may not be as he had always imagined, with her meeting him at the station in London, but he'd be in Durham by Thursday at the latest: in less than a week. He'd borrow his Dad's car and drive over to her house; it might just work out all right.

By Monday evening Gary was deeply weary, having worked at the limits of his endurance through the weekend including on HMS Avenger. He hadn't slept at all, instead tossing and turning in his bunk imagining what he would say to Lesley, picturing a scene of reconciliation, the tears and the apologies. He had packed his bag and it only remained for him to throw in his wash kit and last few things in the morning. There wasn't so much to carry this time - he had already sent most of his clothes home because he never used them.

"Everything sorted, Gary?" asked Steve from the other side of the room. "Didn't take you long."

"Nope; it's easy, isn't it, when you just have to shove it all in. No decisions to make. Here, does anyone want my other rucksack? If I pack everything down tight in this one I reckon I could manage without it. Rob, you've always had your eye on it."

Rob's eyebrows rose, his chin tucked in. "Too right, it's good kit."

Gary held the bag out by one of its straps, buckles and webbing trailing onto the floor, the squashed canvas as flat and empty as he felt inside.

"Here, take it."

Rob ambled across and held out his hand. Gary lifted the sack a few inches and hooked the strap over Rob's wrist. "All yours, mate." He left it hanging there, swinging gently from his friend's grip. He turned to the bulging pack on his bunk, put one hand inside to compress the contents down further.

"We'll have to meet up again," said Rob. "I'll be going home in five weeks, and Steve a month after that."

"Some of the lads were talking about getting together for a holiday, maybe in October when the last of them are back," said Gary. "Let's swap addresses."

The green book was on the table, the penguins on the cover looking a bit faded, its edges slightly knocked and beginning to curl.

That night after a final game of cards in the canteen at which he beat everyone, Gary wrote his last diary entry in the green book. It seemed strangely formal, this finishing of the story, the moment of signing off.

Coastel 2

Room 4531

RAOC/EFI

c/o F.I.L.O.G.

BFPO 666

F.I.S.A.

Today is Monday 8th July and thank God I am leaving. I will never regret coming here, but I will never regret leaving early.

So fare well,

Gary Shewan.

And as if to underline just how final the entry was, he allowed himself a double flourish, side to side across the page under his name. That really was it. Over. All that remained was to check in with Dita at the office the next morning and then to get a lift to Mount Pleasant Airport.

Tuesday. It was a misty winter's dawn in Stanley and during the walk along the harbour path to FILOG the heavy air clung to Gary's cheeks and dampened his hair, pushing down on him like an old Durham fog. He arrived at the office cold and slightly breathless, warmed from inside only by the prospect of going home. Everything was ready – he had said his goodbyes, packed his bags and spent all of this month's money on presents at the Kelper Store.

"Gary, come in and sit down." Dita approached so closely that Gary could feel the breath on his face.

His boss's hand was firm on his shoulder, it squeezed hard and propelled him into the office, directed him towards the chair then pressed down to make him sit. The man was shorter than Gary but it made no difference, Gary could feel the authority and it was surprisingly powerful.

Dita swung away around the desk and sat down firmly the other side, staring him straight in the eye with that ice-blue gaze under the blonde lashes. With both elbows on the desk, he pressed his fingers tightly together against his top lip then took a breath.

"I'm really sorry, Gary, but there's a problem."

Silence.

"You can't go today. It's out of my control and out of the Major's as well. In fact he has been fighting your corner all morning with the Colonel."

Gary blinked, his body paralysed, unsure whether he had heard what he thought he had heard.

“The thing is, Gary, the Colonel says it’s against Army rules to allow anyone to go home without sufficient reason or the proper notice period. And apparently your reasons are insufficient for us to let you go this quickly. The trouble is, we are the first EFI ever to be sworn into the Army, so the Colonel insists on doing everything by the Army book. He’s not going to let you go.”

The bullet penetrated with a sting of deception. Gary sat numb in the chair.

“Look, I’m really sorry, Gary. Believe me, the Major and I recognise that we’ve had more than our money’s worth out of you; you’ve worked incredibly hard. We also know what a blow you suffered with your grandfather’s death and now this upset with your girlfriend. We think that you deserve to go home and we’ll go on fighting your corner. We’ve asked the Colonel to make an exception but he says he can’t for the very first case. You have to understand it’s an awkward situation.”

Gary’s blood pumped in his ears but seemed to have deserted his limbs. Without the chair, he would have collapsed. He found himself staring at the top of Dita’s desk, noticing how badly the surface was scratched and a few grey patches like fuzzy felt where dust stuck to ancient coffee spills.

“Listen, I’m sure it’s just a question of time until we can find a way through this and at the very worst it’s only ten weeks until you finish your contract. We’re behind you, Gary, but you’re going to have to steel yourself to be patient until we can get things sorted out.”

Gary lifted his eyes to meet Dita's gaze. "But I've packed and everything."

"Listen, if it was up to EFI, you'd be going. But since we all had to swear in, things have changed. It's the first time the Army's been involved in an EFI personnel issue, so that makes you a guinea pig. It's a question of which side gets to make the final decision."

Gary's head was bursting. He rubbed his forehead with his hands. "I said at the time I didn't want to swear in, I never trusted it. I didn't want to join the Army."

"I know. Listen, I'll do everything I can to keep pushing."

"What am I supposed to do?" Gary was struggling to comprehend what was happening.

"Go back to work, son. It's the only thing you can do."

Gary started the walk back to the coastel, his vision blurred by tears that flowed freely down his cheeks in acknowledgement that the opportunity to resolve things with Lesley was slipping out of his hands. From time to time he stumbled over a stone or scuffed the toe of his boot, barely lifting his feet as he struggled with his thoughts, desperate for a solution that would persuade her to wait until he got home.

In the room, he unpacked again into his locker, and then sat for a while at the table with his green diary in front of him. He turned the pages and took a deep breath.

Today is Tuesday 9th and I don't half regret what I wrote on the previous page because I have been told the CO FILOG does not think my reasons are sufficient. So God only knows when I will be going home.

But the sooner the better.

There was nothing for it but to go and open the shop.

The queue outside the telephone box that evening was longer than ever and Gary chewed anxiously at his stubs of fingernails until every single one of them was down to the quick. Although they hurt, he couldn't stop pressing at them with his teeth, tearing at any edge where he could gain purchase.

When it was his turn he piled coins on top of the phone as usual. He hoped his parents would be in; he'd had to wait a long time and they might have finished their tea and gone out.

Down the line, a distant click and ringing. Please be in.

"Dad!" He could feel emotion rise in his throat.

"Gary! How are you, son? Everything all right?"

"No." How he wanted to be home. "Everything's gone wrong." Hysteria rose as he spoke. "Lesley's seeing someone else, Dad." Hot tears streamed down his face; words poured out. "She just getting back at me, I know it. She never wanted me to come away. I'm desperate to see her but the Colonel won't let me fly home and I'm going mad because I am dying of overwork here and I need you to go and talk to her for me, Dad, and tell her to wait for me, it's only a few weeks longer and then I'll be back and…"

"Hold on, son, hold on." His father's voice was calm but insistent. "Start again, son, breathe properly and tell me slowly."

Gary took a deep breath and explained the whole story between gulps and sobs and wiping his nose on his sleeve.

"Dad, you and Mum have got to go and talk to her for me." Having reached the end of the narrative he felt better, certain that help was on its way. His parents would go and see her, persuade her to wait.

"Well now, hang on a minute," his Dad's voice sounded less than reassuring. "I don't think it would be right for us to get involved. I know it's hard for you being away and everything, but really it isn't up to us to go and see Lesley, you know."

"But you've got to." Gary couldn't believe it. "You're my only chance."

"I'm sure that's not true."

There was a pause, so long that Gary could hear his heart beating.

“Listen, son, you made your decision and now she's made hers. You’ve got to fight your own battles, sort it out between you. The only person who should speak to Lesley is you. It wouldn’t be right for your Mam and me to intervene.” The tone was firm now.

He could hear fumbling as the receiver changed hands. “Gary?” His Mam’s voice came down the line. “Listen, love, I'm sorry if things are going badly for you. I didn't catch all of that, but your Dad’s right. You know we only want the best for you but you have to speak to Lesley yourself. Why don’t you phone her?”

They just didn’t understand. He couldn’t have some stupid, stilted conversation down the phone from eight thousand miles; he wouldn’t be able to stay calm and all he would do was cry. The tears started again now, this time hot with frustration and despair. He hiccupped down the phone, his breath catching in short gasps.

“I hate to hear you so upset, love." His Mam's voice cracked and his father came back on the line.

"Gary? Look, we’re on your side, son, but really there's nothing we can do. Perhaps you could ask for special leave or something, just for a week or two and then you could go back and finish off. You must be due a lot of holiday with that commendation and so on."

"But you don't understand, that's just money, you don’t actually get any time off. I’ve tried but it’s a total shambles. The rules changed when we had to swear into the Army. The EFI bosses, they think I deserve to leave early, but the Army Colonel says I've got to stay until the end of my contract. I don't know who else to ask, who might be able to put in a word for me. The only person I can think of is the Major at Wingham. He might be able to pull some strings. Listen, will you find out the number and ring him? Please. Please help me get out of here."

There was muffled talking at the far end, he could hear his mother.

"Mam? Are you there?" He held his aching forehead in his hand.

The voice came back down the line, clear as if from next door. "It's your Dad, son, I'm just discussing it with your mother."

They continued whispering then Dad's voice returned.

"OK, son, we'll see what we can do. But don't go getting your hopes up. We'll give Wingham a call and explain what's happened, see if they can't at least find out who should make the decision. After that it's up to them. Here's your mother."

Gary felt exhausted, his energy gone. He leaned his head against the wall of the cubicle.

"Gary, love?" His Mam's voice soothed him. "I know it's hard dealing with this when you're a long way from home but you need to keep going. We'll make the call but it's bound to take some time to sort out. You've got to stick at it, go on working like you have been."

He trawled words up from his very depths. “Mam, you have no idea what it’s like.” A tide of anger began to rise, dry fury pounding at his temples. “You never did like Lesley, did you? Well, I hope you’re happy now.” And he slammed the receiver down, hands shaking.

Scooping the spare change into his pocket he kicked his way out of the booth, face so hot that his cheeks pulsated. He avoided the looks of the lads in the queue, crashed out of the main door of the coastel and ran into the chilly blackness of the night, down the causeway to the shore, with wind and sea spray beating at his aching head.

There was a time he ran away from home as a young boy, absolutely convinced that he was adopted. His childish threats to leave for good were met only by encouragement from his Mam and Dad, who quietly ignored him while he packed the little suitcase and even helped him make up a brown paper bag of sandwiches. It was only after the front door had clicked behind him and he had dragged the suitcase along the pavement a few hundred yards that he stopped to think about what he should do next. Night would soon fall and the escape plan had no objective, direction or purpose. His motivation, that he was a misfit who did not belong in the Shewan family, had quickly faded only to be overtaken by a realisation that apart from home, he had nowhere to go. All alone in the twilight he had no ideas and nobody to ask. After eating the sandwiches and skulking around the park for as long as he could stand it, he crept back into the house and, too mortified to climb the stairs, slept the night in the dog's bed. The worst thing was his parents knew all along that he would come back and had let him learn his own way. It felt to him that behind their normal faces the next morning they must be laughing. Nothing was said.

Looking out now across the oily darkness of Stanley Harbour, he knew that his parents were again leaving him to deal with the consequences of his decisions. A sense of injustice stung him to the core. It was as if his parents, the Army and Lesley had conspired together to create this hellish situation, so that he would crawl home humiliated and grateful to resume life and work exactly where he had left off. It was their punishment for his spur-of-the-moment decision to escape from Durham.

He kicked his way along the water's edge, his boots overturning stones and seaweed, finding purchase between slippery surfaces. The wind gradually cooled his hot cheeks and took away the pain in his head, and slowly the tension in his back and shoulders eased and he could look up again, peering to make out the horizon.

As his eyes grew accustomed to the dark, he found a dry boulder to sit on and scraped up a few pebbles to throw one by one into the water. The movement was calming. Soon he was looking for flat stones and seeing if he could make them skim across the surface, to disappear hopping into the dark.

The more he thought about it, the more he knew that the situation was hopeless. The Army was not about to change its rules for a minnow such as him; there must be thousands of military lads all over the world who had good reason to want to abandon their posts, who faced distress with their jobs and difficult family circumstances. The EFI might have listened and made an exception, but the Army definitely would not.

His thoughts turned to Lesley. The lads were right: he had taken too big a risk. With her good looks it was inevitable that someone would try it on. Maybe she had resisted, held out for him, and only given in eventually because, momentarily, she had forgotten that she loved him. If only he could believe that was true.

He had always found it incredible that he had such a gorgeous girlfriend. He had missed her and dreamed about her and written to her, he was so proud of her and just recently he had started to think that they might have a future together. But that niggling sense of inadequacy he had always felt was the truth: he was not enough for her and he had been an idiot to imagine she would wait for him.

Somewhere across the water a door clanged. Gary realised that he had not moved for quite some time, that his whole body was cold and stiff and that his backside ached from sitting on the boulder. The more he sat and thought, the more miserable he became and the more helpless and dejected he felt. And although in some ways it would have been good to teach them all a lesson by freezing to death out here by the harbour, frankly he was too uncomfortable to hang about any longer.

ELIZABETH

After Gary had slammed the phone down on her, Elizabeth was left holding the receiver, staring at Mattie in shock.

"Come on, put the phone down," he said, taking it from her.

"I've never heard our Gary so distraught; he's in a terrible state. Things must be really bad for him. It's not just Lesley; he's been worked into the ground and he isn't over Grandad, you know how upset he was about that even though he put on a brave face. It must be terrible for him, being so far away from home."

She stopped, tears pricking her eyes, wishing she could comfort her son.

"You're right, love, it must be tough for him," said Mattie. "I've never been one to give him much guidance. There's never any point telling him what to do, he only goes off and does the opposite. It just seems best to let him work things out himself. You know, back at the start I thought he was crazy to fly off to the Falklands on this wild-goose chase but he's made a good go of it, and he's proved himself and they all appreciate him. It could just be the making of him, give him something to look back on that was a success, all on his own merit for once. He's never had that before. I can't say I'm surprised that Lesley did the dirty, but it sounds like the months of hard work have finally got on top of him and I think he's worn out."

Elizabeth looked at her husband's blue eyes and saw the man she had fallen in love with decades earlier. The thick hair swept back from his forehead was still black and lustrous, the eyebrows still strong. Mattie was her rock and she knew that he would find a way to help Gary.

"So what can we do?" she asked. "We promised to phone the Major at Wingham."

"And that's what we will do," replied Mattie. "But not tonight, it's too late now. And we will need to find the number."

While Mattie went out to the Coal Hole for a pint and a game of dominoes, Elizabeth fetched the box containing Gary's letters from under their bed. She didn't hold out much hope of finding the number of the EFI headquarters at Wingham amongst them, still less the name of the Major in charge, but it would be enjoyable to read through all the letters while sipping a sherry.

Paula was out for the evening but would want to know what all the fuss was about when she got in. She was expecting awful exam results but with her place at college secure she was enjoying the freedom of the summer holidays, pursuing boys and fashion and pop music, in fact so many boys that Elizabeth couldn't keep up with who was who. Elizabeth wondered if perhaps they shouldn't have a serious talk before Paula went to Blackpool with her mates in August, but there was plenty of time for that. For the time being, she knew that Paula would be furious when she heard that Gary was unable to come home and would pester until the phone call to Wingham was made and Gary's return was secured.

She started to sift through the letters, working backwards from the most recent, reading through each and laughing at his stories and ridiculous comments, punctuated with so many exclamation marks and questions. His spelling was atrocious, but you could hear him joking and teasing, his voice coming through the writing, a little immature maybe but so funny and intensely likeable. And he was never embarrassed to say he loved his family, which melted her heart every time.

After an hour she knew the search for information was fruitless and went out to the kitchen where the dog glanced up from her basket, sleepy after an earlier walk.

"What would you do, Schweppes?"

The animal looked at Elizabeth quizzically, head tilted on one side, tail half wagging in a lazy but expectant way.

"Brilliant!" exclaimed Elizabeth. "You are the most amazing dog. Directory enquiries, why didn't I think of it myself?"

A couple of days later, before they needed to leave for work, they tried the number. To their surprise, they were put through to Major Anderson, the man in charge.

Elizabeth deferred to Mattie on such an important errand, so had to strain to hear the responses that were coming back down the phone. It took a little while to explain who they were and why they were calling, but the Major was attentive and very soon said, "Ah, yes, Gary Shewan. Great lad, I gather he's been working very hard and got a commendation. He did a marvellous job in the gardens here, I seem to remember. Now, how can I help you?"

It was a case of explaining the whole story, in particular the issue about not knowing which was the right authority to appeal to, the EFI or the Army, and then asking what the options might be for getting Gary home early. The Major listened until Mattie had run out of explanations and questions.

There was a silence, during which Mattie's eyebrows were working up and down and Elizabeth could not help whispering, "Is he still there?"

"Hmm," at last came the voice down the phone. "Under the old regime this would be an EFI decision and doubtless there would be no argument, an exception would be made and he would be permitted to come home early, especially in light of his excellent service. Unfortunately however the regime has changed and it's not clear who has the authority for such a decision, not clear at all. And of course any action now will set a precedent, so of course the Army will be nervous about that."

"I see," was all that came from Mattie. Elizabeth didn't know what to expect.

"Listen, I will make a few checks and put a word in if it will make any difference but I have to say, to me it's not very hopeful. There may be no option and Gary will probably have to see his contract out."

There was nothing else to say. Mattie thanked the Major and hung up.

That evening, after work and dinner and washing up, Elizabeth sat down at the kitchen table to write to Gary.

How are you? Hope you are keeping calm. We phoned Major Anderson up and had a good talk to him, he seems very nice and understanding but you must realise you are on six months' contract. Even if you have to finish your six months, nine weeks left that's not forever. We all love you and want you home but if you have to finish your time do it the right way, not full of hell. You've had good times, think of them not just the bad times. You committed yourself to six months and you will only make your life a misery if you have a chip on your shoulder. Major Anderson is going to check out what is happening... he will see what he can do.

She didn't want to raise Gary's hopes. Elizabeth took a deep breath and carried on writing.

Gran looks better than for a long time. Paula's taped Live Aid - watched it until four on Sunday morning. Miners Gala Saturday was not very busy, just lads with cans of beer.

She wished she could give him better news about the shop, to take away any guilt he was feeling and regrets he might have.

And listen, don't worry about the shop. We know you have been feeling bad about leaving us with it but we've managed for five months and another few weeks waiting for it to sell won't make any difference now. You just get back to work and keep your chin up. We love you.

GARY

In the next postbag there was a letter from his old Durham mate, Paul, who he had known through secondary school. He had replied to Paul's previous letter, the one that had arrived the day he learned about Grandad's death, and it came as a surprise to see another one now. Although Gary was sociable, he had never thought of any of the lads from home as particularly close friends. Paul and a few others were regular features in a murmurating crowd of local youngsters who sometimes skipped school or hung around the park of an evening, chatting up the same girls until they hooked up into relationships and changed their focus to going steady. In Gary's case he had barely seen any of their faces since that skiing holiday when he met Lesley, and of course now they all were following different paths in the world of work, whether finishing apprenticeships or starting from the bottom in other occupations. Some had even gone into the Forces.

Sorry for not writing earlier but I've been away on my hols! I've been to Majorca with Ted and Finna and a great time was had by all. We went with Club 18-30 and even though we had a good time it's nothing like the papers make it out to be.

I don't know if you had heard but me and Angela finished and I'm now going out with Julie C. I'm now working as a plumber with the council and I am quite enjoying it but I could not imagine working there all my life. It has its ups and downs but you've got to take the rough with the smooth.

I was talking to Kingy down Durham the other night and he says he is not going back to the Falklands and Stewy is in Germany at the minute so we don't know what he is doing. I sold the Capri and have now got a little Fiesta which is more economical and I'm starting to save some money. You'll have to let me know when you are coming back so all the lads can go out on the town and get drunk.

I am playing for Gateshead FC now which is the highest level of non-league football in the north east. We were in the Gola League but we were relegated into the Northern Premier which is still a good level of football. I was also Player of the Year for Gateshead so it was quite a good season for me even though we went down. I might also have an outside chance of playing in Greece in the next few years so keep your fingers crossed for me, you might get a cheap holiday in Greece.

Durham is still the same old boring place but I would not swap places with you!! Well, it's Saturday and I'm wondering where to go tonight. It cannot be much fun where you are if there's only two pubs, in fact it sounds a little bit like Durham.

Anyway, keep the good work up and keep the money rolling in and I hope to hear from you as soon as possible so I can keep up to date with the news. All the lads are asking after you so don't think we've forgotten about you.

All the best.

The letter was chatty and amiable but somehow that just made Gary more miserable; he felt lonely and homesick and all he wanted was to go and get drunk with a whole crowd of familiar, cheerful faces and have a few laughs and maybe chat up a few girls. How could he endure the weeks until his release?

The July days ticked by interminably and he dragged himself through the gruelling routine with no interest or enthusiasm. He agreed with the Major that he would work alternate weeks at the coastel and the outstations to keep everyone happy. The three thousandth haircut merited a note in the green notebook but more as a record of his suffering rather than by way of achievement. Wayne had already asked to go home but that was not going to be an option. Even with him taking some of the load, Gary's own meter was clocking around faster than ever, haircut after haircut. There was no prospect of stopping.

He received a welcome at each of Mount Kent, Mount Alice and Byron Heights as well as FIPASS and FILOG but the familiarity and warmth did little to lift his morale; he found every day depressing. The helicopter rides had become mundane; he barely looked at the mountains and scenery which once had held him in rapt attention and the trips offered only more grinding drudgery. One night after working at Mount Kent he crawled into a bunk, plugged in his headphones and wept himself to sleep with hopelessness rather than joining men he knew at the bar.

It was all he could do to force a smile and speak to anyone. A gloom had come down upon his spirits and, unlike the ever-changing Falklands weather, it was sticking heavily.

When he returned to the coastel at the end of the week and Rob asked him how he was doing, Gary could barely remember where he had been and what he had done. He had to look at the green notebook where the name of each day's location sat alone on the page, with no comment or score. With his motivation so low, even small things had become a massive effort.

Back at the shop he remained professional, cutting hair as efficiently as ever, taking the money, managing the books, but he had lost all his spontaneity. By the time work finished each day he was overcome with exhaustion, every ounce of energy drained by the effort it took to put on a brave face. After eating in the canteen, he would drag himself back to the room, where he would plug in his headphones and play the same yearning track over and over again, staring blankly at the ceiling or sobbing into his pillow.

On a Saturday evening at the beginning of August, lying prone in his bunk and gazing blindly upwards with the same tune playing yet again through the wire, Gary felt a rough shaking.

"Hey, Gary lad." It was Rob. "Listen up!"

Gary slowly focused his eyes on his roommate and pulled the headphones down.

"I've had an idea. You know I'm qualified to go home after five months because I'm married? In two weeks' time? I don't mind doing a swap, hanging on here an extra month; Dita really needs the manpower. You could take my flight home. What do you say?"

What? Had he heard right? Gary shut his eyes and opened them again.

"Gary? Are you listening to me? I said you can take my flight home. I know the Army has said no but that's assuming they are the people to make the decision. If I offer to stay on instead of you, that might give Dita and the Major a bit of ammunition to reopen negotiations and maybe even force the issue. What about it?"

Gary stared at him, speechless.

"Well?"

Then hot tears welled up in Gary's eyes and he could do nothing but hold his arms up like a child, and the comforter who was Rob stood close and wrapped him in a hug while Gary just cried.

After a while Gary took a breath and pushed himself away to speak through the mucus and the tears and the darkness that was drowning him. "I just can't believe you could even think of it. I know you've enjoyed yourself out here but you've been missing Susan and your kids, and you keep saying how ready you are to go home."

Rob's calm hand weighed gently on his shoulder. Gary fumbled in his pocket for a handkerchief then blew his nose, twice, and took another deep breath. "I mean, how could you sacrifice your flight for me?"

"An extra month, Gaz, it's all about the money."

Gary was not sure that was entirely the truth but a glimmer of hope, faint, watery, somewhere in the back of the darkness of his brain, was emerging. "Honestly, Rob, I am so lucky to have you guys as friends. I know Steve is mad and all that, and he still seems to think he can make Paula keen on him even though he hasn't got a cat in hell's chance, but he's a good laugh and genuine. And you, well…" He gulped. "Rob, I don't know how I'd have managed without you. Really. You've been a mate and, well, better than a mate."

Rob continued to say nothing. Gary paused and thought and the light seemed to grow as he slowly pulled himself together.

"I am so, so grateful to you for offering me your ticket home, I can't tell you. And maybe the Army won't let me use it. But if it is possible, it would be fantastic."

"Good decision. I'll go and talk to Dita." And Rob went into action.

Dita came and found Gary early the next morning at the barber shop, where Gary was facing another day's grind despite its being a Sunday. The pale eyes twinkled as Dita told Gary that the Major had argued strongly about NAAFI terms and conditions and fairness. And then under additional pressure from himself about the genuine level of concern that everyone, especially his colleagues, felt for Gary's wellbeing, and what a deserving case he was, the reluctant colonel had finally conceded and had given way. The operational trade-off didn't even come into it.

"You can go home after all, Gary," he smiled. "And there's even better news. There's a TriStar due out this afternoon so if you can be ready in time, they will let you aboard."

It was all Gary could do not to hug his manager. He let out an enormous breath somewhere between a sigh and a whoop and made to shut up shop. A couple of frantic hours were barely enough to pack his things, celebrate with his friends and get to the new international airport at Mount Pleasant.

This time there was no ferry to endure and no stop at Ascension Island, instead he shared a plane with a lot of

Gozomers and a few Kelpers and the skiffle group who had performed the Friday entertainment just two nights before. It was an eighteen-hour flight which, had his original hopes been realised, should have filled him with intense excitement at the anticipation of seeing Lesley but instead he slept profoundly most of the way, rocked by the motion of the aircraft and the simple relief of knowing that his trials were over.

They touched down at RAF Brize Norton and a few hours later he was back at Wingham.

Before his debrief and final medical he found the old phone box and called his astonished parents to announce that he was in England. His mother could barely speak.

"Gary, you'll never believe it but we've got great news, too. The sale of the shop is going through after all, we've exchanged contracts. Upstairs Downstairs will be off our hands."

Another massive weight fell away.

"Gary, call us when you get to the railway station so that we can collect you. Oh, we're so glad that you are nearly home!"

ELIZABETH

Early the next evening Elizabeth was watching television distractedly with Mattie and Paula while they waited for Gary's call. It was some costume drama that she had wanted to follow but she was unable to concentrate for thinking about the quickest way of driving to the station. They didn't know which train he would be on but time was ticking by and each minute heightened her anticipation of the phone's ring.

Outside a car pulled up but they ignored it; people often parked on the street and it was probably just a neighbour or someone going in to visit next door. Then Paula squeaked, "Mam! Dad! Look!" A tall figure was peering through the sitting room window, with the widest grin on an unmistakeable face. "It's Gary!"

GARY

The reunion with his family of course made him cry. And laugh and sing and cry a lot more and there was so much to say. They talked for hours while Mam dished up his favourite dinner and afterwards, when they all were exhausted and it was time for bed, his own room had never seemed so spacious or so comfortable.

The next morning Mam drove him over to see Gran in Whitburn. While she was parking the car, he rushed up the pathway of the house and knocked eagerly at the door. When Gran answered he was amazed at her appearance: of course she was the same, yet she was so different. She looked well, with colour in her cheeks and a softness in her face, and her hair was lovely. It was almost as if time had reversed while he had been away and she had grown younger. Her smile radiated sunshine. He hugged her tightly at the doorstep and they went in to catch up on all that had happened.

BET

It was wonderful to hear her grandson so grown up, confident and assured and he looked different, still handsome but broader, not a boy. For hours she and Elizabeth could hardly get a word in but she didn't mind. They laughed and wept as he told his stories, the good times and the bad, the amazing adventures and his experiences across the ocean; they heard about the unspoilt landscapes and the wildlife and the alien environments at the outstations. He enthused about the wonderful friends he had made and the reunion that they planned for when they were all back, and she could sense, too, just how much he was looking forward to seeing his old Durham mates for a drink and to establishing a new kind of normality. He had saved up enough money to buy a car, would find a job that had absolutely nothing to do with hairdressing and was ready to make a new start.

And then of course Gary wanted to know all about his Grandad so they reminisced about Tom and she and Elizabeth told him how things had gone although they managed to avoid the worst of the details and the three of them cried a great deal more.

Gary said how dreadfully he regretted being away during those last months. But she had no difficulty reassuring him that nobody could have done more and that Gary had been right to take his chance and live his own life. Grandad's suffering was over and it was all for the better.

In loving memory of Tom and Bet Davison

Printed in Great Britain
by Amazon

58725970R00224